Adolescence and Delinquency

The collective management of reputation

Nicholas Emler

and

Stephen Reicher

BLACKWELL
Publishers

First published 1995

Blackwell Publishers Ltd
108 Cowley Road
Oxford OX4 1JF

Blackwell Publishers Inc.
238 Main Street
Cambridge, Massachusetts 02142
USA

British Library Cataloguing in Publication Data
A CIP catalogue record for this book is available from the British Library.

Library of Congress Cataloging-in-Publication Data has been applied for.
ISBN 0–631–13802–1 (alk. paper)
ISBN 0–631–16823–0 (pbk.: alk. paper)

Printed in Great Britain by Hartnolls Ltd, Bodmin, Cornwall
This book is printed on acid-free paper

Adolescence and Delinquency

Social Psychology and Society

General Editors: Howard Giles and Miles Hewstone

The aim of this series is to channel the constructive attempts of psychology to deal with social issues. Its concern is with life outside the laboratory and with realizing the immense potential of the discipline in understanding and confronting contemporary social problems.

Nuclear Energy and the Public
Joop van der Pligt

Interpersonal Accounts
A Social Psychological Perspective
John H. Harvey, Ann L. Weber and Terri L. Orbuch

Children and Prejudice
Frances Aboud

Adolescence and Delinquency
Nicholas Emler and Stephen Reicher

Contents

List of Tables

Preface

This is the book that delinquents tried to suppress . . . in a manner of speaking. The night before we were to hand the book over to our publishers, thieves broke in and stole our only final copy of the manuscript and the only disk with our final copy of the files. If there was a certain irony about this, we certainly didn't feel it at the time. Nevertheless, we persevered and this is the result.

However, were our thieves unwittingly doing everybody a favour? Does the world really need another book about adolescent delinquency? After all, it must sometimes seem as if academic pronouncements on the subject appear with about as much frequency as government initiatives to fight crime – and with about as much use. What is more, just as the political debate can be broadly characterized as a see-saw between ritual condemnations of sin on the one hand and assertions that 'society is to blame' on the other, so also, with a few honourable exceptions, scholars tend to stick within the deep ruts of individual–social dualism.

The former camp, largely inhabited by psychologists, sees transgression as deriving from some flaw in the psyche of the delinquent. It may be acknowledged that these flaws derive from upbringing rather than reflecting original sin. None the less, however formed, delinquent character will out. The latter camp, more associated with sociologists, gives causal priority to some aspect of social position – be it class, gender, neighbourhood or whatever. While these two approaches may appear to be polar opposites, they have one important characteristic in common. Both portray delinquency as a reflection of irresistible forces. They may come from within the adolescent or they may act upon the adolescent. But, whether glove puppets or puppets on a string, actors are ultimately moved around by forces beyond their control.

That which has been noted many times of the social sciences in general is therefore also true of the study of delinquency. There is a glaring paucity of attempts to address the inherently social nature of individual action – the fact that to be an individual is to exist in a social structure, and that social structural factors affect individual behaviour only through the ways in which they impact upon the rhythms of mundane existence. In the case of delinquency, this means an analysis of the ways in which transgressing – and, equally, not transgressing – has implications for everyday experience. How does it affect the ways in which others see us, how they treat us, what we can do, who we are allowed to be and not to be? In other words, for all the rows of texts and monographs and journals on library shelves, the social psychology of delinquency is notable mainly for its absence. That is our excuse for sacrificing a few more trees (quite a lot of trees, we hope) to the delinquency literature.

Of course, there are countless forewords where brave conceptual claims are made in order better to ignore the issues in the ensuing text. As Charles Morris noted some 60 years ago in his introduction to G.H. Mead's *Mind, Self and Society*, many are those who announce that they have shown how the individual is produced out of the social without actually ever performing the trick. Moreover, to invoke the name of social psychology is hardly to ensure that one has avoided the perils of reductionism. There are many social psychologies, and the mainstream has always been resolutely individualistic. It is therefore worth being more specific about the approaches we have brought to this study.

In fact, we started from somewhat different positions. One of us (NE) began from an interest in reputation and reputation-management theory. The other (SR) had previously worked on group processes from the perspective of social identity/self-categorization theories. What both theories have in common is a concern with the ways in which that most psychological of constructs, the self, is constructed through social processes. However, reputational models look largely on the way in which who we are depends upon how we are (and suppose ourselves to be) recognized by others and the attempts we make to influence the judgements others make of us. The social identity tradition, on the other hand, has been more concerned with the way in which selfhood is bound up with the nature of those groups to which we belong and their relations with groups to which we do not.

In a phrase, if the former approach focuses on the strategic dimensions of self processes without asking who is of strategic relevance, the latter can be said to trace the sources of the self in specific group relations while ignoring the active strategies through which social identity is claimed and maintained. We would see each theory having the wherewithal to remedy the omissions of the other. We therefore see the combination as providing a powerful conceptual tool. In the present case, we have sought to show how committing or refusing to commit delinquent acts is a powerful way of laying claim to social identities that are particularly important in the social world of young people. Whether the various debates, arguments and compromises which marked both our work and writing, re-writing and re-re-writing of this book represent a creative synthesis, or whether we have merely ended up with a camel, is not entirely within our power to say.

Whatever issues of detail may arise in relation to our model, there is one aspect of the work on which we would insist. It is this: if one wishes to understand the significance of delinquency – or indeed of any activity – in the lived experience of adolescents, then one must start from the evidence of that experience. Simply, one must listen to and take seriously what adolescents have to say about their lives. It may be a remarkably simple point, but it is something that is not simply excluded but actively ruled out by mainstream analysis. For, if delinquency is the expression of forces beyond individual control and if individuals are denied any part in the creation of their own lives, then there is little point in giving any priority to what actors have to say. At best, an individualistic psychology might listen to delinquents for evidence of the pathology which drives them to transgress. But that is not to listen to the meaning of what is said, but rather to use what is said as evidence of lack of meaning – hardly a respectful attitude!

If we have managed to go any way towards understanding what adolescents are doing when they are being delinquent or refusing to be delinquent, it is because they were prepared, to some extent, to talk to us. Therefore it is right that our first acknowledgements should go to the hundreds of anonymous young Scots who participated in our research. We can only hope that we have done some justice to their many lively and fascinating accounts. We must also thank the various schools and youth clubs which allowed us access and spent many hours organizing the systems we devised to ensure absolute confidentiality to our respondents. Perhaps it is wrong to single out one person out of the many who helped us. However, it is hard to resist thanking Mrs Sturrock whose ceaseless good humour in the face of our ceaseless irksome requests still baffles us.

Then there are those who helped us design, carry out, and analyse much of the work reported here. These include Barbara Boyle, Julie Dickinson, Suzanne Heinz, Derek Honour, Julie Pehl, Stan Renwick, Bridget Ronson and Andy Ross. It is customary to credit them for anything that is good about the book and exclude them from all blame for what is bad. It must be a custom since it goes against all we know about attribution theory. However, in the case of a jointly authored book let it stand. We always have each other to blame.

Lastly, there are our series editors and several successive staff editors at Blackwell Publishers who have despaired of this book ever being produced, who have had to witness more than one phantom pregnancy (to the extent of announcing the delivery date in their catalogues) and who have shown remarkable patience through the entire process. Well, here it is at last. Was it worth the wait?

Nick Emler
Steve Reicher

1

Introduction

To each generation youth presents both a promise and a threat. On the one hand, the values and structure of a social order can only survive beyond the present generation through the socialisation of the next. On the other hand there is the ever present threat that instead of continuity there will be rupture. The socialization process may fail and if it does youth will destroy society rather than perpetuate it. Consequently, any evidence of youthful dissent can signify not only a disruption of the present but the denial of a future. As Samuel Smiles put it: 'the worst of youthful indiscretions is not that they destroy health so much as they sully manhood. The dissipated youth becomes a tainted man; and often he cannot be pure even if he would' (1903, p. 335).

Cohen (1972) makes the point that particular groups may be elevated into 'folk devils' and become the subject of 'moral panics' to the extent that they or their actions feed wider collective insecurities. Those youth whose deviant forms of self-expression appear to step beyond the limits of civilized social conduct are perfect candidates for demonization. Unsurprisingly then, Cohen (1985) notes that one of the most regularly repeated moral panics in Britain since the war has been associated with the emergence of various forms of youth culture. Yet collective panic about youth is nothing new. For as far back as one cares to look, crimes by juveniles have evoked lurid fantasies and acute fears (Pearson, 1983).

Nor is this tendency to dramatize youthful misconduct confined to the popular imagination and its regular consort the popular press. In 1925 Burt published his highly influential psychological treatise on 'The young delinquent'. The book opens with the following description: 'One sultry August afternoon, in a small and stuffy basement kitchen, not far from Kings Cross station, I was introduced to a sobbing little urchin with the quaint alliterative name of Jeremiah Jones. Jerry was a thief, a truant and a murderer' (p. 1). While acknowledging that this is his only case which has gone beyond 'mere threats and wild attacks' to involve murder, Burt none the less gives it considerable space as a typical example.

This preoccupation with the exotic and the extreme is even more pronounced in studies of group delinquency. Two years after Burt, Thrasher's classic study of 'The gang' appeared. In places the introduction reads more like a trailer for a Hollywood blockbuster than an academic treatise: 'Here are comedy and tragedy. Here is melodrama which excels the recurrent "thrillers" at the downtown theaters. Here are unvarnished emotions' (Thrasher, 1927, p. 3). As the topic is introduced in more detail the style become recognizably that of the Western: 'the feudal warfare of youthful gangs is carried on more or less continuously. Their disorder and violence, escaping the ordinary controls of the police and other social agencies of the community, are so pronounced as to give the impression that they are almost beyond the pale of civil society. In some respects these regions of conflict are like a frontier; in others like a "no-man's land", lawless, godless, wild' (1927, p. 3).

The language of recent texts may be more sober but they are equally packed with dramatic incident, whether it be joy-riding (Sherif & Sherif, 1964), gun duels (Short & Strodtbeck, 1965), or razor fights (Patrick, 1973). Even writers who explicitly challenge the idea that delinquency is a threat to 'civilized values' and who present it as resistance to oppressive institutions (e.g. Humphries, 1981; Willis, 1977) have been criticized for overly romanticizing both the actors and their actions (Cohen, 1985; McRobbie & Garber, 1976). Cohen in particular rejects any attempt to replace the image of delinquent as desperado with that of revolutionary hero. One can accept that delinquency arises out of a rejection of the social order without sharing in illusions about the level of challenge it represents for that order. Delinquent action is rarely creative, frequently self-destructive, mostly mundane and still a minority pastime among adolescents as a whole.

Of course, even if over-represented or occasionally distorted in the scientific literature, there is no denying that serious delinquencies do occur. Lest we be accused of missing the obvious, we readily acknowledge that young people do occasionally take part in serious crimes, including thefts of private property, violent attacks with deadly weapons on innocent victims, wild, reckless actions causing the deaths of bystanders, and even cold-blooded murder. It is the extreme and the exceptional that attracts public attention. It is also perhaps part of the business of the media to give public expression and legitimacy to the outrage and distress felt by the victims of these crimes. But it is the duty of the social scientist to put them in perspective. If one researches among the small minority of youths whose delinquencies have led to incarceration by the State, the extremes will be found with some regularity. However, the reader who is looking for spectacularly outrageous exploits or underworld heroes will not find them in this book.

This is a book about mundane delinquency. Though it is not simply a report of a research project, and it draws upon data collected by ourselves and others over a prolonged period, much of the original evidence for our argument was collected from a series of studies involving approximately 1,000 12–16-year-olds attending Dundee schools in the 1980s. The schools were all in the State sector and children from working class backgrounds were heavily represented in the samples. In one study several of the sample failed to answer a question as to whether teachers give preferential treatment to pupils with 'posh' accents on the grounds that there were no kids of this kind in the school. Our aim was to study ordinary young people. As will be shown, there was much evidence of delinquent behaviour. However, almost exclusively it consisted of relatively minor forms of misconduct: being rowdy, getting into scraps, writing names and slogans on walls with spray paint, smashing the windows of derelict buildings, stealing sweets from shops and so on.

Of some 5,000 delinquent acts described to us, the most extreme case came from a boy who had supposedly started a riot. On closer examination it became clear that he and a few friends had decided to see what would happen if they filled a milk bottle with petrol, stuffed a rag in the top and set it alight. This home-made 'Molotov Cocktail' was then thrown at a derelict and deserted garage door. The act was spotted and the boy was arrested. It was only because this had happened in 1981, in the midst of Britain's inner city disturbances, that the event became news and led to Dundee's inclusion on a map of British 'riot cities'. Once again, the drama is less to do with the qualities of the act itself than with the way in which it fits with a larger agenda.

It is important to stress, however, that even if individual acts are rather mundane it does not follow that the phenomenon is without interest. Indeed, we will argue that it is precisely the commonplace character of adolescent delinquency which makes it such a fascinating matter. Or, to be more specific, it is the fact that delinquency of this kind becomes an ordinary occurrence for a short period of life which broadens the significance of its study.

Early in adolescence, at around 11–12 years, the incidence of delinquent acts rises sharply. Later in adolescence, after about 16, there is a gradual decline. There are delinquents younger than 12 and it hardly needs saying there are criminals over the age of 16, but there is no other period of life in which such a substantial proportion of the age group is regularly involved in delinquent activities (Ageton & Elliot, 1978; Farrington, Biron & LeBlanc, 1982). What is it, therefore, about adolescence which makes it pre-eminently the criminal age? And what is it about delinquency which makes it so attractive in adolescence?

These twin questions run as central themes throughout this book. They are not, however, the only questions we address, for there is more to be explained than the age profile. While there are serious doubts about some of the statistics (Box, 1981), the balance of evidence indicates that boys are more likely to be involved in delinquency than girls, black youth more than white youth, working-class youth more than middle-class youth, and those resident in the inner cities more than those in the suburbs and small towns. In other words there is a strong social shape to the distribution of delinquent action.

In order to avoid misunderstanding, an aside is required at this juncture. There are those who contend that to point out the uneven social distribution of delinquency is to impugn the moral character of particular groups and classes. For instance, during the 1992 General Election campaign in Britain, the Prime Minister, John Major, asserted that those who attributed rising crime to rising poverty were casting a slur upon the poor. It is a conceptual sleight of hand to conflate an attack upon the circumstances that shape action and constitute group membership with an attack upon the character of those individuals trapped in these circumstances. As Sherif and Sherif (1964) observed of car theft, the fact that working-class adolescents are more often responsible than middle-class adolescents is less a testament to the shining character of middle-class youth than it is a reflection of the fact that they are more likely to possess cars of their own.

Though social categories differ in their propensity for crime there are still marked individual differences in delinquent activity within any social category one cares to consider. Even those authors who romanticize male working-class rebellion so as to make it seem almost natural have to concede that male working-class conformists lie equally thick upon the ground (cf. Jenkins, 1983). We have to address both the social contours and the individual variability of delinquent conduct. This is what we term the 'double character' of delinquency, and it is this character which constitutes such a challenge to the analyst. On the one hand, one must be able to explain the social determination of delinquency without being socially deterministic. On the other, one must be able to account for individual variability without succumbing to individualistic reductionism. What is required, then, is an account which specifies how broader social structural factors feed into the proximal process by which individual actions are produced. In other words, we require a social psychology of adolescent delinquency.

There is one further aspect of the phenomenon which buttresses the call for a social psychological approach. It is commonplace that observers impose their values upon those they observe. Hence, those who have regarded delinquency as shameful have tended to see it as something of which delinquents will be ashamed. Out of this, psychology has elaborated the myth of the 'secret sinner': individuals will break the rules when they are alone and unobserved and will then attempt to conceal all traces of their guilt. The reality, however, is very different. Delinquencies are generally committed in the company of selected others (Emler, Reicher & Ross, 1987; Erikson, 1971; Shapland, 1978). Offenders also go out of their way to communicate the details of their delinquent exploits when these others were not present to witness them (Reicher & Emler, 1986). Delinquency is normally a product of small group interaction; it is largely performed in groups, it is talked about in groups, and it is communicated to group members.

These observations are not in themselves inconsistent with all traditional psychologies of deviance. On the contrary, there is one perspective in particular with which they appear to be entirely compatible. As Brown (1988) has argued, the individualism of modern Western psychology is yoked to a distrust of all things collective. Groups are held to be bad influences. Individuals become submerged and anonymous within the group, and individual rationality is replaced with mass emotionality. This in turn generates negative, aggressive, socially destructive behaviour. Nowhere is this more clearly stated than in the work of Le Bon (1895). Crowds, he said, are only powerful for destruction. It is therefore hardly surprising that delinquency should be added to the long list of charges laid against the social group. Moreover, given that adolescence is widely represented as a period of crisis in which personal identity is in flux (Coleman, 1980; Erikson, 1968; Hall, 1904) it is equally unsurprising that this should be a period in which the individual is especially vulnerable to the malign influence of the group. The temporal pathology of adolescence combines with the generic pathology of the collective to produce an upsurge of anti-social behaviour.

Quite apart from the general discredit into which such negative views of the group have fallen (Brown 1988; Hogg & Abrams, 1988; Turner, 1991; Turner et al., 1987), this analysis has at least two inevitable flaws. In the first place, while delinquency may be a group activity, not all groups are delinquent. As we will show, in many cases the collective context considerably diminishes the likelihood of delinquent action. Therefore it is plainly untenable to assert that there is some general feature of group process which promotes deviance. Secondly, what seems to be important to group members is that they be known and identifiable to one another as the authors of delinquent acts. The emphasis given to the physical presence of others as either releasing deviance or submerging individual identity is misplaced. Rather we need to explain why certain adolescents go out of their way to be seen to be delinquent by their peers.

Such an explanation must begin with more precision about what is meant by delinquency. One response, what has been called the 'positivist' perspective, is that delinquency is an objective, self-evident category of conduct; common sense alone tells us what kinds of behaviour present a danger to orderly social existence. There is, however, another view: what we take to be common sense in this matter is a socially constructed product. According to this latter view, variously represented as societal reaction theory, labelling theory and 'the new criminology' (Archer, 1985), what we need to understand are the power relations within a society which cause one particular definition to prevail and allow it to be applied successfully to certain people and their actions. Thus Oplinger (1990) has argued that deviance is not a quality which inheres in particular acts, nor does any given action of itself define an individual as deviant. Rather, 'deviance is to be conceptualised as a social status that is determined by those in power. This status may be ascribed to individuals on the basis of being discovered engaging in an act that is threatening to the powerful' (Oplinger, 1990, pp. 24–5).

There are two important aspects of this argument. First, deviance can only be defined by reference to the moral codes that are propagated by particular social groups and enshrined in particular social institutions. In line with this we treat delinquency as the violation of those codes promoted by the institutions of which young people have experience. We are thus concerned with the regulations and laws applied to the conduct of young people in schools and other public places.

The second part of the argument is that deviance confers upon individuals the status of being outside of the relevant social order. Philips (1985) makes the point that this is not just a matter of defining moral boundaries so as to warn any waverers against transgression. It also legitimates certain reformatories and practices intended to resocialize errant individuals as 'true children', that is, to bring them back into the institutional fold.

However, such arguments risk becoming one-sided. If one presents institutions as constructing definitions and imposing them upon individuals so as to allow inclusion or force exclusion then the individuals themselves are liable to be seen as passive pawns, moved around a board by outside forces and according to external rules. It is appropriate to acknowledge the power and inertia of institutional forces, but it is equally important to recognize that people may also adapt, shape and seek to use for their own ends the definitions thrust upon them.

For delinquency as for other matters, meaning is always a two-way traffic. Labellees retain some form of negotiating power with labellers, however marked the power differentials may be. Hence if institutions can use delinquency to define individuals as 'insiders' or 'outsiders', so individuals can use delinquency to define their relationship to institutions. The more the school and the wider society succeed in making certain acts grounds for excluding young people and attributing bad character to them, the more young people can utilize such acts to signal their rejection of school or the social order which stands behind it and to parade their badness before teachers, police and peers.

Starting from this position, our argument has three main elements. First, the need for individuals to define how they relate to the institutional order only arises as they enter this order. The education systems of most Western societies involve rather different provision for children and adolescents. In Britain, children leave the more intimate and personal domain of the primary school to enter the more formal world of secondary education at 11 or 12. Consent and obedience begin to shift away from attachments to individual teachers and towards acceptance of an implicit institutional contract: 'give up your time and freedom, defer to the regulations of the school and you will be equipped with the skills to make something of yourself in the world'. Knowing how to respond to this, whether to give consent, whether to accept direction, whether to invest effort in assigned tasks therefore depends upon acknowledging the validity of this contract. Hence it is essential for the young adolescent to define his or her relationship to the institutional order.

Second, commission of, or abstention from, delinquent action is the principal means by which adolescents lay claim to oppositional or conformist identities. Delinquency is a form of self-presentation though which young people manage their public reputations. This applies in a double sense. It is not only that delinquency confers a reputation as antagonistic to school or law-abiding society. It also provides a reputation to deal with the consequences of such a position. If one rejects school rules, teachers, laws and the police, one can no longer rely upon them for protection. Hence to be delinquent is also a means of communicating a dangerous identity: 'I am hard and violent; don't mess with me.'

If delinquency is reputation management, the same is true of its absence. In choosing not to offend, adolescents signal their allegiance to social institutions and also show themselves as worthy of the support and protection of its functionaries. It may be true that conformity attracts little attention while non-conformity occupies the limelight as soon as it is seen to become a social problem. However, this should not obscure the fact that psychologically the absence of delinquent action is every bit as interesting as its presence. To avoid or turn away from opportunities to fight, vandalize or thieve is as saturated with social meaning and communicative intent as it is to participate. Consequently it is as important to ask why some young people are not delinquent as to inquire why others are. We shall argue, however, that these different choices of identity contain different problems of expression.

The third and final aspect of our analysis has to do with the importance of social groups in the construction of delinquent and non-delinquent reputations. It would be very difficult for any single person, let alone an 11- or 12-year-old, to work out by him or herself the character of his or her institutional world. Such understandings are more likely to be cultural and to be conveyed through social relationships. The ideological models which determine the identities that individuals assume and the reputations that they seek are derived from their collective involvements.

To suggest that individuals define their position by constructing reputations is to imply that collective support is important in another respect. Reputation is an inherently social phenomenon. It concerns the way in which individuals are appraised by others. For a person to assume a particular identity, that identity must be confirmed and validated by others. It is difficult to see oneself as, for example, defiant of authority if others are unwilling to concede that one has ever significantly defied authority. It is even harder to see oneself as conforming if others see one as a trouble-maker. Self-definition, we shall argue, depends on the reputations an individual is able to negotiate with significant audiences.

There is one further way in which the group is important, especially for those who pursue an oppositional identity. It is difficult to sustain any position, let alone one that is deviant, in the face of united and unanimous opposition. The tacit approval of at least some others is indispensable to the maintenance of a deviant line of action. And the more deviant or delinquent the activities are, the more crucial is the support provided by willing co-conspirators. Thus the reputations young people are able to sustain depend in no small measure upon acceptance into a group of like-minded peers. Consequently, whether we are talking about the ideological basis for identity, the validation of identity or the practical expression of identity, the peer group is indispensable.

Putting it all together, we seek to show in this book how defining one's place in society is a central task of adolescence, how this task involves the negotiation of reputations, and how the conceptual as well as practical support which enables individuals to define a social position for themselves comes from the set of social relationships in which they are embedded. What is more, it is in specifying how the individual–society relationship is mediated by the processes in face-to-face groups that we will explain how delinquent action displays social form, how it retains individual variation and how it cannot be reduced to either.

The remainder of the book is structured as follows. Chapter 2 shows how many contemporary approaches to adolescence and to delinquency are rooted in foundations provided by nineteenth-century mass society theory. This body of theory equated threats to the prevailing social order with a breakdown in any form of social order. Two things flow from this. First, the social life of subordinate groups is portrayed as at best a series of transitory and superficial bonds. Second, any challenges to dominant mores are dismissed as consequences of this fragmented pattern of social life, as symptoms of moral decay within subordinate groups. Hence, delinquency becomes a form of pathology to which those in the biologically vulnerable phase of adolescence are particularly prone.

Chapter 3 examines some of the major psychological and sociological perspectives on conformity and deviance in more detail. The aim is not to review the huge literature that has accumulated in this area. Rather we seek to show how, despite their obvious differences, such diverse approaches as bio-genetic theory, psychoanalytic theory and cognitive developmental theory share some underlying similarities. In effect they are linked by the assumptions of mass society theory. In this chapter we also explore theories of adolescence and consider why adolescence is characterized in these theories as a period of life in which the individual is particularly inclined towards crime. Two kinds of explanation emerge. One interprets adolescence as a period of emotional uncertainty for individuals trying to redefine their roles and identities as they sever childhood attachments. The other represents adolescence as a period in which the autonomy of the personality has still to be achieved.

Chapter 4 outlines what is indicated about delinquency from research evidence. After considering various strategies of research and their impli-cations, we illustrate what we have called delinquency's 'dual character': the incidence of delinquency varies systematically across different social categories but at the same time there are clear individual differences within socially and demographically homogeneous categories. These patterns pose a challenge to which no theory has yet risen with complete success. The problem, we shall argue, resides in the common model of society which still in some degree underpins them all.

Chapter 5 provides a reappraisal of this model. We show that, far from living either as social isolates on the margins of society or as isolated individuals in an atomized society, adolescents inhabit social environments in which they are chronically identifiable. It is because this is the normal condition of life that reputations assume importance. We examine a range of alternatives to the proposition that conduct is sensitive to considerations of reputation and show why none is entirely satisfactory. We conclude with a consideration of the requirements of reputation management and the conditions that shape the reputations young people are able to negotiate with those around them.

Chapter 6 goes on to relate reputation management to the ways in which adolescents adapt to the institutional order. We consider why it is important for young people to define their relationship to parochial and societal institutions during this period and why some might define themselves as 'oppositional' while others define themselves as 'conformist'.

Chapter 7 considers the centrality of the social group to the process of self-definition and reputation management. We show the importance of social support in the everyday lives of adolescents, the clear division between delinquent and non-delinquent groups and the importance of adhering to the group position on delinquency in order to ensure continued acceptance in the group. Thus reputation management is as important as a means of regulating the micro-social world of adolescents as it is in their relationship to the macro-social world.

In chapter 8, we set the same criteria for our approach as we earlier set for others: to what extent does it allow us to make sense of the observed empirical pattern of delinquent action. We argue that this approach does provide distinctive explanations for the gender, class, racial and residential patterns as well as for individual variability in behaviour. We conclude with a consideration of the wider implications of the foregoing analysis for our understanding of social order and social control.

2

The Historical Context of
Delinquency Research

2.1 Introduction

Our excuse for a chapter on history is simple: the past explains the shape of the present. Present explanations of crime and delinquency all have a history: they evolved from earlier explanations. If one is to explore an intellectual territory one really ought to be acquainted with the routes taken by previous expeditions. And it is helpful to appreciate why ideas were eventually discounted and abandoned. What justifies our attention to the evolution of ideas, however, is not just that there is some economy in knowing where we have been, theoretically speaking, so that we can avoid unnecessarily retracing earlier footsteps. These reasons are important enough in themselves to justify an historical excursion but there are other, perhaps even more important reasons in the case of juvenile crime.

Quite a lot of theoretical baggage has survived the journey to the present without passing through the rigorous procedures that scientific method supposedly supplies to police the frontiers of knowledge. Much of the baggage dates from the turn of the century and some from a great deal earlier. Among the items it contains is an analysis of civilization and modern society, and the dangers they supposedly face. It is an analysis which continues to exert an influence on theorizing about juvenile crime out of all proportion to its correspondence with the facts.

The analysis to which we are referring here is familiarly known in the social sciences as the 'mass society thesis', by virtue of what it takes to be the key feature of society in modern times. Its claims have been widely discredited and in most areas of the social sciences it is no longer regarded as a plausible model of society or social relations. The study of criminal and anti-social behaviour has been almost alone in proceeding as if its central claims and assumptions still held good. In this chapter we will examine those claims and the agenda for theory and research to which they gave rise. We shall argue that part of its continuing attraction is its resonance with more long-standing social anxieties about youth and the survival of social order.

The reader familiar with arguments about crime and deviance developed within sociology over the last 30 years might protest that we are not breaking any new ground here. The ideas developed by Erikson (1962), Kituse (1962), Becker (1963) and many others are, after all, hardly faithful reflections of the mass society thesis or its particular interpretation of the threats to social order. But – and we shall argue this point in more detail in chapter 5 – neither do these ideas represent a complete emancipation from the legacy of this thesis.

2.2 Threats to Civilization

The period from 1890 to 1920 was one of unparalleled innovation in social theory. Three of its greatest exponents, Freud (1856–1939), Durkheim (1858–1914), and Weber (1864–1922), were at the height of their creative powers and their intellectual attentions were focused upon the same central questions: could civilization survive the changes which had been transforming the economies of Europe for the previous hundred years.

The fears were for a particular form of civilization which had evolved in European society from the seventeenth century – what had become known as the Enlightenment – a progressive and rational emancipation from superstition, ignorance and human misery guided and supported by the equally rational and triumphant forward march of science, a humanitarian, intellectually sophisticated civilization which enjoined respect for the individual, tolerance of individuality and due regard for individual rights. What seemed to put this progressive civilization at risk was the accelerating process of mass urbanization. The problems to which this gave rise were seen to expose civilization to the destructive forces in human nature.

2.2.1 The loss of community

Through the eighteenth century in Great Britain and subsequently in continental Europe, there was a dramatic shift in economy, popularly described as the industrial revolution. Technological innovations transformed manufacturing processes. Coal-fired steam engines multiplied productive capacity to the point where economies of scale forced cottage industries to give way to the factory system. The consequence was that people too had to leave their cottages and move nearer to the factories. A shift in settlement pattern which had begun in Britain with the land enclosure movement was accelerated by the logic of industrialization; populations concentrated as never before in rapidly mushrooming urban centres.

For scholars like Tonnies (1887) the most significant consequence of this movement and concentration of people was, in Wellman's (1979) apt phrase, 'the loss of community'. The economy of feudalism in Europe had been associated with a much closer mingling of the lives of persons from different levels of society. At the same time the poorest members of society, those who did the manual work, were geographically dispersed. Typically they lived in small-scale communities in which everyone knew everyone else, in which all transactions were between relatives, neighbours or other acquaintances, and in which individuals were bound to one another by ties of loyalty based on kinship or marriage.

Some writers were prone to romanticize the pre-industrial community, representing it as a natural rhythm of life, allowing a proper attachment to place, meaningful labour and enduring, satisfying emotional ties. For others, its principal significance was that the social relations in a community supported the social control of individual conduct. Thus Durkheim (1893) was to argue that the solidarity of communities took a particular form. He called it 'mechanical', by which he meant that similarities were emphasized – similarities in beliefs, manners, values and behaviour – and all deviance was ruthlessly condemned and punished. The proper standards were defined and promulgated by religious authorities who, in medieval Europe, wielded a degree of power that is virtually incomprehensible today. Absolute conformity could be enforced because every detail of a person's conduct was subject to constant scrutiny by neighbours and acquaintances who were quick to envy, and primed to resent any display of difference. But finally, firm control of the populace could be maintained because their lives were directly supervised by their social, and it was assumed moral, superiors. Parishioners dwelt directly under the eyes of their priest, as did servants under masters and peasants under landlords.

The new industrial cities seemed to be the opposite of rural communities and small towns in every respect, not just economically but also politically, socially and morally. Throughout history cities have been reckoned sinful places, the breeding ground of vices and wickedness, the natural habitat of confidence tricksters, alcoholics, gamblers and prostitutes. The stereotype which country folk the world over hold of city dwellers almost universally stresses the venality, guile and deviousness of the latter (Levine & Campbell, 1973). These were qualities that the special conditions of social life in the city were presumed to produce, namely that people deal with one another impersonally, as strangers. Exchanges were, in the words of Wirth (1938), 'transitory, segmented, formal and impersonal'. But mass urbanization had made matters much worse; it had exaggerated the anonymous and isolating character of city life, and introduced into it vast numbers of peasants used to the very different ways of the village or hamlet.

Steadman Jones (1981) argues that, at the beginning of the nineteenth century, masters and workers tended to be united in opposition to those who made their money through political privilege. However, by the mid-century 'class' had gained its modern meaning: those who sold their labour considered their natural adversaries to be the owners of capital. Steadman Jones shows that the division was social as well as political. At the beginning of the period the pattern of day-to-day life brought people at different economic levels of society continually into close proximity. Even in the city, master and artisan would generally live under the same roof. By the mid-century this had changed. The combined effects of coal-fired industries and prevailing westerly winds meant that those who could afford to do so monopolized the more desirable residential areas up-wind of the filth and pollution pouring out of factory chimneys. In other words, the industrial revolution also produced a physical segregation of economic classes.

These two changes combined to cause considerable concern to the ruling strata. Not only were they faced by a potentially powerful enemy, but this enemy was no longer under their supervision, let alone their control.

Occasionally social commentators would make forays into working-class areas, but these only served to highlight the mysterious and shadowy nature of working-class existence. Clarence Rook, a journalist on the *Daily Chronicle*, talks of his trips to meet a working-class boy in the following terms:

> I was in a sense a pilgrim. Good Americans, when they come to London, may be seen peering in Bolt Court and eating their dinner at the Cheddar Cheese. I was bound on an expedition to the haunts of a more recent

celebrity than Dr. Johnson. My destination was the Irish Court and the Lamb and Flag. (Rook, 1899, repr. 1979, p. 1)

It is necessary to add a third detail to this picture. It was not just that the existence of a working class separated off from bourgeois eyes constituted a potential threat to the existing hierarchy. That threat was made real in collective working-class action. This was a period in which trades unions were legalized and grew in membership. It was also a period in which political organizations of socialists and anarchists came into existence. The result was seen both in a rising tide of strikes and in political demonstrations. These were viewed with special alarm by the bourgeoisie. For months prior to the first May Day demonstration in France there was speculation as to whether this would mark the moment of revolution.

Throughout Western Europe, then, there was a perceived crisis. For some, particularly those who romanticized rural communities, the roots of the crisis lay in the direction that industrial civilization was taking, producing squalid living conditions, alienating conditions of work, and a degenerating impoverishment of the human spirit. Matters could only be improved by tearing down the 'dark satanic mills', dismantling the mass and returning to nature. One finds this view expressed by social theorists like William Morris and by aesthetic movements such as the Pre-Raphaelities. It is perfectly captured in Blake's 'Prologue to the Wanderers':

> Forget six counties overhung with smoke,
> Forget the snorting steam and piston stroke,
> Forget the spreading of the hideous town,
> Think rather of the pack-horse on the down,
> And dream of London, small and white and clean,
> The clear Thames bordered by its gardens green.

The response which won the day theoretically speaking, however, was less inclined to romanticize the pre-industrial era. It accepted that the cities were here to stay, but treated the crisis as primarily one of social control. The old social ties which bound subordinates in their place had been disrupted, and the subordinates threatened to get out of hand. This was the paramount social reality in which modern social theory was formed. It was popularly supposed, and certainly accepted by Durkheim and his contemporaries, that the new urban working class, physically separated by the structure of industrial cities from the moral leadership of the ruling class and lacking the restraint of constant supervision, would be out of control. There would be nothing to restrain them from riot and crime. Contained in this conclusion is an assumption so important to what followed in psychology that it needs to be set out quite explicitly: people will break the law and commit crimes when conditions render them anonymous.

There are echoes in this conclusion of two key ideas familiar to nineteenth-century scholars. One is the idea of a state of nature prior to the state of society, in which humans had been presumed to live a solitary and barbarous existence before they saw the advantage of coming together and submitting to a common authority. In other words, certain natural forms of behaviour are intrinsically destructive and the social contract was an arrangement between people to regulate these behaviours.

The other is the assumption that human nature is inherently self-serving: people are disposed by their make-up to be selfish and pleasure-seeking. Once Darwin had persuaded the intellectual community that *Homo sapiens* was another animal species it seemed entirely reasonable to conclude that, barring the intervention of civilization, humans would behave like animals. If religion asserted they were born as sinners, evolution seemed to suggest they were born to fight and to copulate, both socially destructive proclivities if uncontrolled.

In making sense of the social thought of this period, however, it is important to understand the Englightenment views which intervened between religious and Darwinian notions of human nature. Beccaria (1738–94) and Bentham (1748–1832) had prompted significant judicial reforms with their secular interpretation of humans as rational beings endowed with freedom of choice. Explaining crime was no problem for this theory: if people break the law it is because they have made a free and rational choice based on the perception that this has greater utility for them than not breaking the law. Prevention of crime was therefore a matter of revising the law and organizing its enforcement to ensure that individuals would more often make the opposite choice. This could be achieved by ensuring that punishment was certain, prompt and rationally graded according to the severity of the offence.

Classical theory urged attention to sins and not sinners. Beccaria and Bentham argued that individuals are all the same, all endowed with free will and reason. This being so, crimes cannot be explained in terms of the peculiarities of the people who commit them, but only in terms of the circumstances which made each crime a rational choice at the moment it was committed. This is essentially the plot logic of a certain genre of crime fiction: Inspector Bentham solves the murder by deducing the rational considerations which led one member of the cast of suspects to commit it. The assumption is always that the culprit is like everyone else, differing only in that the circumstantial web of relations in which he or she is embedded leads logically to murder.

Although the classical view appeared to provide a straightforward explanation for the criminogenic character of city life, in the event it proved unsatisfactory in social theory, if not murder fiction, for a variety of reasons. One was the general scientific assault on notions of free will and rational choice, led by Freud, Durkheim, Le Bon and others. Another was the pessimistic prognosis for modern society offered by the classical view. It recommended the social control of crime but modern social conditions seemed to rule this out. On the other hand, those same social conditions seemed to produce rather less crime than the classical view required. The inhabitants of cities were neither permanently running riot nor universally involved in crime. In other words, not all urban inhabitants were pursuing self-interest even when this appeared to be the rational thing to do. The inevitable conclusion, and certainly the one to which Freud and others came, was that behaviour is not under rational control.

Over a century earlier, social and political philosophers had foreseen that changing social conditions would necessitate a shift from social control to self-control (cf. Adam Smith, *The Wealth of Nations*, 1776). Smith had argued that self-control would require the moral socialization of the populace, and this in turn implied the dissemination of improved methods of child-rearing. The model for such methods, of course, was to be found in the families of the ruling class. The fact that, by the late nineteenth century, social life in the cities had not broken down entirely seemed to confirm that such methods had been made to work for a wider segment of the population. Psychologists could then set to work explaining how these methods produce their effects while criminologists and others could link crime and civil disorder to local failures of the socialization process.

In the next chapter we will examine theories of socialization and the role of socialization failure in the production of crime. Before that we will look in a little more detail at the political agenda behind the mass society thesis and at the emergence of adolescence as a special category of problem for social order.

2.2.2 *The great disappearing trick*

When one tries to measure mass society theory against the phenomena it seeks to explain, the most significant feature is not what is present so much as what is missing. What most disturbed the intellectual establishment of the day was the mounting challenge of the working class to bourgeois social control. In other words, the issue was conflict between groups with fundamentally different interests. However, look where you will in mass society theory, you will not find any discussion of the role of the ruling class in that conflict. Examine accounts of increasing lawlessness and you will read only of the internal organization of the masses. Even in studies of direct confrontations in which crowds of workers clashed with the owners, the police or even the army, the theory is written as if crowds were acting in a vacuum (cf. Reicher, 1987; Reicher & Potter, 1985). In other words, working-class action has been abstracted from its social context.

We have argued elsewhere (Reicher, 1987) that this act of decontextualization has several political consequences. It means that the role of the ruling strata in the generation of social conflict cannot be questioned. It also means that the reasons for working-class dissent cannot be understood. Finally, if disturbance is internal to the masses, it allows for outside intervention – either repressive or paternalistic – as a solution. Given the power of this ideological cocktail, the appeal of such views to bourgeois scholars, to the institutions in which they work and to the organizations through which their work is disseminated, is understandable. However, our concern here is not so much with this political dimension as with the consequences of decontextualization for the nature of theory.

We can best approach this issue with an analogy. Imagine, for instance, filming two people in the midst of an argument and then removing all trace of one of the protagonists from the final product. If an observer were subsequently to try and explain events which had been edited in this way, three things would follow. The first is that acts could no longer be understood as arising out of the relations between people; they could only be explained as a property of the one remaining individual. This is precisely what has happened with the core premise of mass society theory: communities have given way to aggregations of anonymous individuals. The notion of anonymity is, in fact, an inherently relational concept. That is, it does not make much sense to say that someone is anonymous. The real issue is: to whom is he or she anonymous? Now, we have already seen that the concern of the bourgeoisie was that the working class had become unknown to them. Working-class areas had become like a foreign land (Rook, 1899, for instance, notes of his foray into the Lambeth Walk that 'there was not a well-dressed person to be seen, scarcely a passably clean one'). Yet, for mass society theory, this has become an assertion that anonymity is an inherent quality of the mass. This clearly does not follow. To say that two groups are anonymous with respect to each other does not mean that group members are also strangers among themselves. Indeed one of our major arguments will be that this image of social life provided by mass society theory is highly misleading.

The second consequence of decontextualization concerns the attempt to make sense of behaviour. Returning to our example of the argument, the observer would see the isolated protagonist suddenly gesticulating and then becoming calm, showing anger and then perhaps laughter. In the context of the argument in which these actions occurred, they would be perfectly coherent, communicative acts. But remove the other, obscure the communicational dimension of action, and it loses all sense. So it is in mass society theory. People do not break laws because they might have something to say about standards of legality any more than they demonstrate because there are matters about which they wish to protest. Their behaviour is simply the blind consequence of internal forces.

This takes us to the third point. If behaviour is both a reflection of internal qualities and lacks any sense then it must reflect internal pathology. Our lone actor's shouts and cries have become ravings and the diagnosis is madness. The same is true of mass society theory except that, right from the beginning, there was some dispute about the level on which the pathology operated. Thus, in the first debate on crowd psychology, between Gabriel Tarde and Scipio Sighele, the issue under consideration was the nature of criminal responsibility in mass disorders. Could anyone get swept up in mass hysteria such that none could be held responsible or was it that only criminal deviants would be prepared to go along with the crowd (cf. Barrows, 1981; Reicher, forthcoming)? To put it more crudely, are we dealing with mob madness or with individual immorality?

In fact, despite the fervour with which the debate was conducted, in the end it fizzled out as those involved reached an unacknowledged compromise. They converged on the position that those of weak character are particularly liable to succumb to group pressure. Either aspect, individual character or group influence, may be emphasized, therefore, but there is no inherent contradiction between them.

We can summarize these various effects by saying that mass society theory turned social disturbance into evidence of psychological disturbance. However, it is not only in its general relevance to delinquency that the theory is of interest to us. It also has something specific to say about the nature of adolescence.

2.3 Mass Society and the Danger of Youth

It is not surprising that mass society theory, given its preoccupation with the maintenance of social stability, should be concerned with youth. If a society is to survive from one generation to the next, it is necessary that children grow into adults who accept and fit into established patterns of social relationships. The transition to adulthood always heralds the possibility of disruption. Consequently, while on the one hand youth may stand as a metaphor for renovation and progress, on the other it contains a constant possibility of turmoil and social crisis.

Pearson (1983) provides a delightful illustration of this in his 'history of respectable fears'. Starting in the 1980s he shows how present panics about youthful disruption are contrasted with nostalgia for the previous generation when Teddy boys may have been exuberant but posed no fundamental threat. He then goes back to contemporary accounts of the 'Teds' which in turn saw them as a cause for profound concern as against the golden age of the 1930s. And so the account proceeds backwards, revealing a pattern in which the youth of each period are set against those of the previous age in a contrast between danger and familiarity. In other words, once social reproduction has been successful, past generations of youth can be read in the light of that success; the Teds can be viewed fondly for their assertions of patriotism and love of the monarchy. With contemporary youth, however, things remain in the balance and the task of ensuring a desirable outcome leaves no room for sentiment.

Indeed, the troublesome nature of youth seems to have been a perennial preoccupation from the dawn of civilization. Aristotle, for instance, characterizes young people as 'in character prone to desire and ready to carry any desire they may have formed into action . . . they are passionate, irascible and apt to be carried away by their impulses . . . they regard themselves as omniscient and are positive in their assertions; this is, in fact, the reason of their carrying everything too far' (quoted in Conger & Petersen, 1984, p. 4).

Yet it is too easy to be blinded by superficial similarities of tone to profound differences in the way the problem of 'youth' has been conceptualized over time. For, if the concern with youth reflects a generalized anxiety about social reproduction, then the focus of that concern will be reflected in the precise nature of the transition to adulthood. Thus, various writers point to the emergence of a modern concept of adolescence in Western societies only during the second half of the nineteenth century and coinciding with the progressively extended character of the transition from child to adult status (Baumeister & Tice, 1986; Demos & Demos, 1969; Gillis, 1974; Kett, 1977).

Baumeister and Tice (1986) argue that among the supposed attributes of the individual in this newly identified phase in the life-cycle were awkwardness, indecisiveness and vulnerability. Young people came to be seen as in need of constant supervision by adults even in leisure activities, and so there emerged such adult-sponsored institutions as the Boy Scouts, the YMCA, the Boys Brigades and so on. To understand the full force of the reforming zeal which demanded that adolescents be constantly monitored, supervised and involved in 'improving activities', it is necessary to look at the place of youth within the fears which generated mass society theories. If it was true, in general terms, that 'the rootless mass' was prone to criminality and riot, it remained the case that degrees of rootlessness could be envisaged. The more marginal the individual, the greater the possibility of succumbing to the mass. Not surprisingly then, groups whose social incorporation was incomplete were likely to be a particular focus of anxiety.

In this context, an emerging concern over the identity choices which adolescents might make, if not suitably guided, became linked to the struggle to defend bourgeois values. Childhood, being an age of uncertainty, was a dangerous age and children had long been regarded as key members of the 'dangerous classes'. As Chevalier (1973) shows in his study of the urbanization of Paris, children were virtually equated with criminality. Hugo, for instance, talks of the Paris urchin as aged seven to thirteen and living in gangs. As the popular saying went, 'gangs of children, gangs of thieves'. But children were more than just a threat to bourgeois property, they stood at the forefront of a more general assault on the social order. Thus Chevalier quotes the reminiscences of Canler, a former Prefect of Police, on the insurrection of 1832: 'everyone knows the race of Paris urchins, who have always raised the cry of sedition in our meetings, carried the first paving stone to the barricade in our riots and fired the first shot' (p. 116). Or again, Tocqueville, describing the days of February 1848: 'it is the Paris urchins who usually start insurrection and they usually do so merrily, like schoolboys on holiday' (quoted in Chevalier, 1973, p. 116).

The threat to public order posed by children might be contained by adequate parental supervision, but youth seemed to present a different order of problem for which different remedies would be required. Consequently the theme of youth was to the fore in discussing the dangers of the urban mass. Considerable concern was voiced at what happens to young people when, in the words of Morrison, writing in the 1890s, 'the restraining eye of the village community is no longer upon them . . . (and

they belong) to no social circle in which their conduct is either scru-
tinized or observed' (quoted in Humphries, 1981, p. 8). The fear was
that unless new forms of social control were imposed, young people
would reject conventional norms, reject traditional authority and be
influenced by 'subversive' ideologies. In France Durkheim (1925/1961)
regarded universal state education as the most promising means to
counter these centrifugal forces. Similar hopes had been expressed in
the British context, though with much less conceptual subtlety and
still with some confidence, that religious authority could be reasserted.
Corrigan (1979) illustrates the point by quoting from a *Times* leader of
1854:

> While we are disputing which ought to be considered the most beneficial
> system of education, we leave the great mass of the people to be influenced
> and formed by the very worst possible teachers. Certain teachers, indeed,
> could be called instructors for evil. . . . In the very heart of the apparently
> well-ordered community enough evil teaching was going on to startle, if
> not alarm, the most firm minded. Systems the most destructive of the
> peace, the happiness and the virtue of society, are boldly, perseveringly,
> and without let or hindrance, openly taught and recommended to the
> acceptance of people with great zeal, if not with great ability. Cheap
> publications containing the wildest and the most anarchical doctrines
> are scattered, broadcast over the land, in which religion and morality
> are perverted and scoffed at, and every rule of conduct which experience
> has sanctioned, and on which the very existence of society depends, openly
> assailed. While in their place are sought to be established doctrines as
> outrageous as the maddest ravings of furious insanity – as wicked as
> the most devilish spirit could possibly have devised. . . . Only in one way
> could this great danger, this great evil be counteracted. The religious sects
> must bury their differences. Let the prudent spirit of conciliation enable
> the wise and the good to offer to the people a beneficial education in the
> place of this abominable teacher. (pp. 32–3)

Corrigan goes on to argue that the birth of mass state education was
directly tied to these fears of insurrection, and that it had four distinct
aims. These were: to provide bourgeois 'fact' which would counter
revolutionary ideas and those resulting from working-class experience;
to provide a bourgeois moral and religious code; to create a disciplined
and punctual workforce; finally to construct a hierarchy of civilization,
legitimated by all, through which the working classes would accept their
place at the bottom. As Kay-Shuttleworth put it rather more directly in
1868, education should promote 'the diffusion of that knowledge among
the working classes which tends beyond anything else to promote the

security of property and promote the maintenance of public order' (quoted in Corrigan, 1979, p. 36).

However, if the internal threat was not motive enough, there was also an external threat. The final years of the nineteenth century were marked by the rise of European imperialism and an associated increase in rivalry between the imperial powers. In Britain, for instance, the spectre of German domination cast an ominously growing shadow. This gave rise to an additional fear concerning the nation's youth, namely that their indiscipline and their physical and psychological deterioration would mean British imperial demise. Thus Sims, another writer of the 1890s, talked of the child as the vital factor in the future of the British Empire, and held out the prospect that, without deliberate effort at improvement, race suicide would result (Humphries, 1981). The remedy lay in an improved schooling system which therefore became a vital bulwark against domestic subversion and international competition.

Of course, if such a project were to be successful, it could not be presented overtly as an act of ideological domination. Therefore, rather than characterizing education as imposing middle-class values, it was sold as a generalized improving influence. Young people were supposedly deprived as a consequence of a brutalizing background, deficient cultures and inadequate homes. Schooling therefore served to bring higher standards and the possibility of advancement (Dale & Esland, 1977; Humphries, 1981). Thus the liberal ideology of education depended upon the idea that youth was at risk, vulnerable and in need of constant and careful adult supervision.

All this is highly reminiscent of the treatment of social unrest. The difference is that crowds and criminality were the overt behavioural evidence that control had broken down while youth were a social category who had the potential of getting out of control. Thus the reaction was not so much to pathologize youth as to portray them as in a period of crisis, a reaction which justified the paternalistic intervention of state agencies into young people's lives. The argument was that without such intervention the crisis might well result in pathology.

Despite this difference, in its fundamentals mass society theory approaches deviance and adolescence in much the same way. In both cases, an issue of class control is obscured by talking of a general social problem. Here, a concern about the reproduction of class relations has been transformed into a concern about the condition of youth. Therefore the possibility that behaviour might have something to do with the reluctance of working-class youth to be socialized into bourgeois norms is not even countenanced.

All that was needed in order to complete the trick was an explanation of just why youthful development should result in an inevitable period of crisis, of vulnerability and of danger to the self. In the next chapter we will show that theories of adolescence have indeed taken this to be the fundamental question.

2.4 Conclusions

We have now examined how the mass society thesis deals with both deviance and adolescence. In the first case dissent is turned into the pathology of the mass. In the second a potential break in the reproduction of class authority is turned into a generic problem of adolescent adjustment. The power of the thesis flows from a particular view of the nature of the subject. Just as the key political question of the mass society analysis is to separate behaviour from context, so the key conceptual step is to separate the individual and social domains. However, to argue that individuality is devoid of social context is not to deny that the operation of this personal construct may be affected by social conditions. Indeed all that remains to be decided is precisely what these effects might be.

3

Deviance, Socialization and the 'Crisis' of Adolescence

3.1 Introduction

In this chapter we will consider some theoretical accounts of deviance. We will then turn to look at the literature on adolescence with a particular view to understanding why this should be seen as the delinquent age. In neither case is our aim to be comprehensive. Thorough reviews have been published elsewhere of both areas (for delinquency, see Box, 1981; Empey, 1982; Feldman, 1977; Rutter & Giller, 1983; for adolescence, see Brake, 1985, and Coleman, 1980). In addition we do not intend to describe all the intricacies of the various theories nor will we examine the evidence upon which these theories are based. Rather our aim is to give some flavour of the range of influential theoretical positions and, above all, to examine the premises upon which these approaches are based.

In the case of the deviance, our argument is that most theories continue to reflect the key assumptions of mass society theory. In brief, we propose that, however diverse the deviance literature, it agrees on one thing: since modern industrial society has destroyed the bases of external control then adherence to the social order depends upon the development of internal controls. Conversely, deviance must be related to the nature of these controls. Of course, different theorists have looked at the relationship between deviance and internal controls in very different ways.

In very broad terms, psychologists have tried to specify the nature of the intra-psychic structures which ensure control. Sociologists, on the other hand, have looked to the social factors affecting the internalization of control. However, between them, the two disciplines tend to rip the social fabric apart – either looking inside the head or to broad social conditions. What is largely absent is any focus on the way in which the immediate social relations within which delinquent acts are committed shape individual actions.

In the case of the adolescence literature, we argue that theorists tend to see the teenage years as a period of transition between childhood and adulthood in which internal controls are inadequate to cope with the external demands placed upon the individual. As a result, individuals are particularly vulnerable to delinquent suggestions. Again, psychology and sociology tend to look at the picture from different sides with the former examining the bases of intra-psychic weakness and the latter looking to the origins of excessive social demands. None the less, for both, the picture frame excludes much the same things as deviance theories.

3.2 Psychology and Deviance

3.2.1 Models of biological determinism from Galton to Eysenck

The simplest way to explain differences in human capacities is by invoking biology. Some people are simply born with more developed 'moral' capabilities (or else the capability to acquire them). One can trace the derivation of this idea in psychology from Darwin's theory of evolution through Galton's contention that individuals inherit different degrees of intellectual giftedness. The translation of this from assertion to scientific finding was facilitated by Binet's development of a means for measuring intellectual differences.

Although it was no part of Binet's own intention, his scales were used to 'prove' that intelligence was a biologically fixed quantity. If scale scores could be related to criminality, it could then be asserted that the propensity to crime stems from being born with a deficient intellect. Goddard (1914) first took this step in the United States and he was shortly followed by Burt in Britain (Burt, 1925). If, today, crude concepts of inheritance have been replaced by the more sophisticated terminology of genes and chromosomes the idea remains essentially the same: criminals differ from other people because of something that they acquired at conception and not because of any influence of the environment in which they grew up or now function. Moreover, their difference or peculiarity is ineradicable; it is built into their bodies as unalterably as eye colour or stature.

In fact, early hypotheses did actually link criminal behaviour to stature as an inherited characteristic as well as to innate intellectual inferiority. To post-Darwinian Victorians, it might have seemed natural that intellectual, physical and moral degeneracy would go together. From there, it was easy to explain the resistance of indigenous peoples to the colonial enterprise as representing the greater criminality of primitive 'races' (Lombroso, 1912). The subsequent genocidal history of such crude notions of biological degeneracy has been well documented (e.g. Muller-Hill, 1988) and goes a long way to explaining their demise. This is not to say genetic explanations of criminality have disappeared but rather that more recent incarnations do not use them to the exclusion of all else.

Most modern biological theories argue in one way or another that genetic make-up affects the way in which we deal with environmental events. Thus Mednick and Christiansen (1977) suggest that genetically influenced chemical imbalances in the brain can incline people to react aggressively to circumstances which cause only mild annoyance in others. Others (Schalling, 1978; Trasler, 1978) argue that there are genetically determined sensitivities to socializing events that may, in turn, affect later propensities to crime. However, perhaps the best known and most widely researched example of such theories is Eysenck's (1964) theory of crime and personality.

Eysenck's theory, an unusual blend of genetic and learning theories, is based upon three key ideas. First, anti-social impulses are restrained by conditioned anxiety. Second, this conditioning occurs over the course of childhood. Third, the process of conditioning is under the control of genetically determined characteristics. These are cortical arousal and reactivity of the autonomic nervous system. Criminal dispositions arise either because the individual is biologically incapable of acquiring conditioned responses or because the environment (normally meaning the parents) provide the wrong conditioning experience. If Eysenck (1964, 1970) mentions both possibilities his focus is on the former. Delinquency is largely explained in terms of the genetically determined personality traits of extraversion and neuroticism. In contrast, conventional learning theory, unencumbered by Eysenck's biological baggage, tends to focus on the environmental contingencies which determine our learnt responses.

3.2.2 *Learning theory and environmental determinism*

Another way of contrasting Eysenck with orthodox learning theorists is that the former looks at differences in the extent to which people are capable of learning while the latter assumes that people are equally capable and so examines differences in the content of what is learnt. Yet the learner him or herself has no part in this story. This is not learning in the sense of deliberate application on the part of an individual to master some skill or body of knowledge, whether it be by rehearsal, repetition, practice, directed and deliberate observation and reproduction or any other manner by which individuals may be the authors of their own destiny. If biological determinists make human beings the helpless victims of forces within, learning theory makes people the helpless victims of forces without. It is a theory of environmental determinism whereby internal connections automatically flow from external coincidences.

Both classical and operant conditioning models have been used to explain delinquency. According to the former, the repeated association of transgression with inherently aversive stimuli (in other words, punishment) eventually leads the individual to anticipate distress simply by contemplating transgressive behaviour. Moreover, by withdrawing from contemplated crimes distress is decreased and hence conformity is endlessly reinforced. So, if mother and father provide the right conditioning experience, in time they can turn their backs and remain confident that the child will remain law-abiding even when beyond all possible detection or punishment. Should parents fail to provide the necessary experiences the child will never become anxious at the mere thought of offending and hence transgressions will come more easily.

According to this account, individual action is determined entirely by the environment as opposed to fixed biological predispositions. However, the weight of environmental influences lies in the past. It is conditioning history which largely determines responses rather than the immediate contingencies. At best, these can only exert a small influence on the future of the conditioned reflex. Quite apart from the fact that there is no place for conscious judgements, for calculations of consequences or judgements about right and wrong, it is very one-sided. The emphasis is entirely about learning to be anxious about sanctioned activities rather than learning to embrace approved activities. For the latter, operant conditioning appears to provide a basis of understanding. The basic premise is that behaviour is driven by consequences. Those behaviours that are rewarded are more likely to be repeated, those that are not rewarded or punished are less likely to re-occur. Thus, by structuring environmental contingencies appropriately, parents can shape the behaviour of their children. However, if they fail to do so, then the wrong lessons may be learnt. It is even possible that negative behaviour may be learnt because they are inadvertently reinforced (Bandura & Walters, 1959). Thus a boy who attacks his sister may be rewarded with parental attention and hence repeat the action, much to the bemusement of his parents who cannot see that a few moments of their concern is more important than the harsh words which accompany it.

While showing the strength of operant conditioning approaches, this example also points to some of its weaknesses. First of all, if we had to wait to experience personally the consequences of actions before learning how to act our education would be a very slow process indeed. As well as the boy learning something from parental reaction to the attack upon his sister it is highly likely that the sister would also learn, as would any other siblings. In other words, as social learning theory proposes, we learn from the consequences of actions to others and we may imitate even in the absence of direct reinforcement (Bandura,1969; Bandura, Ross & Ross, 1963).

Yet the concept of imitation only exacerbates a second weakness. The issue has to do with what aspect of a stimulus should be taken as significant; in the case of harsh words from a parent, is the consequential thing that the words are harsh or that they are words from a parent? Once we move on to consider issues of imitation, especially as they pertain to complex and extended stimuli such as media products, the problem becomes far more acute. There is ongoing concern about the effects of media on children; everything from graphic comics to violent television to horror videos to combat video games is held to corrupt our youth. But why should children imitate the anti-social products and not the pro-social ones? And, within the same product why should children learn from the law-breaker rather than the law enforcer, the act of aggression rather than the act of kindness? Moreover, will everybody watching the same thing learn the same lessons from it? Critics can never seem to agree on the significance of any film, book or television program. Are ordinary viewers any different?

Once the significance of stimuli is no longer self-evident to the subject then the attempt of learning theory to exclude all organismic variables from the explanation of behaviour is fatally undermined. It becomes essential to introduce some basis for the selection and interpretation of stimuli (Danziger, 1971). There are a number of ways of doing this. One is to argue that subjects imitate particular people rather than segments of behaviour. We must therefore look at how individuals identify with others which, in turn, depends on the question of how their own identity is defined. A concern with the dynamics of identification clearly leads in the direction of psychoanalytic theory. A second path is to examine the ways in which internal cognitive development affects the individual's understanding of complex issues in the external world. A concern with cognitive development points us to the Piagetian tradition and, more particularly, Kohlberg's work on the ways in which different levels of cognitive complexity affect moral reasoning and moral action.

3.2.3 The psychoanalytic tradition

The question of delinquency is not just one of the many issues about which psychoanalytic theory has something to say. Rather, it goes to the very heart of Freud's enterprise. One of the key questions which guided him was how can civilization be sustained when the natural inclinations of humans are selfish and socially destructive? Put more bluntly, Freud shared the essential worry of all mass society theorists: how can the social order survive? His answer also accords with the tenets of mass society theory.

For Freud, the social order must be implanted within the psyche of the individual. This structure, the superego, can then police impulses from the id towards the gratification of sexual and instinctual desires. Hence the superego incorporates both cultural proscriptions against uncontrolled behaviour and also self-punitive tendencies to ensure compliance with these prescriptions. An overly developed superego will lead to neurosis since guilt will be experienced out of all proportion to conduct. Conversely, a weak or imperfectly formed superego will lead to continued self-gratification irrespective of social norms, lack of guilt and hostility to authority. An understanding of delinquency therefore depends upon an understanding of the dynamics of superego formation.

Freudian theory relates early personality development to the way in which successive centres of bodily need and satisfaction are managed. After focusing on oral and then anal gratification, the child enters the 'genital' phase where erotic desire is experienced for the opposite-sex parent. Such feelings conflict with earlier attachment to the mother or father. More dangerously they might invoke the ire of the same-sex parent who is clearly much more powerful than the infant. Indeed, Freud argues that, around the age of five years, boys begin to imagine that their fathers will castrate them as punishment for their incestuous desires (Freud, 1913). There is therefore a major tension provoking serious anxiety. This is resolved when boys internalize an image of their father, renounce conscious desire for their mother and repress all conscious recollection of these events. The internalized image of the parent as authority figure is the superego.

For girls, the story is somewhat less straightforward and less elaborated. The crisis is driven not by castration anxiety but by the rather less intense fear that they will be abandoned by their mothers. Since the strength of the superego will be directly proportional to the strength of the anxieties that preceded its formation, the implication is that girls will have weaker and less exacting consciences than boys.

This account may seem unconvincing in a number of ways – quite apart from displaying a strong masculine bias. However, its importance lies not so much in the details as in the way it has set the agenda for much subsequent work on moral psychology. On the one hand Freud contributed a meta-theoretical frame to the research which, if not entirely original, was at least elaborated into a coherent and enduring edifice: social order depends upon the development of internalized personality structures to curb excessive appetites and we need to look back to the early history of the individual to understand the later form of these structures. Understanding social relations, especially with the parents, is essential to this understanding. However, by the end of infancy the structures are relatively fixed and determine social relations rather than vice versa.

On the other hand, and of more obvious influence, Freud contributed a range of concepts upon which researchers continue to draw in order to make sense of social development and the occasions of its apparent failure. These include attachment, identification (especially the problems of male identification), deferred gratification, styles of parental control and relations with authority figures. Bowlby (1969), for instance, draws attention away from five-year-olds to the very early problems of attachment. The lack of a stable mother figure or else the presence of an unaffectionate mother will lead the child to lack emotional responsiveness. This leads to an inability to form attachments in later life, an incapacity to empathize with others and an insensitivity to their feelings. In extreme forms it leads to psychopathy. Other researchers have been less concerned with any particular critical period but have emphasized the general problems of internalizing moral concerns deriving from cold unloving parents, harsh or erratic discipline, an absent or indifferent parent or poor parental supervision (Glueck & Glueck, 1968; Hoffman, 1970; McCord, McCord & Zola, 1959; West & Farrington, 1973). The precise processes of internalization are therefore a point of considerable controversy but the dependence of moral action on internalization is not.

3.2.4 Cognitive developmental theory

Along with Freud, Piaget stands as one of the most influential psychologists of the twentieth century. Moreover, at least since his death, Piaget also compares with Freud in that the general tenets of his approach retain their influence even if the specific details are increasingly disputed. This approach was explicitly opposed to the mechanistic models of behaviourism in which each individual essentially only reacts to the surrounding environmental forces – in much the same way that a billiard ball only moves when struck. For Piaget (e.g. Piaget, 1950) humans, like any other organism, are inherently active and constantly striving to adapt to their environment, adaptation being characterized by a state of equilibrium between the actions of the organism and the actions of the environment. However, our expectations of the environment are continuously contradicted by our experience of it. This leads to cognitive conflict which energizes attempts by the intellectual system to re-establish equilibrium through reorganization of internal cognitive structures. Consequently, cognitive development comes about through the activity of problem solving. In Piaget's own words: 'intellectual development is none other than the outcome of intellectual functioning'.

A central assumption of the approach has to do with the qualitative rather than simply quantitative character of successive cognitive reorganizations. It is not that younger children are somewhat worse at thinking in the ways of older children. Rather they look at things in fundamentally different ways, employing a fundamentally different logic. In order to understand the ways in which the child will go about problem solving we must examine the cognitive procedures that children use in their own terms. This argument is not restricted to children's interactions with the material world but is also applied to their dealings with the social world of rules and norms (Piaget, 1932). What counts is the child's ability to deal with the logic of the task as a function of the stage of cognitive development that he or she has reached. All tasks of similar logical structure should be treated in exactly the same way. In short, the individual acts like a bio-cognitive automaton. The possibility that performance may depend upon the symbolic significance and social meaning of tasks is not even entertained (Donaldson, 1978).

Piaget was once asked if he was a true Piagetian. He is reputed to have replied that he might not be, but Mr Kohlberg certainly was. Kohlberg (1963) argued that moral reasoning can be divided up into a series of stages which directly parallel and build upon stages of intellectual growth. As children mature intellectually, so they are capable of more complex forms of moral reasoning and this is directly reflected in the way that they solve and act upon moral dilemmas. Moral development is the discovery of increasingly comprehensive, rational and consistent principles of justice. Moreover, moral development occurs for the same reasons and in the same way that intellectual change in general occurs. Children continuously confront moral problems and their intellectual attempts to solve these successively reconstruct the ways that they are able to think about them. Moral development is therefore an inherent tendency of the intellectual system.

The implications of this model are that culture, social conditions and individual experience may affect the rate of development from step to step and how far individuals progress up the ladder (Snarey, 1985), but not the sequence of steps which is universal, invariant and irreversible. There is only one developmental sequence irrespective of any social factors. Similarly, there are absolute, rational and universally valid moral principles as well as a hierarchy between different principles of morality. Kohlberg can therefore claim that some forms of moral reasoning are better than others on the grounds that they reflect more advanced stages of intellectual development. These implications are not accidental. Kohlberg designed his model as a critique not only of behaviourism but of psychoanalysis as well. He rejected the assumption that people's commitment to morality is based upon an irrational process and that the precise moral standards they come to apply are fortuitous, ultimately relative and culturally defined.

Kohlberg (1963) proposes that there are three broad periods or levels of moral reasoning, each of which contains two separate stages, a total of six stages. In the preconventional period moral issues are looked at from the perspective of the individual who is involved. However, at stage 1 they simply consider an act wrong because you get punished for it. By stage 2 punishment is to be weighed against other pros and cons in light of what one needs. Moreover, there is some recognition of the fact that different individuals may have different interests such that a moral solution may consist of the different parties striking a deal. Of course, where there are irreconcilable conflicts of interest or where agreement cannot be obtained such an approach to 'the good' is inadequate. The only solution is to move to the second level of reasoning which sees shared standards of virtue lying behind separate individual interests.

The two stages of so-called 'conventional' moral reasoning are as follows. Stage 3 is a matter of defining morality in terms of the extent to which individual claims match against collective notions of what is nice or decent. However, for Kohlberg this still involves a limited concept of convention since what is right or fair is defined by how much individuals adhere to standards in their interpersonal relations. It cannot cope with the possibility that people behaving with all the virtues of good group members may still be in conflict with others doing likewise. What happens when the unemployed father seeks to care for his family by stealing from a shop? In stage 4, standards are related to a social system that is more general that any particular set of relations between individuals. Moral action is defined in terms of adherence to these rules.

Thus morality is no longer a function of interpersonal relations but of the relation between the individual and society. Disputes are resolved in terms of what is necessary first and foremost to maintain society.

This still leaves open a number of questions. For instance, what are one's obligations to those outside the society? Moreover, how does one create laws or change them once they are formed? If conventional morality is entirely dependent upon the conventions of the society one happens to find oneself in at the present then one can make no claims to their superiority over those of other societies or of one's own society at a different point in time. The only solution is to seek non-relative principles which define good societies in general and upon which one's own society can be modelled. If old laws violate these universal moral principles they are bad and deserve to be broken. New laws should accord to such principles: they should be democratically decided, recognize diversities of interest, be based on a rational hierarchy of rights and obtain free consent from rational individuals. When one reasons in these terms (what Kohlberg, 1976, calls a 'prior to society' moral perspective) one has reached the post-conventional level of moral reasoning. The differentiation between stages 5 and 6 need not concern us here in so far as no clear stages of stage 6 have yet been identified in research samples. Indeed according to Colby, Kohlberg et al. (1987) few people get beyond stage 4 even when well into adulthood.

If the distinction between conventional and post-conventional reasoning echoes the contrast between conservatism and bourgeois liberalism this is more than mere coincidence. Kohlberg (1984) regarded his enterprise as part of the tradition of the liberal enlightenment. His particular contribution was to enshrine the superiority of liberal ideals by translating an ideological difference into a cognitive hierarchy. The reason why people are conservative is that they lack the intellectual development to apprehend liberal arguments. It is not that they might use particular forms of moral reasoning because of their ideological stance, let alone that forms of moral reasoning may be purposefully used to signal their conservatism or liberalism (Emler, Renwick & Malone, 1983; Markoulis, 1989; Reicher & Emler, 1985b).

The implications of Kohlberg's argument are enhanced by the fact that he draws a tight connection between moral reasoning and moral action. Admittedly, he allows two processes to mediate between the two. The first is a judgement that one has a personal responsibility to act in accordance with one's judgements as to what is right (what Frankena, 1973, calls an 'aretaic' judgement). The second is the possession of the non-moral skills to follow through a moral decision (what Kohlberg, 1984 calls 'ego control'). However, as the stages progress so aretaic judgements are more likely to be made and ego control is more likely to be present. If the translation of reasoning into actions is not perfect it is none the less pretty intimate. Certainly no individual can be expected to act beyond their levels of moral development (one cannot expect principled actions from conservatives) and precious few will act below the highest level that they have achieved (liberals are most unlikely to be bound by convention).

In addition to its clear implications for political practice, this tight linkage of reasoning and action provides a clear basis for the understanding of trangression. At a pre-conventional level individuals will transgress because it benefits them personally. Conventional reasoners will transgress either in pursuit of good intentions (at stage 3) or else to uphold what they perceive to be the state interests (at stage 4). One could, for example, interpret the actions of those involved in the Watergate cover-up in these terms (Candee, 1975). Finally, post-conventional reasoners will transgress in the pursuance of higher moral imperatives. The applicability of this idea to explain the upsurge of civil disobedience and opposition to State policy in 1960s America contributed considerably to the popularity of Kohlberg's ideas (Sampson, 1971). It is, perhaps, even more congenial to see one's protests as a mark of superiority than as a statement of principle.

Even if some transgressions are possible at all stages of development, it remains true that the greatest tendency to break the rules will occur in the pre-conventional period. Most of those who are in this period are children who lack the means to inflict much criminal damage and who anyway tend to be under the supervision of adults. However, should individuals linger in this period then their transgressions will become more serious. Delinquency is ultimately a consequence of moral retardation. This raises the obvious question: what determines the rate of transition from one stage to another? According to Kohlberg (1984) a number of factors may be involved, including intellectual retardation, limited social experience or the failure of institutional arrangements to present appropriate moral choices. Indeed Kohlberg, Scharf and Hickey (1972) argue that the most popular forms of crime control are organized around the principle of 'obey the rules or risk punishment' which only reconfirm the wisdom of stage 2 morality.

It would therefore be wrong to accuse Kohlberg of ignoring social influence. Yet, like those occasions we have encountered in which psychologists are willing to countenance the importance of the social, it is only at a distance. One's experience in the world may affect progress from stage to stage, but in the immediate context internal structures operate without reference to external social relations. Indeed, perhaps more clearly than anyone else, Kohlberg provides a way of mapping the specific structures of internal control onto the commission of delinquent acts.

3.3 Sociology and Deviance

3.3.1 The influence of Durkheim

Before pointing to the differences between psychological and sociological theories of deviance it may be best to start off by pointing to their similarities. One way of doing so is to compare the figures of Durkheim and Freud, given that the former's influence on subsequent sociological enquiry mirrors the influence of the latter in psychology. Both Durkheim and Freud started from a concern with how social order was maintained. They both assumed that human nature, left to its own devices, would become destructive – both to self and others. Something extra was therefore needed in order for civilization to survive. What is more, their particular concern – resting on the core assumption of all mass society theory – was what that something might be in a period when the industrial revolution seemed to have destroyed the close ties of community. As Giner (1976) puts it, Durkheim's 1893 treatise on 'The Social Division of Labour' (trans. Durkheim, 1984) set out 'to investigate the nature of social cohesion in a world no longer dominated by *Gemeinschaft* bonds'.

Durkheim's explanation, however, starts from very different assumptions and proceeds in very different directions to that of Freud. The sociologist does not see the civilizing process as something painful in which the personality represses itself more or less successfully. Indeed he makes no assumptions about the inherent structures of mind but rather looks to the way in which social conditions shape the human psyche. In this he is like most others in the discipline who, either by commission or omission, imply that human nature is almost infinitely plastic and ready to assume any form that social forces impress upon it. If there is any assumption about human nature it is that people are inherently social: one therefore doesn't have to enquire as to why people exist in society for it is their natural habitat. They can only be driven out.

Durkheim, however, has a particular notion of the social. Unlike much of classical theory as well as dominant psychological models of collective phenomena (cf. Moscovici, 1976) he does not view society as reducible to an aggregate of contracts between individuals. He insists that there is an edifice of traditions and practices – of 'social facts' – that, even if it is itself a human construction, predates the existence of any given individuals and constructs their personalities and human natures. The implication of this is that, if one wants to look at the forces that bind people to society, one should not examine the structure of individual minds or even the relations between individuals. Instead, one needs to address the forms of social organization into which people are born and the institutions in which they exist. As far as criminality is concerned, this translates into the question of how a social environment produces conformity or else nonconformity rather than a psychological focus on the forms of intra-psychic structure that are implicated by the presence or absence of criminal action.

While Durkheim went along with his predecessors in recognizing that the developing forces of production had profoundly altered forms of social organization – that the intimate bonds of village life had given way to the formality of urbanized industrial existence – he did not accept that this meant a loss of social cohesion. His argument was that the basis of social solidarity had changed rather than vanished. To put the matter rather more precisely, Durkheim agreed with Tonnies (1887, trans. 1957) that *Gemeinschaft* had given way to *Gesellschaft*, but he did not agree that this meant a shift from organic communities to merely mechanical aggregates. This was reflected in his very terminology since the term 'organic solidarity' was used to characterize the bonds of industrial societies while 'mechanical solidarity' was used to describe 'primitive' clans.

Durkheim argued that the very features of industrial organization which others decried as breaking the social bond – especially increasing divisions of labour – are in fact essential to its construction. To quote Giner (1976) once more: 'the centrifugal force that tends to separate individuals as their tasks and occupations become more specialized also engenders a centripetal force, as a consequence of their increased need to depend more than ever before on the whole' (p. 97). Division and specialization of labour only worked, in other words, because it was also more thoroughly integrated within a single system.

There are, according to Durkheim, three facets to organic solidarity. The first is discipline, which refers to reliable and predictable performance of specialized roles. This stems from socially transmitted rules and a socially constructed hierarchy of command. The metaphor is unmistakably military: each soldier-citizen clearly knows his or her place. This is true in both senses of the term. Not only are individuals aware of how to carry out their roles, they also accept the limits which the roles impose: 'the trick of social control was not to give people what they want . . . but to persuade them that what they have is about all they morally deserve' (Box, 1981, p. 98).

The second facet is attachment. In order to transcend the merely mechanical performance of tasks, it is necessary that individuals should feel a bond with the collective and its aspirations. This makes performance more than drudgery. A necessary enthusiasm is added, a spontaneous emotionally felt commitment. For Durkheim the collective body towards which attachment should be felt in the modern world was the nation – another echo of other mass society theorists such as Le Bon whose political project was to replace what they saw as damaging class conflicts with a unifying nationalism.

Durkheim's third facet of organic solidarity is autonomy. Individuals must make a free choice to conform based on an intellectual appreciation of the necessity of their society's particular moral order. This autonomy does not involve each individual going his or her separate way and so causing the fragmentation of society. Instead it engenders a more profound and principled commitment to the collective. All in all, then, organic solidarity overcomes the social entropy that might result from idiosyncratic action or the decay of role performances. It also provides a strength to overcome external threats. A population of nationalistic soldier-citizens is far less likely to be invaded by its neighbours. Again, like Le Bon, much of Durkheim's theorizing seems to be marked by the trauma of the Franco-Prussian war.

Not surprisingly, therefore, Durkheim is also heavily concerned with the weakening of solidarity. One sign of this was the loss of attachment to the social unit due to the sheer scale of industrial society, its impersonal character, and the degrading character of the industrial process. This he terms alienation. The other sign is anomie, which literally means normlessness and refers to aspirations running out of control, undisciplined by clear limits and unregulated by rules of conduct. This again results from the conditions of mass production, especially the fact that workers are outside the moral supervision of their employers or other purveyors of society's codes.

An increasing concern with alienation and anomie, and a fear of the ways in which they may lead vulnerable individuals to anti-social behaviour, to mental illness and even to suicide (Durkheim, 1897), led Durkheim back to the idea that the organic solidarity of modern industrial society was not enough to underwrite the social order (Durkheim, 1915). Instead something of the quasi-religious rites of earlier societies – mechanical solidarity in his own terminology – was necessary. People need to come together in regular rituals in order to reaffirm their commitment to, faith in and passion for the collective. Whether such mechanical solidarity was possible under the conditions of mass society remained in doubt.

For us, the first thing to note about Durkheim's approach is that anti-social acts are still explicable in terms of internal deficits: norms and attachments to the social order. Durkheim may see the relevant psychological variables as entirely socially constructed and therefore concentrate his attention on the social organisation that succeeds or else fails in implanting them. However, society still relates to delinquency at a distance. The immediate social context of anti-social behaviour continues to be ignored. The second point is that, as should be clear by now, there is a central tension running through Durkheim's work. On the one hand he provides a positive vision of society as inherently cohesive, where even those elements that might tear it apart actually serve to bind it together. On the other hand he suggests a more pessimistic vision of modern times in which the self-same conditions tear people apart, dehumanizing them and rendering them out of control. Despite his early break with the notion that modern times threaten social collapse, Durkheim ultimately leaves us worrying about the ways in which the social relations of industrial cities generate lawlessness and cannot sustain the necessary palliatives. Crime may be thought of with insouciance in terms of the optimistic vision. However, it is more likely to be treated as a sign of impending catastrophe.

There are those who argue for a more radical reading of Durkheim (e.g. Taylor, Walton & Young, 1973). They stress that, in his work, deviance may be a means of realizing the true collective conscience against the prevailing moral climate. Moreover, they highlight the fact that Durkheim saw the existence of inherited wealth and the division between rich and poor as the prime sources of a corrupt moral climate. Their Durkheim is one for whom plebians are functional rebels. For us, whether they are right or wrong is beside the point. We are concerned primarily with the subsequent impact of Durkheim and, as Taylor et al. admit, it is the conventional reading which has clearly prevailed.

The notion that all aspects of society contribute to its cohesion, even those that might be supposed to undermine it, was further supported by subsequent research both in the industrializing West and elsewhere. The experience of the United States, in which a society composed almost entirely of refugees, colonizers and less willing émigrés from all round the world seemed not only to work but to thrive, suggested that powerful tendencies towards cohesion are intrinsic to social units. Anthropologists who went back around the globe to document less developed societies returned home with accounts of an ever more bewildering variety of social forms. However, each one seemed to work, to be a stable and unified whole. Thus it could be assumed that whatever structure there was must be contributing to its persisting solidarity and survival. The structure must be functional (cf. Radcliffe-Brown, 1952).

This functionalist perspective could be used to explain virtually all phenomena, including crime. While crime might be thought of as an attack upon society, it can be argued that it actually reinforces the social unit. From a Durkheimian perspective it is not so much the crime itself that is important but the opportunity it provides for the public rituals of trial and punishment. Moral boundaries can only be marked by contrasts. Only when people transgress and step outside is it possible to show where the line is drawn. Thus the rituals provide regular reminders to all members of society as to which standards are acceptable and which are not. Whereas classical theory had it that punishment is instituted to influence rational decision making by the potential offender, Durkheim (1925) argued that its significance is symbolic: it serves to reconfirm societal standards and to reassure non-offenders that their choices are valued. For symbolic confirmations to be possible, crimes must occur. Society needs its villains to sustain its moral solidarity.

Functionalism also allows for the more pessimistic view of of anti-social behaviour. From this perspective, crime is evidence of some form of decay in society. This is the premise of most sociological theories of deviance. Like Durkheim they share the premise that human nature is essentially plastic. They therefore also see human personality and behavioural inclinations as socially constructed. Where they differ is in the analysis of precisely how society gets it wrong.

3.3.2 Some modern sociological theories of deviance

Society could fail properly to socialize its members in four ways. First, it could be that particular forms of social organisation fail to implant individuals with any standards to guide their behaviour. Criminals are not following deviant norms, they are behaving without norms. Second, society could implant the wrong standards in individuals, such that criminal behaviour is compatible with the norms they hold. Third, society could implant the right standards in all individuals but do something to stop certain individuals acting on these standards. Such individuals would be those prone to criminality. Fourth, there could be something in the dominant norms themselves which facilitates delinquency.

Of course, to pose matters in these terms is to define them from the perspective of the social order, to see its maintenance as something desirable and to see deviants as having done something wrong. All these stances are contestable, whether from the Marxist perspective that so-called criminals are actually involved in struggling against an oppressive order (cf. Hall & Jefferson, 1976; Humphries, 1981) or else the more Foucaultian argument that delinquency is not a self-evident thing whose social causes are to be analysed. Following Foucault (1977) the category of delinquency may be seen as a social construction in itself, bound up with the more general ordering of people in society. It is the emergence of the category 'delinquent' which should therefore be studied rather than taking it for granted in the more usual study of what makes delinquents. None the less, most mainstream sociological theories of deviance do take one of the four forms identified above, although – as we shall see – variations can be found within each of them.

(1) *Delinquency as a lack of norms*: this position can be seen to derive from the social ecological theories of the so-called 'Chicago school'. As the ecological metaphor suggests, society is conceived as an organism which is fundamentally in equilibrium. Yet the thorough-going empirical tradition of the school (which is usually associated with the journalistic training of Robert Park, one of its founders) forced an awareness of social diversity and of disequilibrium. As Brake (1985) notes, the challenge was much like that which confronted Durkheim: how to reconcile the model with the reality without resorting to notions of individual pathology. The answer lay in the existence of social pathology or, to be more specific, social disorganization.

Any community is seen as involving both cooperative and competitive social relations. The cooperative relations are those by which equilibrium is achieved and conflict minimized. At the same time, however, individuals are seen as involved in a struggle against others for resources. If the community becomes disrupted by such factors as rapid migration, then the competitive forces will gain the ascendancy over cooperative forces. This will then lead to normlessness and to delinquency. Empirical support for these ideas came from the work of Shaw and McKay (1931, 1942). They started off by showing that, in Chicago, delinquency was higher in areas where population transitions were greatest. They then replicated the findings in a number of other cities. With such a weight of evidence behind them, Shaw and McKay felt confident in arguing that it is disintegrative forces alone which prevent the community from acting to impose social control and which are responsible for the absence of any accepted set of cultural standards. Other factors, such as poor social conditions, are consequences rather than causes of disintegration.

Given the empiricism of the Chicago school, a powerful objection to this model is that it is basically tautological: delinquency is explained in terms of social disorganization, while delinquency in turn is the main criterion of social disorganization! However, there are a number of conceptual problems as well (cf. Taylor et al., 1973). In particular, why should a lack of norms lead to any behavioural inclinations, let alone criminal ones, if one isn't prepared to accept explanations in terms of individual pathology? One obvious answer, which we have already encountered in Durkheim and of which echoes persist in social disorganization theory, is to accept the Freudian premise that human impulses are inherently destructive and will express themselves as such unless somehow socialized. Another way out is to argue that delinquent areas are marked not so much by a lack of norms as by different norms. This represents the second position outlined above.

(2) *Delinquency as a commitment to unconventional norms:* already there are traces of this position in the work of Shaw and McKay who, while starting from the loss of common standards, also accept that new norms which are supportive of delinquency are found in disorganized areas. None the less the stress remains upon loss and upon social *disorganization*. In contrast Sutherland (1939, Sutherland and Cressey, 1970) placed the emphasis on differential social organization. The underlying distinction was between the earlier vision of a single social consensus and Sutherland's notion that there are many different forms of consensus in society. In other words, his model is one of cultural diversity with some cultures stressing violation of the law and others stressing conformity to it. Whether one becomes criminal or not depends upon whether one has more exposure to the former or the latter type of culture. This is the essence of Sutherland's differential association theory.

In its grounding of criminality in alternative bases of social control, as opposed to the loss of social control, the differential association approach dispenses with the need for assumptions about human nature. According to this view, people are entirely motivationally empty. They are simply vessels to be filled according to the experiences they happen to encounter in society. There is no room for purpose or choice in this vision. In all these characteristics the echoes of learning theory are unmistakable – even if the focus here is on the nature of society which fills the human vessel as opposed to the means by which the filling takes place. Correspondingly, it should come as no surprise that the objections run along similar lines: what determines the way in which the complexity of experience is made sense of and affects the individual. It is notable that sociologists, like psychologists, have turned to the concept of identification to help them out. Thus Glaser (1956) suggests that a theory of differential identification might profitably replace differential association theory. None the less, despite the problems associated with it, the work of Sutherland is an important precursor of subcultural theories of deviance (for a review, see Brake, 1985). By insisting that delinquents may follow different norms rather than being anomic, differential association theory opens the way to studying the cultural world of the delinquent in its own terms.

However, there is an important distinction to be made in subcultural theory. The traditional of Sutherland himself is to argue for a plurality of cultures, some of which may happen to be oppositional. Cohen (1955), on the other hand, argues that delinquent culture is a simple inversion of the dominant culture being actively formed in opposition to it. His argument goes that all young people are subject to a single measuring rod in achieving success in society. The values by which everybody is judged include self-reliance, good manners, respect for property and so on. Some youth, especially those who are working class, will not have the means to pass according to these criteria. They will therefore suffer from status frustration and this will lead to a process of reaction formation whereby everything that is rejected by the dominant society is accorded value. In Cohen's own words: 'the delinquent subculture takes its norms from the larger culture but turns them upside down. The delinquent's conduct is right, by the standards of his subculture precisely because it is wrong by the norms of the larger culture. "Malicious" and "negativistic" are foreign to the delinquent's vocabulary, but he will often assure us, sometimes ruefully, sometimes with a touch of glee or even pride, that he is "just plain mean"' (Cohen, 1955, pp. 28–9).

In many ways, Cohen's approach might be seen as an instance of Merton's strain hypothesis (Merton, 1938, 1968) according to which delinquency results from an inability to succeed in terms of dominant social norms. While he claimed influence from Durkheim, Robert Merton (like Sutherland) rejected the remnants of biologistic reasoning that survived in the notion of normlessness as leading to crime. Indeed he openly attacked any invocation of what he scornfully termed 'man's imperious biological drives'. Instead Merton argues that most people share in the dominant values of society. In the case of the United States, this meant a commitment to the American dream, to ever greater success in financial terms and the ever greater accumulation of material goods. Problems arise not so much from those few who reject these values (although some psychotics and rebels may do so) as from the many who, while fully sharing in the dream, lack the means of fulfilling it. They turn to illegitimate means of achieving desired material success. Such 'innovation' is the source of most deviant activity.

There are, however, two obvious differences between Cohen and Merton. The first is that, while Cohen stresses failure in status terms, Merton is more concerned with material failure. However, the stress on material achievement in Merton is not meant to be a universal, it simply reflects what he sees as essential in American society. It could even be said that it is money that confers status. The distance between the two theorists on this point is not as great as it might seem. The second difference is less easily bridged. Cohen himself contrasts his own theory, which lays stress on the destructive zest of delinquent subcultures, with Merton's utilitarianism (Cohen, 1955). Conceptually, Cohen feels it necessary to invoke a set of negativistic norms to explain delinquent action while Merton has no place for such norms in his account. Even in their delinquency, people remain committed to societal norms. They are just realizing them in different ways. Hence Merton provides the source for the third of the positions that we have identified.

(3) *Delinquency as meeting conventional norms by unconventional means*: Cloward and Ohlin's work on 'delinquency and opportunity' (Cloward and Ohlin, 1960) starts, like Merton, from the assumption that crime may signify acceptance rather than rejection of dominant norms. However, in different types of neighbourhood, there will be different means of achieving the commonly desired end. Those who live in middle-class areas can succeed by following conventional paths and therefore one would expect little delinquency. Those living in stable working-class neighbourhoods may not have the education, the connections and the wealth to succeed conventionally, but they do have access to adult criminal models, to teachers of criminal skills and to 'fences' for stolen goods. This can support a 'criminal subculture' as an alternative means of sharing in the 'American dream'.

Thus far, the argument sounds like pure Merton. However, Cloward and Ohlin also suggest that, in disorganized working-class areas, there will not even be the presence of criminal models and resources. Therefore young people will spend most of their time with peers, giving rise to gangs and a 'conflict subculture'. What is more, for those who are so unfortunate as to have neither criminal resources nor even peers to provide the opportunity for illegitimate action, then escape into drugs – the 'retreatist subculture' – is the only remaining option.

Clear echoes of social disorganization theory exist in these latter parts of the theory. The difference is that such disorganization leaves people so devoid of means that they don't even have the resources to be criminals. Thus, while Cloward and Ohlin retain the Chicago school's distinction between the normative and the anomic, they are original in placing criminals on the normative side of the line. This has a number of further implications for our understanding of the issues at hand. To start with, it splits the more general phenomenon of delinquency apart. While the organized working class thieve, the disorganized working class fight and the isolated lumpenproletariat take to drugs. Such differing types of delinquency are not only distinct to different people, the model also suggests that they are found in different areas. Another implication is that a rejection of dominant values only occurs amongst those without any means. The organized working class are explicitly excluded from contesting the nature of society – something that is hard to reconcile with a century of socialist and syndicalist agitation. Moreover, the evidence is that such collective agitation was dependent upon the existence of settled working-class communities (Tilly, Tilly & Tilly, 1975). Perhaps because of the rigidity of their distinctions, the difficulty in countenancing such things as retreatist subcultures of the privileged or else claims to political and social inclusion by the most dispossessed, the influence of Cloward and Ohlin's position declined as the 1960s progressed. Hence Taylor et al. suggest that: 'it would be amusing, for instance, to conjecture what Cloward and Ohlin would have made of the Black Panthers or the hippies in their typology of subcultures' (1973, p. 135).

(4) *Delinquency as an expression of dominant norms:* thus far, the approaches that we have dealt with in this section generally take a socially deterministic approach. The positions in which people find themselves in the social structure (whether this be analysed in terms of class or social organization) are used to explain the internal structures (whether these be norms or orientations to the fulfilment of norms) which lead individuals to conform or deviate. Such approaches therefore characteristically move from a general analysis of society to an analysis of the general differences between people in different social locations. Both of these tendencies are targets in the work of David Matza.

Matza (1964) begins with the premise that analysis should start from the meanings of actions in the world of the actor. He therefore urges investigators to adopt a naturalistic perspective, by which he means as accurate a description as possible of phenomena in their own terms. With such a perspective, one will move away from the view of delinquents as impelled to transgression by social forces beyond their control and begin to appreciate the purposes, motives and fears which shape delinquent action. Matza's first 'naturalistic' observation is that delinquents are not as calm about their offences as one might expect if they really had no truck with dominant values or else see themselves as reasonably pursuing dominant values in unconventional ways. In fact they are often guilty and ashamed about their actions. Matza concludes from this that delinquents remain within society's normative bind even as they commit delinquent actions. This is possible for two reasons. First of all, societal norms are themselves ambiguous and involve elements (such as the search for excitement) that sanction transgression at the same time as they outlaw it. Secondly, the significance of delinquent acts can be diminished by using techniques of neutralization such as denying one's responsibility, denying that any injury was caused, discrediting the victim, condemning those who might object and so on.

It follows that rather than thinking of delinquent subcultures that exist outside society, we should turn our attention to the subterranean delinquent dimension of mainstream culture. In acknowledging its existence we see that individuals who commit delinquent acts do not need to break with mainstream society. Rather they inhabit the space between convention and crime – toying with both but committed to neither. If they do commit delinquent acts these are short-lived interludes and commitment to the social order is immediately reconfirmed by applying the various techniques of neutralization. This portrait of the social world of the delinquent is summed up by the concept of 'drift'. It implies a much greater convergence between 'delinquent' and 'respectable' cultures than is normally allowed. What is more, it is not just that delinquents are constantly asserting their delinquency. The ambiguity of social norms ensures that the converse happens as well. Thus Matza notes that even surviving puritans create a false biography of transgression or inflate their trivial misdemeanours to a status of glamorous danger. Note, for instance, how the Conservative Prime Minister John Major sought to contest his boring image and enhance his popularity by letting it be known that he referred to internal critics as 'bastards'.

As with so many of the theories that we have encountered, the details of Matza's position have been widely rejected – even to the extent of the author himself criticizing them as a confused jumbling of views (Weis, 1971). His empirical assertions concerning guilt in adolescents are open to doubt (Hindelang, 1970; Hirschi, 1969). The notion that so-called 'techniques of neutralization' are recommitments to the social order rather than critiques of it closes off the possibility of delinquency as rebellion or resistance. The concept of 'drift' itself drifts between determinism and free will according to the precise explanation of how bouts of delinquency originate and are maintained (Taylor et al., 1973). None the less, Matza's work does stand out from other sociological (and indeed psychological) work on deviance and it does retain its value in three respects. First, attention is finally shifted away from the creation of general behavioural predispositions to the microsocial contexts in which specific acts occur. Second, care is taken to look at things from the perspective of the individual in so far as the understandings people hold are crucial to their behaviour (whatever the accuracy of these understandings may be). Third, delinquent and non-delinquent actions are understood in terms of the same general processes. Even if nothing else survives of Matza's own theories, such assumptions allow for lines of theorizing that have effectively been closed off by the lingering influence of mass society theorizing.

3.4 Models of Adolescence

3.4.1 Adolescence as a test of socialization

The general drift of the theories of deviance that we have considered can be summarized in the words of Aronfreed: 'the young child's behaviour is initially highly dependent on its experience of external events . . . But its behaviour gradually comes to be governed, to a considerable extent, by internal monitors which appear to carry out many of the functions of the external controls originally required to establish the behaviour' (1968, p. 263). While there may be differences as to the exact nature of these monitors, the ways in which they are formed and whether anything exists in the absence of control, the overall argument is that adults follow rules because their own conscience obliges them to do so while the origins of conscience are to be found in childhood. If childhood fails in some degree to equip an individuals with the appropriate internalized controls over conduct, whatever the precise form those controls take, then as external controls over behaviour are withdrawn more anti-social and criminal conduct can be expected.

As we indicated in chapter 2, the overall concern of mass society theory lay with the collapse of external control in society at large. The particular concern with adolescence is to do with the fact that this is an age at which adult surveillance is diminished at the same time as the physical and intellectual power to do serious damage emerges. For the first time, only internal controls are left to hold back a surge of criminality. Thus adolescence is the first 'road test' for conscience. Will socialization prove to have been successful? Will these apprentice adults exercise the desired degree of self-control? Will this generation prove the future or the nemesis of society? These are some of the issues which made adolescence such a topic of concern.

However, if crime were simply a matter of decreasing external control, then one might expect rates to increase gradually into adulthood as individuals become more and more autonomous. So why the particular concern with adolescence? One response would be to argue that if parental control declines into the teenage years, new forms of external control begin to be imposed as individuals emerge from their teens. Delinquency exists in the temporary gap between. We will explore this possibility in a later chapter. However, it is not a path taken by most theories of adolescence. They tend to argue that there are conditions intrinsic to adolescence which can temporarily or more permanently weaken or undermine the effects of socialization in childhood. The basic lines of enquiry therefore match those of deviance theories: concern returns again and again to those factors which affect the moral resilience of individuals. In psychology, the main approaches are of psychoanalytic inspiration and address the ways in which physical changes associated with puberty provoke or else reawaken crises of identity. In sociology, the focus shifts to the way in which role changes – especially changes of economic role – test out the resilience of actors. What both approaches share is the notion that peer groups will be of particular importance in helping individuals through the crisis of adolescence. However, this is viewed as akin to falling from the frying pan into the fire, for inherently pernicious collective influences only exacerbate the temptation to offend. We shall presently examine these various arguments in more detail. However, to start with, we shall outline the origins of the idea that adolescence is a period characterized by turmoil and crisis.

3.4.2 *Inventing the crisis of adolescence*

As Freud stands to psychological models of moral action and Durkheim stands to sociological theories of normative behaviour, so G. Stanley Hall stands to explanations of adolescence – even if his name is all but forgotten today. Hall was the first American to gain a doctorate in psychology, the first president of the American Psychological Association and the founder of the Child Study Movement in the United States. Despite this pre-eminence in the discipline, he originally trained in divinity and later came under the influence of German idealist philosophers, particularly Nietzsche. These influences remained and influenced Hall's psychological concerns. Thus his ambition was to contribute to the creation of supermen where pity would be abolished because of its role in perpetuating the survival of weaker beings. His particular interest in adolescence was due to the fact that this is a period in which even the potentially gifted are in danger from pernicious influences. His explanation of this in the preface to his two-volume study on 'Adolescence: its psychology and its relations to physiology, anthropology, sociology, sex, crime, religion and education' (Hall, 1904) invokes what should be by now the familiar cast of seducers and saviours in mass society theory. Thus youth are described as under threat from, amongst other things, the 'temptations, prematurities, sedentary occupations and passive stimuli' (1904, p. xv) of urban life, as opposed to the healthy active outdoor life. They are described as particularly vulnerable because they 'lack some of the regulatives they still have in older hands with more conservative traditions' (1904, p. xvi).

In order to explain the psychological basis of this vulnerability, Hall employed a model of development which derived from the recapitulationist theories first mooted by the biologist Muller and later popularized by Haekel. The theory is encapsulated by the aphorism 'ontogeny recapitulates phylogeny'. In other words, the development of any individual repeats the stages through which the species as a whole evolved. In Hall's particular adaptation of this idea, the child exists in a state of savagery until adolescence, knowing nothing of such things as reason or 'true morality'. Entry into adolescence is therefore akin to a new birth in which the 'higher' and 'more completely human traits' come into being. This dawning of conscience represents a hope for improvement for both individual and 'race'. Yet, at the same time, it brings to mind conflicts with the past. Consequently adolescence is necessarily a period of psychic tension. In a key phrase, Hall writes that for adolescents: 'development is less gradual and more saltatory, suggestive of some ancient period of storm and stress when old moorings were broken and a higher level attained'. He continues: 'the momentum of heredity often seems insufficient to enable the child to achieve this great revolution and come to complete maturity, so that every step of the upward way is strewn with wreckage of body, mind and morals. There is not only arrest but perversion at every stage, and hoodlumism, juvenile crime and secret vice seem not only increasing but develop in earlier years in every civilized land' (1904, pp. xiii–xiv).

By now, recapitulationist theory is thoroughly discredited and Hall's theory has long fallen into obscurity. It is the tone of his ideas which survives. More specifically, he has left three general constructs which continue to influence the field. The term 'storm and stress' encapsulates the dominant view of adolescence, both in academia and the media. It is a time of crisis, a period of conflict, the 'difficult years' which every child passes through. Even if acknowledgements are sparse, echoes of Hall can still be found much later in the titles of general textbooks such as *The Stormy Decade: Adolescence* (Mohr and Despres, 1958). Hall also presents a model of development as a series of stages which pose psychic challenges to individuals. If they fail to match up to the challenge individuals will fall by the wayside, prey to perversion and to criminality. This suggestion most obviously anticipates psychoanalytic approaches to which we shall now turn.

3.4.3 *Psychoanalytic approaches to adolescence*

Such is the influence of psychoanalysis in this domain that one influential recent text (Coleman, 1980) presents it as the only psychological perspective on adolescence. That said, Freud himself did little more than sketch the outlines of such a theory. His main contribution was to highlight the upsurge of instinctual energy surrounding the period of puberty. This leads to a destruction of the various defences that individuals constructed against their sexuality during the period of infant development and therefore reignites the conflicts of early childhood. Having already dealt with these conflicts at such length, Freud probably felt disinclined to go over them again in the context of adolescence. However, in the *Introductory Lectures on Psychoanalysis* (1917/1963), he does point to two ways in which adolescent sexuality is distinctive. Firstly, it is capable of satisfaction. Secondly, therefore, it needs to be directed outside of the family. Indeed this shift in the targets of sexual gratification is fundamental to adult functioning. Freud therefore talks of the task of freeing oneself from one's parents as the precondition of ceasing to be a child and becoming an adult member of the community. He also stresses that these tasks are laid down for everyone.

There have been two main attempts to transform these snippets into a coherent theory of adolescence. The first and more orthodox stems from the work of Anna Freud. The second is contained in the work of Erikson.

Anna Freud starts, like her father, from the premise that the psychology of adolescence is rooted in the reawakening of sexual desire which inevitably accompanies the biological transformations of puberty. She also accepts that this reawakening does not lead to a direct repetition of infantile conflicts but rather that the conflicts are modified by other maturational developments. So, while infants repress their sexual desires out of fear of punishment, for adolescents the conflict between desire and demands for restraint is internalized. Guilt produces the effects formerly produced by the fear of adults. The developmental task for adolescents is to overcome the guilt surrounding renascent sexuality in order to open up the capacity for finding a sexual partner and having children. Thus, instead of entirely supressing sexual desires, it is necessary to achieve a balance between control and satisfaction (A. Freud, 1937, 1958). Anna Freud is quite explicit in the 1958 paper that this tension between sexual expression and sexual control not only makes turmoil inevitable in adolescence, but also that such turmoil is a necessary part of working towards sexual maturity.

One way of taming excessive sexual desire is through the use of defence mechanisms (A. Freud, 1937). For instance, one could reject all pleasure and adopt an ascetic stance. Alternatively, one could intellectualize sexuality into discussions of free love, religion or revolution. Which defence is selected is a matter of choice. However, when it comes to expressing sexual desire, certain choices are expressly ruled out. Again closely following her father, Anna Freud argues that the infantile resolution of sexual conflict through sexual identification with the same-sex parent is no longer possible in adolescence where sexual gratification could become a reality. One therefore has to remove emotional investments from the family and locate them elsewhere. This process of disengagement is held to be central to behaviour in adolescence.

First, early involvements need to be reanimated if they are to be discarded. Thus adolescents temporarily regress to the infant level. This is expressed, for instance by forming infantile attachments, but this time to figures outside rather than inside the family. Instances of such behaviour include the idolization of sporting heroes or pop stars (Blos, 1962). Second, behaviour is marked by profound ambivalence. The emotional conflict between loving one's parents and rejecting them is reflected in generalized fluctuations between acceptance and rejection, involvement and detachment, independence and dependence. Third, nonconformity and rebellion are an almost universal feature of adolescence. This is partly a consequence of emotional ambivalence but it also acts as an aid to the general process of disengagement. By negating all aspects of home life it becomes easier to distance oneself from one's parents. The fourth and final feature of the process is a feeling of emotional loss and a need for alternative affective engagements. In throwing off parental attachments, youth are left in a state that is almost equivalent to mourning. Before mature emotional attachments are developed, adolescents will do almost anything to gain emotional support. It is revealing to quote Coleman at some length as he describes some psychoanalytic views of what results:

> the adolescent need for intense emotional states, including delinquent activities, drug and mystical experiences, and short-lived but intense relationships may be seen as a means for coping with the inner emptiness. Blos includes here the need to do things 'just for kicks', which he argues simply represents a way of combatting the emotional flatness, depression and loneliness which are part of the separation experience. He also indicates his belief that both 'object' or 'affect' hunger find some relief in the adolescent gang or peer group. This social group is often, quite literally, the substitute for the adolescent's family.
>
> (1980, pp. 5–6)

Anna Freud's faithful rendition of psychoanalytic theory therefore suggests that all youth will display similar behavioural patterns in adolescence as a result of their physiological development. It suggests that adolescence is a period of particular vulnerability where not only is one torn by internal external psychic conflicts but also that this turmoil involves casting aside those very attachments that previously ensured equilibrium. Finally, it sees delinquency as resulting from an inability to achieve a mature psychic state. Thus, in the form of psychoanalysis, the basic premises of Hall's psychology still dominate the psychological understanding of adolescence. Indeed if one replaces phylogeny with the Oedipal complex, and inteprets 'old moorings' as parental identifications then Hall's description 'of some ancient period of storm and stress when old moorings were broken and a higher level attained' characterizes the Freudian view of adolescence as well as his own.

Erikson's revised psychoanalytic account of adolescence (*Identity: Youth and Crisis*) was published in 1968 – a time when the beat generation, the hippies and, probably most significantly, protest against the Vietnam war had made 'youth' a prime topic of political concern. In such a context, Erikson was keenly aware of the need to avoid psychological reductionism and to take account of the social context of adolescence. He argues forcefully that previous psychoanalytic theories fail to conceptualize the environment and, in particular, the way in which the social world is represented within the individual and thereby influences his or her behaviour (a concept captured by the German term 'umwelt'). Indeed, in his intentions at least, Erikson's general arguments echo some of the central themes of this book. Thus he argues for a social psychological understanding of how human beings are moulded in a social sphere. At a more specific level, he argues for 'a psychoanalysis sophisticated enough to include the environment . . . (and) a social psychology which is psychoanalytically sophisticated' (1968, p. 24).

In order to achieve this unity of the individual and the social, Erikson reconceptualizes the significance of basic psychoanalytic concepts. Thus, while he accepts that such things as oral relationship with the mother, bowel training and walking are crucial to the development of selfhood, Erikson argues that the way in which they are important depends on the social meaning accorded to them in particular cultural contexts. So, for instance, whereas Freud talks of the importance of walking in terms of a universal principle (locomotor eroticism) Erikson inisists that we investigate the social status accorded to those who accomplish the act. So, in one culture walking may signify 'one who will go far', whereas, in another, it may signify 'one who may go too far'.

Erikson characterizes the human life cycle as a series of stages in which individuals have to resolve different psychological problems. These start with the need to establish trust in relationships and move on to coping with despair towards the end of one's life. Each problem precipitates a crisis – not in the sense of imminent catastrophe, but rather in the sense of a need fundamentally to alter one's perspective – and each crisis may be resolved more or less successfully. However, the most significant crisis of life occurs in the fifth stage, the stage of adolescence.

The reason for this is twofold. On the one hand, the individual acquires the cognitive capacity to reflect upon both what he or she might have been in the past and what he or she might be in the future (the inspiration for this argument derives directly from Piaget). On the other hand, the young person emerges from the protected world of childhood and has to make crucial selections concerning future roles. In other words, the adolescent simultaneously becomes capable of contemplating possible alternative selves and becomes required to choose between them. It isn't easy to reconcile past, present and possible futures. The ever present danger is that individuals will fail to create or discover coherence in their identity – 'identity diffusion'. However, true to his general principles, Erikson argues that the difficulties are not simply existential, they are compounded in cultures such as our own which demand firm choices, for example choices of occupation.

Erikson sums up the principal theme of adolescence as striving for fidelity: the need for something or someone to be true to. He argues that this can only be achieved in the interaction between individual and society. Thus everyone will go through adolescence in a slightly different way. Crisis will only occur if individuals are unable to assume their social roles. Therefore it is neither universal nor inevitable. However, should individuals fail to assume a coherent identity, the results of identity diffusion are dire. Amongst other things, there will be an inability to achieve intimacy, the loss of a sense of time, listlessness and an inability to concentrate. Some relief from these problems may be achieved by consciously rejecting the standards presented as desirable and choosing everything hitherto regarded as most negative. To have some identity, even one devalued by others, is better than having no identity at all. What is more, Erikson argues, such relief is often sought collectively, in cliques and gangs of social misfits. Confusion is therefore inextricably intertwined with a search for degraded 'fidelity' in the group and hence with delinquent and even psychotic episodes.

Ultimately, then, even if Erikson departs from mainstream psycho-analytic reasoning by insisting that the resolution of developmental crisis depends upon larger social factors, he still presents adolescence as a period of particular vulnerability. Perhaps not everybody succumbs to the crisis as Anna Freud suggests, but people are more likely to succumb at this age than any other. What is more, along with Freud, Erikson sees reliance on the peer group as a result of psychic failure. He also sees delinquency and groups as going together. For orthodox and radical Freudians alike, delinquency is essentially a product of the inherently troublesome psychic tasks of adolescence.

3.4.4 Role change, role strain and the problems of adolescence

Sociological approaches have also tended to treat inner turmoil and outer conflict as inherent features of adolescence, but have tended to attribute this principally to factors in the adolescent's social world. However, before sociology could explain why adolescence and crisis went together, it was necessary to focus concern on adolescence in itself. As we have already indicated, a generalized concern with the socialization of the young goes back well into the nineteenth century. Whether one looks to Hugo's *Les Miserables* or Dickens's *Oliver Twist*, the rootless urchin who becomes prey to criminal influences was a powerful folk devil. None the less the concern remained generalized on the whole. The age range remained unspecified, the reasons why the young should be particularly vulnerable remained relatively untheorized beyond a repetition of the principal themes of mass society theory. A specific concern with the position of those in their early to mid teens had to await the period after 1945.

Clarke et al. (1976) put the emergence of the teenager (itself, a postwar term) down to a number of factors, most notable amongst which was the rising economic affluence and independence of young people. This allowed them to partake of a distinctive youth-oriented mass culture and distinctive youth styles whether in music, dress or whatever. Abrams (1995) pithily summarizes the phenomenon by referring to a 'distinctive teenage spending for distinctive teenage ends in a distinctive teenage world' (p. 10, quoted in Clarke et al., 1976, p. 18).

The shift to a particular concern with older youth is apparent in some of the theorists that we have already encountered. Thus, if Merton is concerned with the general phenomenon of strain and deviance, both Cohen (1955) and Cloward and Ohlin (1960) are particularly concerned with strain and adolescent deviance. The question is, what is distinctive about this age group? Why should strain be any different for them than for older or younger people? The principal answer is much the same as Erikson's with the psychoanalytic baggage discarded: in adolescence there are profound changes in role expectations. Individuals are expected by adults to become more responsible, to consider their future, to think of jobs, to prepare for their place in adult society. In all this there is the threat of conflicting expectations from adults and peers.

One can imagine accommodations to changing role expectations afflicting all adolescents and hence a sociological version of the argument that adolescence is a time of vulnerability for everybody. Some theorists have indeed taken this path. They argue that the commonalities of adolescence are accentuated by being cut off from the rest of society in age-specific high schools (Coleman, 1961). They therefore see age similarities as outweighing class differences or even present adolescence as a new class in itself (Zweig, 1961).

Others, however, addressed the possibility that the stresses of role change do not afflict all adolescents equally. If strain is a mismatch between aspirations and opportunities then it should be greater to the extent that aspirations are higher or opportunities lower. From Merton's perspective the notion that differing groups will have different aspirations is explicitly excluded – after all, everyone is supposedly in thrall to the American dream. On the other hand it is plausible to propose that groups will differ systematically in terms of their opportunities. We live in stratified societies. Adolescence therefore is not just a transition from one role to another, but a movement towards a particular destination in the social hierarchy.

The implication of this argument is that adolescence will only be a problem for those who realize their allocated slot in society will never allow them to meet their aspirations. In effect, adolescence will be a problem for the working classes. We have encountered versions of this argument in Cohen (1955) and Cloward and Ohlin (1960). To recapitulate, Cloward and Ohlin argue that realization of their impending exclusion from the affluent society won't lead adolescents to reject its values. Rather they will turn to the help of others in finding delinquent ways to achieve affluence. Cohen (1955) further restricts the problems of adolescence to working-class boys, arguing that working-class girls have been socialized to expect less and therefore to experience no discrepancy between their lowly opportunities and lowly aspirations. He argues that failure to achieve status in terms of dominant middle-class standards, as first encountered in formal education, will lead working-class male adolescents to invert the values of those who stigmatized them and create a collective contra-culture. Status can then be reclaimed through being good at fighting, stealing and vandalizing.

Subsequent sociological contributions to the debate on youth culture have contested the elements of these approaches. Many, especially those with some degree of Marxist inspiration, have rejected the idea that there is a single ladder to success in our society with middle-class values and aspirations at the top and youth culture as a compensation for those who stay at the bottom (cf. Clarke et al., 1976). They therefore argue that youth culture need not be trapped into the dichotomy of either accepting or inverting dominant values. Instead it is often suggested that youth culture serves as a form of 'problem solving' for the particular problems of youth. There is some question as to whether this problem solving is purely imaginary (for instance Cohen, 1972, argues that 'mod' and 'skinhead' styles are a magical attempt to recover the lost community that existed in older generations), whether it is at least partly functional (so Clarke et al., 1976, suggest that youth culture wins actual space on the street and time for leisure), or whether it really provides some sort of alternative in young people's lives (Brake, 1973; Murdock, 1973). However, when it comes to describing what the problems of adolescence actually are, there is remarkably little dissension. The following quotations from Brake and Murdock (both taken from Clarke et al., 1976, p. 29) make the point. First of all, Brake:

> youth is not in itself a problem, but there are problems created, for example by the conscription of the majority of the young into the lower strata of a meritocratic education system and then allowing them only to take up occupations which are meaningless, poorly paid and uncreative. Working-class subcultures attempt to infuse into this bleak world excitement and colour during the brief respite between school and settling down into marriage and adult-hood.

Then Murdock:

> subcultures offer a collective solution to the problems posed by shared contradictions in the work situation and provide a social and symbolic context for the development and reinforcement of a collective identity and individual self-esteem.

Thus, whether in its liberal or Marxist variants, sociological accounts of adolescence tend to focus on issues surrounding the realization of one's structural position (and opportunities) in society. They tend to see youth culture as some kind of compensatory activity for those who are structurally disadvantaged. They also consider such compensatory activities as inherently collective. So, while the sociologists view adolescent vulnerability in social structural rather than psychic terms they still, like the psychologists, see the group as a prop for those who fare badly. Given this consensus around the heightened significance of the group in adolescence, it is time to examine how group influence is viewed.

3.4.5 The peer group

Beyond general agreement that the peer group is particularly important in adolescence, there is little consensus on particulars. Coleman and Hendry (1990) observe that the terms 'peer' and 'peer group' are given a number of different meanings in the adolescence literature. Peers may be close friends, a set of habitual associates or even a group of relative strangers who happen to be engaged in the same activity in the same setting. In some contexts the terms are only used to describe those who belong to the same significant social category rather than a particular set of people in whose company individuals find themselves on one or more occasions. The only two features of peers that are common to most usages of the term are similarity of age and lack of family connection.

This diversity of usages may be put down to the absence of any single theory of the peer group. Rather the idea that relations with peers – whether these take the form of intimacy with age-equals, time spent with age mates or identification with an age-defined social category – are of greater significance than in any other period of life has the status of an empirical claim. The claim concurs with popular stereotype, informal observation and some research evidence, but it is a description of social relations in adolescence, not an explanation.

This is not to say that there are no theories which accommodate this feature of social life. Indeed, each of the theoretical treatments of adolescence that we have addressed so far and others besides incorporates some means of accounting for the 'fact' of peer group participation. In cognitive developmental theory, it is the achievement of intellectually-based social competencies that allow adolescents to develop closer ties than was possible in childhood. For psychoanalysis , the peer group is a substitute for those with problems of identification. For much subcultural theory, peers are a way of dealing with the dawning understanding that one is and will remain excluded from the world of privilege.

If there are many views of why adolescents are in groups, there tends to be a single perspective concerning the consequences. Brown (1988) summarizes the general message of research on collective behaviour as 'groups are bad for you'. If so, the adolescence literature should provide the rider 'peer groups are worse'. Classically, the group is the germ cell of mass society. It is a domain within which individuals can no longer be identified by others. As a consequence their individual identity is replaced by a group mind. The rational self gives way to the irrational collective and the result is amoral if not actively immoral (Le Bon, 1895). Modern psychology, with its aspirations to sober scientism, does not express itself as dramatically as Le Bon, but the general theme of collective irrationality remains. Thus, in the group, individuals' sense of responsibility is diffused (Latane & Darley, 1970), objective judgement is undermined by social influence (Asch, 1956), 'group think' can lead to faulty decisions (Janis, 1972), choices are generically rash and risky (Wallach, Kogan & Bem, 1962) and – in the most direct extrapolation from Le Bon – deindividuation leads to generically anti-social or at least generically uncontrolled behaviour (Diener, 1979, 1980; Zimbardo, 1969). Indeed, as Oakes, Turner and Haslam (1993) point out, social cognition theory starts from the premise that group-level perception is inherently a form of distortion employed in order to achieve simplification. So, whether on a cognitive level or a moral level, entering into the group is to be led into error.

If groups undermine individual rationality, it follows that they are particularly dangerous for those whose internal psychic structures are already weak. In so far as adolescence is characterized as a period where these structures are in turmoil then, to paraphrase Coleman (1980), those adolescents who spend most of their time with others are more likely to get harm than good out of it. A more graphic account of the vulnerability of adolescents to mindless conformity is provided by Johnson, writing about 'The menace of Beatalism':

> While the music is performed, the cameras linger savagely over the faces of the audience. What a bottomless chasm of vacuity they reveal. Huge faces, bloated with cheap confectionery, and smeared with chain-store make-up, the open sagging mouths and glazed eyes, the hands mindlessly drumming in time to the music, the broken stiletto heels, the shoddy stereotyped 'with it' clothes: here apparently is a collective portrait of a generation enslaved by a commercial machine.   (Quoted in Clarke et al., 1976, p. 19)

Consonant with this picture, the peer group is held responsible for a whole series of ills: not just delinquency but also such unhealthy behaviours as smoking, drinking and taking drugs. The response of health educators in the main is to urge young people to keep away from the influence of peers. 'Just say no' urges a familiar slogan, as if the practice of independence and autonomy will by itself ward off the dangers of the social group (cf. Hopkins, 1994a). There is an irony here. For, according to many of the theories we have described, it is not simply that adolescence is a time of vulnerability, but that the most vulnerable adolescents will seek out peer group support. Those least able to exercise autonomy are represented as those who most need to exercise it in order to escape the collective morass. To portray a connection between adolescent vulnerability and groups is – in terms of traditional theory – to draw a generational connection with delinquency even if the term is never explicitly mentioned.

3.5 Conclusions

Having dealt with so many theoretical positions at such length, we will limit ourselves here to reiterating those general assumptions which we have repeatedly encountered throughout the chapter. At the most general level, we argue that most theories of deviance are united by their shared assumption that the problem of deviance reduces to one of socialization failure – a failure that becomes particularly apparent in adolescence. The conditions of mass society preclude the possibility that social control could be sufficient to maintain the social order. Therefore individuals must be made to police themselves. Thus the major theories of deviance that we have encountered start from the position that internal control of conduct is an essential part of the process of crime control. Crime results when this internal control fails. Psychological models relate this failure either to a hiatus in the process of acquiring internal control or else to inappropriate content being fed into the process of internalization. Sociological models relate this failure to the forms of social organization encountered by those who occupy different positions in the social structure.

The link between delinquency and failures of socialization is also used as a basis for explaining the relationship between delinquency and adolescence. This is because adolescence is generally treated as the central crisis in the socialization process. Those who fail to solve either the psychic or the social process of transition from childhood to finding a place in the social world either directly become delinquent or else fall prey to the social group which itself is represented as the royal road to deviance.

So far we have commented on some of the theoretical problems associated with these positions and also what they exclude – in particular an analysis of the social psychological bases of delinquent action. For, if psychological theories tend to look inward towards general process models and sociological models look outwards towards one's general location in society, very few people look to the immediate context in which delinquent acts are committed (or not committed) and the significance of such action (or abstention) in the social world of the adolescent. However, it is insufficient to claim theoretical lacunae in existing theories. It is also necessary to show that these gaps stop the theories from accounting for the phenomena they purport to cover. It is time to examine the research evidence bearing upon the claims we have encountered in this chapter concerning the causes of deviance and conformity.

4

Colliding with the Facts

4.1 Introduction

In this chapter we will begin to ask in more detail how theories of delinquency accord with what is known about the phenomenon. In the terms of classical scientific method, are hypotheses derived from theories confirmed by the evidence? We shall argue that in certain crucial respects the theories considered in the last chapter do not accord with the evidence. Before proceeding, however, there are two things of which we must remind ourselves.

First, theories are also stipulations as to what is and what is not to count as evidence. Hence, most crucially of all, there has been no widespread agreement on what is a good measure of crime and the history of research in this field is partly one of unravelling the complex and problematic character of measurement. The second is that the sociologies and psychologies examined in the last chapter have posed rather different questions about crime. Broadly, the first have sought to explain criminals in terms of the nature of crime, the second to explain crime in terms of the nature of criminals. In consequence the latter took the nature of crime to be self-evident but human nature to be problematic. The former took it that the more problematic matter was the nature of crime.

So, when it comes to measurement, the respective disciplines have different questions to ask. Sociology wants to know: how much and what kinds of crime are there in a particular society? What are the historical trends and what is the social distribution? Let us call these the sociological questions. Psychology wants to know: how much and what kinds of crime have different individuals committed? How much crime are they capable of? Let us call these the psychological questions.

In our view a social psychology of crime needs to answer both kinds of question. So, in this chapter both the social and the psychological distribution of delinquency will be reviewed, but we must begin with the matter of measurement.

4.2 Measurement Strategies

There are five kinds of answer to the measurement problem: (1) officially defined crime; (2) victim reports; (3) experimental measures; (4) observer ratings; (5) self-reports. The first two and the last have been considered appropriate ways of asking the sociological questions, the first and the third the psychological questions. Observer ratings have not been widely used to answer either, though we shall argue that what they reveal is enlightening. We shall also argue that self-reports shed rather more light on the psychological questions than the discipline has been willing to concede.

4.2.1 *Officially defined crime*

Delinquency is usually taken to be behaviour that constitutes an infraction of the criminal law. From this derives the first and most popular method of measuring delinquency: official decisions. People are convicted and sentenced for committing criminal acts. This has two results of interest to those who would measure crime. It creates official records of the crimes committed and it specifies persons who have committed them.

The latter result is the basis for the most common approach in psychological research concerned with delinquency as such (e.g., Eysenck & Eysenck, 1970; Glueck & Glueck, 1950; Hathaway & Monachesi, 1953; McCord, McCord & Zola, 1959; West & Farrington, 1973). It normally involves one or both of two procedures: firstly, the classification of individuals in terms of the number and/or types of offence officially recorded against them; secondly, the more direct examination of those who have been officially adjudged delinquent in comparison with a standard of normality (constituted by those who have not been so adjudged). In practice researchers have made use of the helpful tendency for society to incarcerate offenders. In simple terms, if one wants to know why crime occurs one studies those people conveniently gathered together in penal institutions.

This practice, however, has several consequences which reduce its value as a way of measuring crime. One is that the researcher encounters the subject not only after his crime but also after he has been apprehended, tried, convicted and incarcerated. Being officially defined as delinquent has its own effects on the individual (Ageton & Elliott, 1974; Farrington, Osborne & West, 1978) as does incarceration (Culbertson, 1975). So if you discover, for example, that an offender admits to liking parties or excitement, have you learned something about the kind of person who is capable of breaking the law, or the kind of feelings that incarceration produces? A second problem is that comparing institutionalized offenders with others, instead of comparing individuals on the basis of a direct examination of official records, produces more extreme differences between groups in terms of actual conduct (Erickson & Empey, 1963). Incarceration does not automatically follow on conviction; this is most likely when offences are serious.

We need next to consider the uses to which sociology puts official records and the problems these raise. Official statistics on crime have been extensively used to establish crime rates for different social groups, whether these are defined by residential area (Shaw & McKay, 1942), class (Reiss & Rhodes, 1961), ethnicity (Wolfgang et al., 1972), age (Tracy, Wolfgang & Figlio, 1990), gender (Wadsworth, 1979) or any other distinguishing feature. Their use has been just as extensively criticized, for providing a distorted picture of the true rates (Box, 1981).

This has become a highly complex debate and we can only pick out a few of the key objections. One is that research based only on official records necessarily excludes anti-social behaviour which does not attract official attention. Another is that different kinds of official record indicate different rates for the same kinds of crime. Crimes known to the police, crimes solved, crimes resulting in a police caution and crimes resulting in convictions each produce different totals. This has prompted the observation that the official records reveal more about the administrative practices through which crimes are defined than about the identity of those who commit them (Box, 1981). It has also produced the assertion that the system responds to the offender as much as the offence; culprits from certain categories are treated more leniently and their cases are less likely to result in prosecutions, convictions or punishments. This is indisputably true in one respect; on the one hand the culprit's age determines whether he is allowed to be regarded as criminal at all, while on the other only his age makes certain activities illegal.

Official records have two further difficulties as measures of delinquency. They can provide only a very crude index of an individual's degree of criminal activity. Though this limitation may be moderated by making counts of convictions per individual, or weighting convictions for seriousness, this is seldom done in psychological research. Even if it were, most people's 'official crime' score would still be zero. This is the second difficulty: official records can only be based on detected crime. There are reasons to believe much crime remains undetected, and so zero scores in many cases may not be true zeros.

4.2.2 Victim surveys

Dissatisfaction with the capacity of official records to provide a picture of the true extent of crime led to a search for more reliable indicators. One source, first adopted on a large scale in the United States in the mid-sixties, is a survey of the victims of crime (e.g. Ennis, 1967). Ten thousand households were surveyed and their occupants asked to indicate the nature and number of the crimes of which they had personally been the victims. About twice as many major crimes were revealed as had been reported to the police. The surveys also revealed wide variations across types of crime in the extent of unreported offences and the patterns provide some fascinating insights into the workings of the criminal justice system. The method also has its own peculiar problems.

Much of this would be a digression for us. However, this research does contain two important messages to which we wish to draw attention. One is that far more crime is committed than ever appears in the official records of detections or convictions. A question which remains is whether the unrecorded crimes are committed by the same people convicted for the recorded offences. Or are the latter merely those too incompetent to evade the law? The other message concerns the identity of the victims, a point we will pick up later.

4.2.3 Experimental measures

Given the assumptions of psychological theory, detection must be a major problem. People commit crimes, according to psychological wisdom, when and because they believe they can get away with it, and if they experience no internal inhibition. So, unless their belief is uniformly and invariably erroneous, how could their culpability be uncovered? Actually, while clinicians and psychologically trained criminologists were studying incarcerated juveniles, those involved in more 'basic' research had been pondering a different question: how can a delinquent disposition be detected, let alone measured? Or conversely, how can one tell whether children have internalized controls over conduct?

Psychology had started from the assumption that to act in a socialized fashion is to act in accordance with rule, law, moral principle or ethical standard precisely and especially when one's actions are not subject to the appraisal or approval of others. Hence the strength of internalized controls can be accurately determined only by assessing an individual's disposition to resist committing sins in secret. This does pose a problem for the researcher. If the sinner is truly successful at keeping his or her responsibility for the sin a secret then, by definition, it cannot be known by any third party whether this person has transgressed or not.

Experimental measures were developed to meet needs for a degree of scientific control over the conditions in which behaviour occurs. And the main conditions to control were those determining an individual's perception of the probability of detection. Notable early examples were the tests of 'honesty' used by Hartshorne and May (1928) with children, and the 'cheating' test McKinnon (1938) devised for use with students. Characteristically, these procedures expose individuals to some behavioural choice that is attractive but forbidden, and do so in a context which appears to permit this choice without any possibility it will be detected by others. In other words, they offer temptations to secret sins. The temptation might be to do well on a test by sneaking a look at the answers (MacKinnon, 1938), lie about or fake scores in a game to win a prize (Grinder, 1961), play with an attractive toy one has been forbidden to touch (Parke, 1967), or cease work on a boring task when left unsupervised.

Of course the wily researcher is able to detect cheating by various ingenious tricks, such as ensuring the task cannot be completed by honest means, or that certain levels of performance are improbable without cheating, or by surreptitiously recording true performance levels. The subject's anonymity of action is merely a compelling illusion, a hoax.

The advantages claimed for the experimental method are that it is based on direct observation and objective recording of actual behaviour and that it allows for tight control of the conditions of measurement. If individuals do not cheat this can only be because internal controls restrain them. The most obvious feature of these methods is that the behaviours sampled by the various tests represent rather trivial kinds of transgression, if they can be thought of as transgressions at all. Succumbing to these temptations is in no case criminal and hardly even morally reprehensible (Turiel, 1983). In some cases actions are only proscribed because the experimenter decrees it so. What is true of trivialities need not be true of more serious offences and we shall see later that the most trivial forms of misconduct tend to be the least representative of an individual's conduct in general.

A related and perhaps more significant point concerns the moral ambiguity of experimentally induced transgressions. The very methodology places the experimenter in a dilemma. To create conditions under which more serious offences might occur would be to connive in them. Moreover, matters regarded as truly serious normally give rise to precautions, obstructions put in the way of rule-breaking. For a person to fail to take precautions against serious mischief would be regarded as foolish and perhaps bizarre. The absence of precautions against cheating in tasks like Hartshorne and May's can be seen as telling the children who take them that the experimenter does not regard these as serious matters. So if children's behaviour also reflects this attitude we should hardly be surprised.

A third peculiarity of these tests is that they operationalize socialization as resistance to cheating rather than to temptation. We may not be able to resist the temptation of more ice-cream for dessert but in this we display susceptibility to vice or weakness, not sin. We become sinful when we also try to conceal the vice. And so crime is conflated with dishonesty. Sinners do not merely break the rules, they also lie about it afterwards. The natural reflex of sinners is concealment.

These ideas take us back to some fundamental notions about the nature of guilt, before Freud persuaded us to see it as primarily an internal, subjective experience. Guilt is firstly an objective social fact, the fact of having crossed a moral boundary, social because the boundary is collectively established. Secondly it is a public acknowledgment by the transgressor that he or she has done so. The unsocialized lack guilt in the sense that they deny it. Freud's twofold embellishment on this idea was to suggest first that honest people are driven to confession by an internalized sense of duty, and second that even imagining the possibility of crossing the moral boundary produces unbearable anxieties.

Once psychology defined socialization as 'not cheating' at the game of life and agreeing to handicap oneself in various ways, it was natural to employ other measures of honesty to assess the progress of socialization. One popular method has been the 'Lie scale' (Hartshorne, May & Shuttleworth, 1930), a device for detecting willingness to confess to transgression. Cheats can also be caught out by projective measures of reaction to transgression (Allinsmith, 1960). They will not admit that they transgress, but they will fail to predict the confession any honest person would make upon breaking the rules. It is interesting that revealing one's transgressions to others should be described as confession and not, for example, as boasting, as if such revelation were tantamount to repentance; even a guilty conscience is after all evidence of a conscience.

In a small community lies can readily be uncovered but the city produces the anxiety that all these strangers will lie to you and cheat you, and you will not be able to detect or distinguish the honest from the dishonest. Conscience provides the reassurance that they will all feel compelled to tell the truth.

One further feature of experimental measures which we believe reduces their relevance to the measurement of crime (and there have been attempts to measure more serious crime in this way – e.g., Farrington, 1979) is that they usually fail to meet basic psychometric criteria. We shall have more to say about this later in the chapter.

4.2.4 Observer ratings

An alternative strategy which has experienced periodic popularity in socialization research is to assess an individual's behavioural characteristics on the basis of ratings provided by others. These ratings may refer to anything from assessments of the frequency with which the individual engages in specified activities to more global assessments of personality characteristics or traits assumed to reflect the relevant behavioural dimensions. Hartshorne, May and Shuttleworth (1930) used measures of this kind as did Havighurst and Taba (1949) in their study of adolescent character development. The latter obtained ratings for their sample from a variety of sources including teachers, parents, peers and research staff. In work more directly concerned with delinquency, Gold (1970) secured details from teenage informants about specific acts of delinquency committed by their acquaintances.

None the less, not everyone has accepted the validity of such ratings, sometimes called reputational measures. One source of criticism was work in person perception and clinical judgement which indicated that people's perceptions and assessments of one another are vulnerable to a variety of distortions and biases. Generally, it was argued, these perceptions are more likely to reflect the characteristics of the perceiver than the perceived (Cronbach, 1955; Mischel, 1968; Passini & Norman, 1966).

More recently some of these criticisms have been answered as it emerged that the distortions they highlighted only occur under certain conditions (Norman & Goldberg, 1966; Weiss, 1979). Researchers have begun to reconsider reputational measures, given their capacity to provide reliable and apparently valid assessments of behavioural characteristics (Wiggins, 1973). The key requirements for reliability and validity would appear to be that the raters are knowledgeable informants, i.e., well acquainted with those they are rating, and that ratings from different sources are aggregated (Cheek, 1982; Moskowitz & Schwartz, 1982).

Necessarily, however, resistance to such measures remains while psychology continues to accept a mass society model of social life. For if society consists of atomized and isolated individuals how can there be knowledgeable informants? And if deviance is covert it should be poorly reflected in observer's ratings.

4.2.5 Self-report measures

Except for victimization surveys which address the 'sociological questions', self-report measures of conduct and misconduct have been far less widely used in psychological research than any of the other strategies considered. The reasons for this neglect are not hard to find. The logic of the method is incompatible with widely held views in psychology about the nature of offenders. The same reservations have not inhibited sociologists.

The self-report strategy uses a data base consisting of the responses individuals give to a list of questions about delinquent and criminal activities. They are asked which of the activities they have engaged in and, depending on the procedure, how often they have engaged in each. Short and Nye (1957) are generally credited with the first systematic use of a self-report procedure to assess delinquent activity, although efforts had previously been made by Porterfield (1946) and Wallerstein and Wyle (1947). The Short and Nye measure contained 23 questions about different kinds of delinquency, although the delinquency scale they developed was based on only seven of these. The measure included questions about minor crimes, acts of disobedience and breaches of regulations. Following Short and Nye's work, self-reports have become a popular method of assessing delinquency in sociological research.

For psychology, however, the objections to this procedure were obvious: individuals would be unable and unwilling to report accurately on their own misdemeanours. Estimates of delinquency obtained in this way would surely be biased by failures and distortions of memory, ego defences, social desirability, and acquiescence response set. But most obvious of all, there is a fundamental contradiction in expecting people to be honest about their dishonesties.

The objections can be answered most directly by reference to research on the reliability and validity of self-report measures of delinquency. Evidence reviewed by Hindelang, Hirschi and Weis (1981) and by

Singh (1979) is quite unequivocal about reliability. Whether assessed by split-half, alternative forms, or test-retest methods, it has proved possible to achieve very high reliability coefficients. Singh's (1979) review cites values between 0.88 and 0.96 while Hindelang et al. (1981) observe that the reliabilities for self-report measures of delinquency often exceed those of measures used to assess psychological attributes studied in delinquency research. Even reliabilities for single items can be quite high. One thing the reliability studies reveal therefore is that self-report data is not simply noise; individuals are not responding randomly. But are such measures actually assessing crime and not something else? The issue of validity is rather more complex and we give it correspondingly more attention.

4.3 The Validity and Meaning of Self-reports

Much of the sociological interest in self-reports lay in what they might be able to reveal, first about the extent of unrecorded and undetected crime and second about the value of official statistics. With respect to the former, self-reports indicated a great deal of undetected or unreported crime, let alone unrecorded and unsolved crime. Indeed the volume of undetected adolescent crime indicated by self-report studies exceeded recorded crime several-fold (Elmhorn, 1965; Short & Nye, 1958). Self-reports and official statistics also provided somewhat different pictures of the social distribution of crime.

In so far as the intention is to measure actual crime rates, then self-reports clearly must satisfy the requirements of face validity: they must sample criminal offences. Although this should in principle be straightforward, in practice it is not. This is partly, as Hindelang (1971) shows, because self-report items are sometimes so worded as to attract admissions when the behaviour in question would not be regarded as sufficiently serious by either the victims or the relevant authorities to warrant official action. Self-report research has also been criticized for using measures in which trivial, and in some cases not strictly illegal, activities are over-represented (Box, 1981; Hirschi & Hindelang, 1977; Elliott & Ageton, 1980). If the goal is only to produce an alternative to official crime statistics so that, for example, official recording practices can be compared with the formal definitions of crime, then these are indeed serious lapses of face validity, raising real doubts about the value of self-report research. The same point would apply to the frequent use of small, unrepresentative samples, to the high non-response rates in some studies, and to the systematic tendency for samples to contain few if any more serious offenders (cf. Rutter & Giller, 1983, p. 31; Hood & Sparks, 1970). Many of the apparent weaknesses of the method, however, stem from a confusion of objectives.

It should be recognized that official statistics will never be representative of all nominally criminal acts, as common sense alone should tell us. Theft is theft whatever the value of the object taken but we know that when the value is low the event is unlikely to receive official attention. Acts within a formally defined category must be viewed as sufficiently serious to justify this attention, and thus have any prospect of appearing in the official statistics, in the interests of distributing finite police resources if for no other reason. The same is true of the individuals responsible for them; official attention is likely to depend on the perceived persistence of the offender and thus the longer-term threat he or she poses to public order.

It has been claimed that self-report research reveals the universality of crime – everybody does it (Schur, 1973) – but this misrepresents what the self-report evidence does show. This evidence indicates, first, that those with official convictions are likely to self-report far more serious and frequent offending than those without convictions (Emler, Heather & Winton, 1978; Erickson & Empey, 1963). Second, it indicates that acts normally considered sufficiently serious to require official attention are still very infrequent within the population as a whole. Hindelang et al. (1981) noted that not one activity in their 'serious crime' index was admitted by more than 20 per cent of their sample of 15–18-year-olds. The self-report strategy has usually relied on samples drawn from the general population. Because serious crime is not widely distributed in this population, very large samples would be needed to detect measurable quantities and the variance would in any event remain low; scores would have a J-curve distribution, heavily skewed towards zero. From the beginning, therefore, the objective of measuring quantity of crime was almost bound to conflict with that of detecting variation in the population studied. Because this was the general population, or some subsection of it such as adolescent males, over-representation of trivial misdemeanours and under-representation of the more serious forms was virtually guaranteed.

We shall argue that this alternative goal of detecting variation within a relatively unselected population is more fruitful than studying crime as such if one wishes to understand delinquency as a widespread feature of youthful behaviour. In effect, it is a shift towards understanding behavioural events whose distribution approximates a normal curve rather than a J-curve. But there are two obvious objections to this, one theoretical and one methodological.

To take them in order, psychological theory traditionally takes deviance to be pathology. Criminality is abnormal; very few people commit crimes. This analysis has depended on the possibility of dividing the world into the tiny criminal minority and the massive law-abiding majority. What we are proposing destroys this categorical distinction. We believe the distinction has hindered rather than helped the psychological understanding of crime. We do not deny that only a minority have convictions for crimes. We do deny they are qualitatively different from those who do not. To anticipate the argument a little, they are simply more likely to be towards the extreme of a behavioural continuum, people who have broken the rules more persistently and seriously than most. This is what the self-report evidence shows (Emler, Heather & Winton, 1978).

The methodological problem is that if the connection between delinquency and crime is weakened in this way, how can self-reports be validated? In particular, can they be validated against officially recorded delinquency? If one accepts the argument that official delinquency represents one end of a continuum, and that those with official records will also have done much that is not officially recorded (i.e., they will be the high scorers on self-report measures), then the answer is 'yes'. More direct validation is possible by checking acts which have resulted in official convictions against admissions of these same actions in the self-report measure.

Available evidence is that self-reports can meet this test (Blackmore, 1974; Erickson & Empey, 1963; Gibson, Morrison & West, 1970; Hardt & Peterson-Hardt, 1977). In this way one can validate the procedure if not all the individual items, because most delinquent acts will not have led to conviction. Another test which can be met is to include direct questions about police contacts or convictions (Hindelang et al., 1981). There are other sources of evidence for the validity of self-reports, such as corroboration by informants acquainted with the subject (Gold, 1970), in effect a test of concurrent validity by cross-checking against the results of reputational evidence.

The sceptic might still object that young people will admit to offences which their acquaintances or the police already know about, matters the researcher could therefore discover from other sources anyway, while denying those that remain unknown to others. But if this were so there should be clearer signs of concealment; why should they admit anything that is not already public knowledge or part of their record? The fact is that far more offences are admitted than are known to the police (Hood & Sparks, 1970). If self-reports are factually inaccurate (albeit that this is not the point) this is as likely to be in the direction of over- as of under-reporting.

We can now consider a fundamental question: what is delinquent behaviour or how does one decide when a delinquent act has been committed? There is of course no single correct answer; it is a matter of interpretation and the answer given will depend on who is doing the interpreting. Though all interpretations draw upon a common core of understanding – almost everyone will agree that theft is a crime, for example – there remains considerable scope for differences of interpretation. Quite apart from the issue of a stolen object's value, there are also frequent ambiguities over such matters as intention – 'did he steal that book or simply forget to return it?' – and ownership – 'was it a gift or a loan?' Similar ambiguities can arise with respect to acts of aggression and vandalism.

Each of the five methods of assessing delinquency – experimental measures, official records, victim surveys, self-reports, observer ratings – puts the interpretive burden in a different place. Experimental measures weigh the balance in favour of the researcher's 'objective' definition of the occurrence or non-occurrence of a transgression. But there has been little overlap between these definitions and methods based on official records; here the balance lies with various institutions and their agents – the drafters of legislation, police officers, courts, lawyers, judges and juries – interpreting specific instances in terms of formally framed definitions. In victim surveys and self-report studies, the balance lies respectively with victims and culprits, each with their own interpretive biases. We know, for example, from research on attribution processes that one's perspective as actor or observer influences the causal interpretation one gives for actions (e.g. Ross, 1977). In the case of 'reputational' measures, the balance is with the observer, and ultimately with collective community opinion which both decides about individual reputations and establishes the standards against which such reputations are judged.

The different methods are used to validate one another, inevitably so given that there is no other 'independent' definition or standard to which one can appeal. Self-report methods have been successfully 'validated' against official records and reputational evidence (Gold, 1970). Reputational measures have been validated against experimental tests (Hartshorne et al., 1930). And so on.

4.4 The Social Distribution of Delinquent Conduct

The self-report method provides for social psychology a particularly useful and indeed relevant way of exploring the psychology of delinquent behaviour since it does after all relate most closely to the interpretations of the young people potentially involved. Given that self-report methods can provide data about delinquency which are reliable and valid let us now examine what it can tell us, first about the social distribution of delinquency and second about its psychological distribution. In the first case, and to some extent in the second, we can look for some convergence with the picture that emerges from the other methods, particularly official records, victim surveys and reputational measures.

4.4.1 Age

The age distribution is the single most conspicuous feature of recorded criminal offences. Wolfgang, Figlio and Sellin (1972) found that among a male cohort born in 1945, arrests were most common at age 16. Official records provided by other sources reveal much the same picture. Recorded police contacts are low at 10 years, climb steeply to the mid-teens and decline, though gradually, thereafter. The Cambridge delinquency study of a cohort of London boys indicates 14–15 as the peak age for first arrests, while conviction rate peaked at 17 (West & Farrington, 1977). These and similar findings are likely to reflect more than an inclination by the police to pick on adolescents.

It is true that few self-report studies have included age as a variable and many have required respondents to indicate which activities on the list they had 'ever' engaged in. However, in a Canadian study, Farrington, Biron and LeBlanc (1982) asked males and females aged 12 to 17 about acts committed in the past year only. Their findings indicated a peak in admissions at around 14–15 years for boys, with a corresponding but slightly less distinct pattern for the girls. A similar study by Ageton and Elliott (1978) indicates a peak in self-reported assault and property crimes between 13 and 15.

We asked some 400-plus high school students aged 12 to 15 which of a range of 22 delinquencies they had engaged in over the previous 12 months. We found that among the boys all the increase in admissions occurred between 12 and 13. Thereafter, there was no overall increase. Admissions among the girls increased steadily across the age range.

There has also been some suggestion that the nature of delinquency changes with age. Loeber (1982) has argued on the basis of his own and other evidence that there is a shift away from 'overt' forms of misconduct such as aggression and defiance and towards 'covert' misdeeds such as lying, stealing and vandalism. Certainly, some evidence indicates offences in this latter category become more frequent between 10 and 15 years

Table 4.1 Age-related increases in self-reported delinquency

Item	Change with age[1]
Played truant from school	Large increase
Stolen things from a shop while it was open	Large increase
Found property belonging to other people and failed to return it	Large increase
Damaged school property on purpose, things like books, furniture etc.	Large increase
Hit a teacher	Large increase
Purposefully destroyed, damaged or defaced others' property	Moderate increase
Broken the windows of empty houses	Moderate increase
Annoyed or insulted strangers in the street	Moderate increase
Stolen from people's clothing or stolen their individual belongings	Moderate increase
Smashed, slashed or damaged public property	Small increase
Deliberately littered street by smashing bottles, turning over bins etc.	Small increase
Used a weapon in a fight	No increase
Thrown things such as stones at other people	No increase
Purposefully annoyed, insulted or defied a police officer	No increase
Involved in a group fight	No increase
Taken a car, motor bike or bicycle and kept it	No increase
Got into someone's home with the intention of stealing things	No increase
Struggled or fought to get away from a police officer	No increase
Broken into a shop, garage or factory to steal things	No increase

[1] Change over a period of 18 months from 12 or 14 years

(Farrington, 1973), but the Cambridge Delinquent Development study also reveals that aggression remains a salient feature of high levels of delinquent involvement throughout the teens (West & Farrington, 1977, pp. 80–108). Ageton and Elliott's study shows a tendency for status offences to show a linear increase across adolescence; 16- and 17-year-olds were more likely than younger respondents to report having run away, truanted, used alcohol or drugs, or been suspended from school. Of the activities we sampled in our own study many of those likely to show increases across age were to do with school (see table 4.1).

Generally self-report evidence does confirm that crime is above all a phenomenon of adolescence. But it also elaborates on this image and raises further questions such as why, for example, do different forms of delinquency peak at different ages?

4.4.2 Gender

Almost as conspicuous as age as are male–female differences in crime rates. The criminal statistics indicate far more convictions for males and also indicate that most arrests of females are for 'female' offences such as running away, sexual promiscuity and parental defiance. Self-report evidence gives a somewhat different picture here. The male-to-female ratio for self-report admissions is rather lower than for recorded convictions though the ratio is greatest for more serious forms of misbehaviour. This has emerged consistently from our own studies with various age groups (Emler & Reicher, 1987; Emler, Reicher & Ross, 1987; Reicher & Emler, 1985a; Renwick & Emler, 1984), and concurs with findings in several other studies (Elliott & Ageton, 1980; Hindelang et al., 1981; Jensen & Eve, 1976). The figures in table 4.2 are typical. As this table also shows, males and females do not engage in quite different kinds of delinquency as the official records imply; the differences are in prevalence. Girls admit to theft, vandalism, and assault, but in smaller numbers than boys. Over a range of delinquencies the average ratio of males to females admitting activities is a fairly constant 2:1.

4.4.3 Ethnicity

One of the truisms of the criminal theory which emerged to make sense of the official picture of crime was that commission of crimes is not uniformly distributed across ethnic groups. Thus official statistics for juveniles in the United States showed a much greater preponderance of arrests among blacks for all categories of serious crime (Empey, 1982, p. 87). The difference however is non-existent for less serious offences. In this area, the picture to emerge from self-report studies has been quite similar (Elliott & Ageton, 1980; Hindelang, Hirschi & Weis, 1981); black–white differences are greater for violent crime but much less for most other kinds.

4.4.4 Social class

The question of social class is the most vexing of all and continues to fuel a lively debate in the journals (see the review by Box, 1981, pp. 75–83).

Table 4.2 Sex differences in admission rates for self-reported delinquencies

Behaviour	Admission rate: males (n=145)	Admission rate: females (n=141)
Done things to people as a joke, like pushing them into water	90	54
Involved in a fight where a weapon was not used	78	46
Thrown things such as stones at people	72	16
Broken windows of empty houses	61	11
Played truant from school	60	46
Annoyed or insulted strangers in the street	55	31
Deliberately littered street by smashing bottles, etc.	51	14
Purposefully annoyed, insulted, taunted a teacher	46	38
Found others' property and failed to try and return it	45	16
Stolen things from a shop while it was open	44	31
Smashed, slashed or damaged things in public places	38	08
Been to an 'X' film under age	37	34
Been involved in a fight using a weapon	36	06
Purposefully destroyed, damaged, defaced private property	34	07
Driven a car or motorbike on the highway under the legal age	32	12
Damaged school property on purpose	32	06
Been involved in a group fight	25	15
Purposefully annoyed, insulted or defied a police officer	29	02
Broken into someone's home with intention of stealing things	14	03
Struggled or fought to get away from a police officer	14	02
Hit a teacher	08	04
Stolen things from people's clothing	06	04
Stolen a car, motor bike or bicycle	03	00

Source: data from Emler, Reicher & Ross (1987). Numbers are percentages.

Much of the debate revolves around the discrepancy between official statistics, which show a strong association between class and crime, and the many self-report studies which show either a much weaker relationship or none at all. The reason for interest in this discrepancy is obvious enough: some of the most influential theories of crime are attempts to explain why it is a working-class phenomenon. Early self-report studies showed that middle-class adolescents were as likely to have committed punishable offences as their working-class counterparts. Where differences were found they were very weak. Such evidence brought into question the whole basis of criminal theory, and simultaneously fuelled arguments about the oppressive and discriminatory character of the criminal justice system.

A perhaps more measured conclusion is that evidence derived respectively from self-reports and from official statistics are seldom strictly comparable, for various reasons. First, those serious offences most likely to lead to recorded convictions are under-represented in self-report inventories. Second, ecological measures, primarily area of residence, have been used as a proxy for social class in some of the research drawing on official statistics. Correlations between delinquency rates in neighbourhoods and mean income levels in those areas can be very high (Shaw & McKay, 1942), but the more direct, individual-level measures of social class which are more characteristic of self-report studies show a weaker relationship (Hindelang et al., 1981).

Finally, official crime concerns the tail of a distribution to a far greater extent than do self-reports. Elliott and Ageton's (1980) widely cited study on the lack of class differences in self-reported delinquency reveals this problem. The mean frequencies of self-reported offences by class indicates a lower class to middle class ratio of almost 4:1 for predatory crimes against the person and almost 2:1 for crimes against property, but in the first case the difference was only just statistically significant and in the second it was not significant. The reason would seem to be that the variances or individual differences within classes were huge compared to the mean differences between classes. There are very high scorers and very low scorers in both categories, though more of the very high scorers in the 'lower class' category; of those reporting 30 or more offences, three times as many proportionately were in this category.

The most reasonable conclusion, then, is that delinquency may be somewhat more frequent, more prevalent and more serious among working-class youth but there are delinquents and non-delinquents in all social classes.

4.4.5 Area of residence

As Hindelang et al. (1981) have pointed out, much of the evidence for apparent social class differences in crime rates which is based on official statistics in fact indicates area differences in crime rates. Two kinds of difference have attracted interest, between the city and the country and between areas within cities. The rural–urban difference was, as we saw in chapter 2, one of the first preoccupations of social theory toward the end of the nineteenth century. Official figures have consistently confirmed the concentration of delinquent activities in urban areas and victim surveys show an identical pattern. Surprisingly few self-report studies have included urban–rural comparisons. One of the rare examples again moderates the official picture; Hindelang (1973) found that young people living in rural areas did also admit offences.

Within cities the differences can be extensive and indeed suggest the area of residence is a far better predictor of an individual's level of delinquent activity than the individual's own social class background. On the other hand, what distinguish high from lower delinquency areas are socio-economic factors. Shaw and McKay (1942), on the basis of their Chicago studies, reported a correlation across areas of 0.89 between delinquency rates and rates of families on relief.

4.5 Some Implications for Theory

The modified picture of the social distribution of delinquency that has emerged in more recent years from comparisons of official figures with self-report evidence and data from victim surveys is forcing a reappraisal of well-established theoretical positions. The clearest casualty is strain theory as formulated by Merton (1938). Developed primarily to account for a characteristic of delinquency that has proved at best elusive – its supposed overwhelmingly working-class nature – it is also difficult to accommodate with the age pattern and sex differences. Other theories which might seem to cope better with these features remain suspect in so far as they also take juvenile crime to be almost exclusively a working-class activity (e.g. Cloward & Ohlin, 1960; Cohen, 1955; Miller, 1958). At this point the most credible survivors of those sociological perspectives we considered in the last chapter would seem to be the advocates of cultural diversity (e.g. Sutherland & Cressey, 1970; Matza, 1964). Yet even they have difficulty in explaining why delinquency rates vary so much within all the social categories that are defined as having delinquent inclinations. Can psychological theories do any better in explaining the pattern of delinquent action?

4.6 The Psychological Distribution

4.6.1 *Individual differences*

One of the most contentious issues in contemporary psychology concerns the existence or otherwise of individual differences in social, and

[handwritten marginalia: This is because how we can label a person or their behaviour]

anti-social, behaviour. The accepted position among many social psychologists is that there are no stable individual differences in dispositions to break rules; whether a person does so is entirely a function of the circumstances in which they find themselves. Behaviour, in other words, is under situational control. This position has come to contain a number of different claims and it is as well to be clear what they are since they are not all logical requirements of the position.

(1) *'There are no stable individual differences.'* This is the idea that those individuals in any set who, for example, break rules on one occasion will not be those most likely to do so on a subsequent occasion. In other terms, individuals have no behavioural inclinations which remain stable over time; people are inconsistent.

(2) *'There are no generalized inclinations.'* This claim concerns the breadth of traits. Hence, if there were such a thing as a general trait of honesty, people possessing this trait in greater measure should display more honesty in all the various forms in which this attribute can be expressed. Those possessing it in lesser measures should consistently display less in all these cases.

(3) *'Different individuals react in the same way to differences in situation.'* If you place people in successive different situations they do not continue to behave in the same way in each; they react differently to each. On the other hand, these situational differences have similar effects on people.

Many psychologists are of the conviction that the concept of moral character, and in particular the idea that there are stable, generalized individual differences in anti-social behaviour, has been so thoroughly discredited that it barely deserves discussion. On what could such a robust conviction be founded? The place to start is with the evidence. To quote Mischel (1976):

> the data on self-control and moral behaviour do not support the existence of a unitary, intrapsychic moral agency like the superego nor do they suggest a unitary trait of conscience or honesty. (p. 461)

Mischel's argument about moral character has been part of a wider critique of trait models of behaviour in psychology. He has asserted that:

> impressive consistencies have been found for intellective features of personality but . . . when one goes beyond cognitive variables to personality

dimensions and when one samples personality by diverse methods, not just by self-report questionnaires, the data change and undermine the utility of inferring global personality dispositions from behavioural signs. (1977, p. 252)

Although Mischel's argument is therefore aimed at a much larger target than theories of moral character, namely the entire enterprise of personality assessment as traditionally conceived, the strongest evidence he adduces for the general case does concern moral character. This is evidence collected through the use of experimental measures of conduct, and the single most important study here is the Character Education Inquiry (Hartshorne & May, 1928). Many of the tests used by Hartshorne and May (1928) in their massive study of children's character development provided opportunities to cheat on typical classroom tasks of intelligence, numerical ability or physical capacity.

Mischel is not alone in the conclusions he has drawn from this study. Aronfreed (1968), Brown (1965), Endler and Magnusson (1976), Kohlberg (1969), and many others have professed themselves convinced by Hartshorne and May's conclusion that there is no stable core to moral character. Subsequent studies did little to modify these convictions. Kohlberg (1969) was able to write with confidence:

no findings have been reported suggesting fundamental revisions of Hartshorne and May's (1928–30) conclusion as to the situational specificity and longitudinal instability of moral character. (p. 367)

Hartshorne and May are cited with similar frequency as having demonstrated that there is at best a modest relation between conduct and verbal support for conformity to moral rules.

We do not believe that Hartshorne and May's evidence can support the conclusions customarily derived from it. We have already commented on the triviality and ambiguity of the misconduct their tests sampled, by virtue of which problems of interpretation arise. But another and more serious objection is that the steps necessary to construct an adequate measure of individual differences were not taken. When writers say that Hartshorne and May's data indicate the situational specificity of conduct, what they usually have in mind is that these data indicate positive but only modest correlations between honesty in one test and honesty in another, an average over all the tests of a little over 0.2. In other words, the children who behaved most honestly in one situation were not necessarily among the most honest in other situations. This is the claim about lack of generality but it is frequently confused with another, that behaviour is under situational control.

Hartshorne and May (1928) noted that the average level of honesty could vary dramatically from one test to another. In other words, whether or not most children behaved honestly or dishonestly seemed to depend on the particular circumstances in which they were placed. It is important to be clear that this is a quite separate point, which has no bearing whatsoever on the existence or otherwise of individual differences in moral conduct. Let us try to make this plain.

There is a common-sense notion of personality and behaviour which includes the following elements. There are circumstances which elicit similar reactions from almost everyone. In these the press of the situation is so great that we do not expect individual characteristics to show through. When the 'no smoking' sign is on inside the passenger cabin of an airliner, we make no inferences about the smoking habits of those present from their non-smoking behaviour. There are other circumstances under which individual reactions will differ. However, not all of these will be equally informative about the personalities of individual actors; in our everyday judgements of character we give more weight to what people do in some situations than to what they do in others. Finally, our judgements are based on observations accumulated over a number of occasions and a variety of circumstances. And we are more confident of our judgements of personality the greater the number and variety of observations on which they are based. Normally no single observation is sufficient; we do not call a man highly creative because he once had a good idea any more than we would call him a fool for once making a mistake (though there is an interesting asymmetry in such judgements, see Rothbart and Park (1986) and Skowronski and Carlston (1989), and one with implications for delinquency as we shall see in the next chapter). Personality concerns the way in which each individual performs in the long run and in general, not his or her isolated reactions to isolated situations.

Psychometric practice accords with this kind of common sense. It requires the selection of items or measures which do not elicit a uniform response, the further selection of that sub-set on which responses covary, and finally the combination of several such items to form a scale. This last step has been called the principle of aggregation; the greater the number of appropriate observations (= item responses) that contribute to an aggregated score the more accurate will be that score.

Burton (1963) has given us some idea of what may be found when these steps are completed. He took scores from Hartshorne and May's study, aggregated over groups of tests, eliminated those scores with low reliabilities and then performed a principal components analysis on the matrix of intercorrelations between the remaining scores. The first principal component accounted for between 35 and 43 per cent of the total variance. Thus, even with this rather unpromising material there was evidence for a single common factor underlying reactions to the various tests of honesty.

Mischel (1976) has taken the view that Burton has only confirmed the very modest degree of consistency Hartshorne and May claimed to have found. He and others appear to regard the low correlations between individual items as more telling than the results of aggregation. Yet there is no reason to expect that one-item tests will make for reliable measurement of any psychological characteristic.

One can accept Hartshorne and May's finding that levels of 'honesty' varied dramatically from one test or situation to another without also having to conclude that individuals show no generalized dispositions. One child can still be more honest than others even if the entire group is more honest in one situation than another. What matters is not the absolute level of honesty but whether the rank order of individuals remains the same across situations.

Some of the weaknesses of experimental measures could be overcome. It would in principle be quite possible to develop scales based on a number of individual measures which satisfy the necessary scaling criteria. In practice, because measures of this kind are cumbersome to set up and conduct they have rarely been used in large enough numbers and with sufficiently large samples to allow the construction of proper scales. The problems associated with the triviality and moral ambiguity of the transgressions elicited would, however, remain.

If experimental measures of rule-breaking will not do, what alternative is there? Of the three options, official records, observer ratings and self-reports, the third would seem to offer particular promise. It avoids the most serious limitations experimental measures have experienced. It can sample non-trivial misbehaviour. It can sample a wide and extensive range of rule-breaking activities quickly and cheaply. Responses to individual items can be aggregated to provide scale scores. And it successfully meets various tests of reliability and validity.

As an indirect assessment of the incidence of crime – the original use to which the method was put – the reliability of individual items is relevant but, as a potential measure of individual degrees of involvement in crime, scale reliability is more important. Short and Nye's measure was constructed according to Guttman scaling criteria, a procedure which invariably produces short scales and which is unlikely to result in selection of good behavioural indicators (Fishbein & Ajzen, 1974).

The Likert procedure on the other hand allows construction of longer scales which are also more likely to have high reliabilities. Researchers have in fact obtained very high reliabilities with self-report delinquency scales. And the use of longer, Likert-type scales is now more popular. Elliott and Ageton (1980) used 47 items, Hindelang et al. (1981) 63 items. But even relatively short scales, if appropriately chosen, can achieve acceptable levels of reliability. Thus an inventory based on our own research and consisting of seven items yielded an alpha coefficient of 0.82 from a sample of 270 boys, higher than those obtained in the same study from well-established personality measures, Eysenck's E and Cattell's Impulsiveness scale (Thornton, personal communication).

The normal strategy in the development of a psychological measure is to employ a procedure to identify a set of indicators that 'scale' with one another. Elementary though this requirement may be, it has been routinely ignored in much behavioural measurement. Research on relationships between attitudes and behaviour have been plagued by the frequently unrecognized inadequacy of using only single behavioural indicators satisfying no more than face validity (Fishbein & Ajzen, 1974).

Application of scaling procedures is a way of testing the hypothesis that a construct, such as honesty or delinquency, corresponds to a psychologically real dimension. That is, it is a way of establishing whether the individual differences predicted by the construct actually exist. To reiterate, personality constructs are about the way that individuals will behave 'in general and in the long run'. But how general and for how long? A minimal possibility is that there are individual differences, for example, among 17-year-olds in the tendency to steal Morris Minors circa 1954. This difference is not related to any other, and will not necessarily last into the following year. This in effect was the kind of prediction that some social learning theorists were disposed to make following Hartshorne and May's work: there is no generality to character because children do not learn to varying degrees to be 'good' in general, they learn a number of very specific habits. One person may have learned not to steal Morris Minors but not learned the same injunction against misappropriating Porsche 911s. In another person these dispositions may be reversed. If this is all there is to find, it will not be very interesting (unless one is a social learning theorist).

So let us start with another hypothesis: there are individual differences of involvement in delinquent behaviour. This still leaves a problem: how is the domain of delinquency to be defined? Should it be restricted to behaviour which constitutes an infraction of the criminal law, for example? Although the objectivity of this strategy is seductive, criminal codes vary between times and places, their application to particular actions is not entirely straightforward, and the category 'crime' has no necessary psychological unity. It is after all an administrative, rather than a psychologically based categorization of action.

A 'moral' definition of delinquency is almost as problematic. If the domain is defined by those actions which attract public condemnation as immoral or wrong, we cannot be confident of our capacity as researchers to reflect public opinion perfectly, even if we can decide which public's opinion matters. (Later we shall need to come back to the consequences of moral and legal labels for behaviour.)

A third alternative is to treat it as an empirical question and so proceed by trial and error. This means discovering by successive samplings what range of activities covary in such a way that collectively they are scalable. It is worth recalling that in 1957 Nye and Short had already undertaken such an exercise. Their original 23 items were submitted to Guttman scaling, with the result that only seven of these items met the criteria for this procedure. Must it therefore be concluded that the evidence of a dimension of 'delinquency' is weak? We think not.

Guttman scaling is based on the hypothesis that a domain, such as delinquency, consists of actions which have a strict order of progression. All people who have robbed shopkeepers at gunpoint have also committed robberies without using weapons, but the reverse will not invariably be true. All people who have committed robberies have damaged public property, but not the reverse, and so on. The scale is likely to reflect seriousness. People who commit trivial offences will not necessarily also have committed serious ones, whereas people who have committed serious offences will almost invariably have committed more trivial ones as well. This is probably true. But precisely which offences, serious or trivial, will be committed is far less predictable than the Guttman procedure requires. There will be an inevitable random element in the extent to which opportunities for different kinds of crime arise. This being so, the Likert procedure for scaling is more appropriate.

Consistent with this, Fishbein and Ajzen (1974) show that those behavioural indicators most likely to correlate with other measures, in their case, attitude scale scores, are those meeting the criteria for Likert scaling and not those meeting Guttman criteria. They also report that most of the behavioural indicators they considered did not meet the criteria of any scaling procedure, a point worth pondering in view of the widespread use of single experimental measures of conduct in socialization research.

The Likert procedure requires that two conditions be met. First there must be some variance; ideal are those items to which half the population of interest respond in one direction and half in the other. Second, scores on each individual item should correlate with the aggregate score; its variance must be related to the overall variance. So long as the item–whole correlations are not at unity, which is to say that each samples some slightly different aspect of the behavioural domain, contributing some unique variance (one assumes that no item is perfectly representative of the domain as a whole), then scores in the population should approach a normal distribution.

The first requirement, however, appears to rule out the application of Likert scaling to delinquency. Serious crimes have, after all, a highly skewed J-curve distribution, so that there would be insufficient variation in response. And any resulting scale would not produce anything resembling a normal distribution. The J-curve distribution of compliance with legal–moral standards is a 'truth' deeply rooted in the folklore of psychology (Allport, 1934). According to this principle, the majority of people will comply with standards all the time, a minority will violate them occasionally, and an even smaller minority may do so frequently. But like many other such 'truths', this one turns out to be misleading in so far as it refers to actors rather than to acts.

Certainly very few people commit murder, rape or armed robbery, and these acts do have J-curve distributions. But among the 15–18-year-old boys in a Seattle sample surveyed by Hindelang et al. (1981), 52–63 per cent admitted theft of small items from a store, 48–58 per cent admitted breaking windows in unoccupied buildings, and 37–42 per cent admitted lying about their age to buy alcohol. Similar examples can be found in the results published in British self-report studies (Shapland, 1978; Gibson, 1971).

Thus a first step for the researcher might be to examine the distribution of admissions for a large number of items. This will provide some indication of the activities which can usefully be sampled in constructing a scale. The results of such an exercise which we performed are given in table 4.4. It appears that some minor misdemeanours, such as trespassing, have admission rates approaching reversed J-curves; almost everyone admits to them. Others, such as robbery using or threatening violence, are very infrequently admitted. None the less, many items can be found which meet the first requirement of Likert scaling, response variance.

It also seems they can meet the second, response covariance. Evidence we have derived from a 39-item inventory of delinquencies and misdemeanours provided item–whole correlations in the range 0.28 to 0.78 (Emler et al., 1983). Fishbein and Ajzen (1974) constructed a Likert scale of religious behaviour based on the 20 items with the highest item–whole correlations; the range for these was 0.38 to 0.66. Selecting the 20 equivalent items from our inventory gave correlations in the range 0.51 to 0.78. Thus we can begin to have some confidence that delinquency is a scalable behavioral dimension and that in this respect it may be even more amenable to scaling than are some other behavioural constructs.

The next step for us was to discover more about the generality of a delinquent disposition and for this we turned to factor analysis. We are by no means the first to have done so. In several investigations, self-report data have been submitted to data reduction techniques such as factor or cluster analysis (Allsopp & Feldman, 1976; Braithwaite & Law, 1978; Ferdinand & Luchterhand, 1970; Gibson, 1971; Gold, 1970; Heise, 1968; Hindelang & Weis, 1972; Kulik, Stein & Sarbin, 1968a; Quay & Blumen, 1963; Senna, Rathus & Siegal, 1974; Short & Strobdtbeck, 1965; Shapland, 1978; Walberg, Yeh & Paton, 1974; Winslow, 1967). The results have been mixed. Those cases in which multiple factors or clusters have been identified unfortunately indicate only the vulnerability of these techniques to the constraints the investigator is free to impose on the statistical procedures. The factors identified have varied in number from three to eleven, with very little consistency in content.

We preferred to consider two more limited and readily answered questions: (1) does factor analysis indicate that there is one major and general dimension underlying delinquency, or alternatively that there are several separate dimensions? (2) is involvement in delinquency versatile and heterogeneous rather than specialized and specific? Specialization and multidimensionality are two distinct alternatives and although they may be rejected on the same basis, the former predicts a dissociative relation between different forms of delinquency – you are involved in one kind or another – while the latter predicts independence – whether you are involved in one kind is not predictive of whether you ar involved in others. Evidence of a single general factor underlying different forms of delinquency would therefore be inconsistent with both specialization and multidimensionality.

The most appropriate test is provided by unrotated principal components analysis, because it involves the fewest arbitrary constraints. Four of the existing published studies of which we are aware provide sufficient details to evaluate the hypothesis, Allsopp and Feldman (1976), Gibson (1971), Shapland (1978) and Walberg et al. (1974). The results quite consistently indicate one general factor accounting for between 20 and 30 per cent of the total variance; the second principal component accounts for 8 per cent or less. This picture might seem rather less impressive in the light of Burton's (1963) results based on Hartshorne and May's data. However, the following should be borne in mind. First, Burton's analysis covered only measures of cheating; the delinquency studies involve much more heterogeneous behaviours. Second, Burton's analysis was based on scores derived in five out of six cases from data aggregated across a number of individual measures; the delinquency factor analyses are based on scores on single items. Finally, the sample from which Burton's data came was quite heterogeneous in terms of age, sex, and social class. If individual differences in conduct are to be of interest, it is important to show they exist in populations that are more homogeneous in these respects, as was true of the populations sampled in the delinquency studies.

Unfortunately, each of the above delinquency studies has one or another shortcoming. Walberg et al. (1974) provide insufficient details and seem to have used Short and Nye's items. Shapland (1978) has small Ns (51 and 54) in relation to the number of variables (27 and 32). Gibson (1971) and Allsopp and Feldman (1976) use dichotomous scoring (see Nunally, 1978).

To try to provide a more definite answer, we collected data from 214 boys aged 15 to 17, all from urban working-class backgrounds. The responses, which were collected in individual interviews with each boy (the procedure is described in Emler, Heather and Winton, 1978), were assigned scores of 0, 1 or 2, depending on claims about the number of occasions on which the act had been committed. Thirty-eight items or variables were included in the analysis. The first principal component accounted for 33.1 per cent of the total variance, the second for 6.1 per cent. Loadings of items on the first component varied between 0.25 and 0.73. This may be regarded as good evidence for the existence of generalized individual differences in delinquent involvement within a fairly homogeneous population.

Further corroboration of this conclusion comes from the study by Braithwaite and Law (1978) which used a variety of non-metric procedures. Their data were based on a sample of 358 males aged 15–20, though heterogeneous in terms of class background. Non-metric factor analysis (Lingoes & Guttman, 1967) yielded a first factor accounting for 60 per cent of the common variance in a 7-factor solution. An estimate for a similar solution from our own data gives a figure of 67.5 per cent.

More recently we have made an analysis of data from a sample of 435 boys and girls, aged 12–15. In this case the first principal component accounted for 31 per cent of total variance. We also tried the equivalent of Burton's procedures, that is, a factor analysis based on sub-scales rather than individual items. We secured answers from 40 boys aged 14 years to questions about 64 different kinds of delinquent activity (Emler, Reicher & Ross, 1987). We then grouped these items into six scales defined by the broad content of activities; these were 'drugs', 'theft', 'aggression', 'vandalism', 'status' and 'minor/nuisance'. Principal components analysis of sub-scale scores yielded a first principal component accounting for 62 per cent of the total variance.

Although these and similar findings are consistent with the view that rule-breaking is a generalized behavioural trait, one could object that the methodology artificially inflates consistency and that anyway self-reports are not equivalent to actual conduct. All the responses are obtained on a single occasion and are of a single type; the results obtained may prove only that at any given moment people will represent their conduct as consistent, not that they are consistent from one occasion or situation to another.

To escape these objections, self-report scores must relate to other indices of conduct. Let us be clear first, though, that the relevant test is whether these scores reflect the relative degree of involvement in delinquent activities, and not whether they correspond to the absolute amount of crime an individual commits; this point is so central to our understanding of delinquency, and not just of self-report measures, that we shall need to return to it. We have already seen that there are several indications of the validity of self-report measures. However, the conclusion that delinquency (rule-breaking) is versatile and heterogeneous, a single and general dimension, rather than multidimensional, specific or specialized, is also supported by evidence based on other methods (Klein, 1984; Farrington, 1991).

There is a similar convergence with respect to the long-term stability of this disposition. Using self-reports we have found correlations over a 12- to 18-month period of between 0.42 and 0.84. Findings reported by Wiatrowski et al. (1982) indicate correlations for American high school students of 0.48 over two and a half years and 0.37 over a four-year period. Others using different methods and over different periods have found similar indications of stability (e.g. Loeber, 1982; West & Farrington, 1973).

The self-report evidence has shown that rule-breaking is commonplace and, in two senses, normally distributed. First, some rules get broken a lot, some moderately often and some very infrequently; second, a few people almost never break rules, many do so occasionally and a minority do so frequently. But the self-report evidence reveals several other things of interest.

First, in so far as there are any delinquent activities which appear to constitute a quite separate dimension or cluster, they are those relating to drug abuse. Braithwaite and Law (1978) found that drug use and alcohol items had relatively low loadings on the first factor. In our first study, one of the 38 items referred to illegal drug use; it was among the eight lowest loading items. Hindelang et al. (1981) noted that the drug cluster identified in a cluster analysis of their data had the lowest intercorrelations with other clusters. In an analysis of a separate sample of boys aged 13–14 (N = 132), we included a number of items referring to different forms of drug abuse; there was some tendency for these to define a second factor. Thus drug abuse would seem to be less characteristic of delinquency as a whole than, for example, theft.

A similar picture emerges when delinquency sub-scales, formed on the basis of manifest item content, are intercorrelated. In the study referred to above (Emler, Reicher & Ross, 1987), the drugs scale has the lowest average correlation with the other sub-scales (see table 4.3; this study also includes a scale of trivial rule-breaking). The drugs scale had the lowest loading on the first factor in the analysis performed on this data.

Table 4.3 Intercorrelations between different forms of delinquency and anti-social behaviour

	Aggression	Vandalism	Status	Minor/ Nuisance	Drugs
Theft (8 items)	0.75	0.77	0.76	0.46	0.48
Aggression (13 items)		0.83	0.66	0.47	0.41
Vandalism (9 items)			0.56	0.52	0.43
Status offences (8 items)				0.18	0.17
Minor/Nuisance (10 items)					0.36
Drug use (8 items)					

Source: data from Emler, Reicher & Ross (1987), *n* = 40.

Another quite consistent result was that many of the lowest loading items on the first principal component referred to trivial activities. Similar findings are reported by Braithwaite and Law (1978) and by Gibson (1971). In other words, delinquent inclinations will be more marked with respect to relatively more serious delinquencies and less marked with respect to minor and trivial delinquencies. Serious misdemeanours are more typical of delinquency as a whole.

This difference between the serious and the trivial has four implications. First, it confirms the inadvisability of generalizing from experimental measures of trivial misconduct. Second, group differences should be more marked with respect to serious delinquency. In an earlier study (Emler, Heather and Winton, 1978) we had created sub-scales of trivial and serious delinquency. We compared the scores on each scale of samples of 15–17-year-olds who were respectively incarcerated in a

Table 4.4 Admission rates and factor loadings for specific self-reported delinquencies

Behaviour	Admission rate %[1]	Loading on first principle component[2]
Written on walls with spray cans	49	0.732
Smashed, slashed, damaged public property	49	0.729
Attacked an enemy in a public place	40	0.716
Stolen things out of cars	28	0.695
Broken into a shop or store	22	0.678
Stolen things from small shops etc. while they were open	61	0.671
Stolen goods, money from slot machines etc.	34	0.668
Used some kind of weapon in a fight	46	0.664
Bought cheap or accepted stolen goods	51	0.663
Struggled, fought to escape from a police officer	41	0.665
Carried a weapon in case it was needed in a fight	54	0.651
Stolen from a large store while it was open	61	0.650
Belonged to a trouble-making group	47	0.645
Got into fights at football matches	57	0.626
Obtained money by false pretences	40	0.623
Broken into a house and stolen things	22	0.593
Annoyed strangers in the street	71	0.591
Joyriding	26	0.589
Malicious littering	39	0.587
Stolen from a deserted house	32	0.579
Stolen a bicycle	23	0.576
Stolen from people's clothes	16	0.564
Trespassing	93	0.524
Attacked a police officer trying to arrest someone	12	0.521
Let off fireworks in the street	77	0.517
Broken windows of empty houses	86	0.505
Stolen school property worth more than 10 pence	53	0.503
Robbery using or threatening violence	03	0.500
Driven a motor vehicle under the influence of drink/drugs	09	0.499
Gone to adult-only film under the legal age	47	0.460
Driven motor vehicle on public highway under the legal age	31	0.455
Ridden bicycle after dark without lights	87	0.399
Deliberately not paid fare on public transport	77	0.373
Taken illegal drugs	11	0.357
Gambled	66	0.353

Table 4.4 (continued)

Behaviour	Admission rate %[1]	Loading on first principle component[2]
Taken money from home with no intention of returning it	45	0.351
Drank alcohol in bars under the legal age	44	0.336
Smoked under the legal age	81	0.328
Truanted from school	85	0.254

Source: [1] data from Renwick (1987) and Emler, Reicher & Ross (1987): males, aged 14–15, $n = 77$; [2] data from Emler et al. (1983): males, aged 15–17, $n = 214$

young offenders' establishment and who had no official record but were otherwise equivalent in social background and area of residence. The scores were in a ratio of 2:1 for the trivial scale but more than 4:1 for the serious scale. Losel (1988) reports a very similar pattern in a German study. This is also consistent with findings that gender, ethnic group and social class differences are most apparent for serious forms of delinquency.

A third and related point is that, in so far as delinquency is related to other individual characteristics as represented, for example, by personality dimensions, correlations will be stronger for more serious forms of misconduct.

Finally, this distinction has implications for the construction of self-report measures and thus for an operational definition of delinquency. We can now be confident that delinquency as a meaningful behavioural dimension is most prototypically defined by involvement in activities that are normally regarded and treated as criminal offences, even if relatively minor ones (malicious damage to public property, various forms of theft, getting into fights in public and using weapons, resisting arrest). Rather less prototypical are status offences such as smoking, gambling, under-age drinking or truancy, but also the Mala Prohibita offences of drug use. Unusually serious crimes with very low commission rates, such as robbery with violence, are also inevitably less prototypical (though when we included an item of this kind it still loaded 0.50 on the first principal component). Fishbein and Ajzen's findings are generally replicated, therefore, in that the items most definitive of differential delinquent involvement are those with response distributions close to a 50/50 split. The exceptions invariably describe more serious offences (see table 4.4).

4.6.2 *Individual differences – theoretical implications*

We are now in a position to reconsider some of the popular theories of delinquency and socialization. First, the situationist critique that there are no stable or generalized individual differences in conduct is hard to reconcile with the evidence considered above. Likewise the assertion of social learning theory that behavioural habits are quite specific is difficult to sustain. Indeed a central problem for delinquency theory must be to account for the pattern of covariation in delinquent activities: why are some offences more prototypical than others?

The evidence also contains difficulties for sociological theories, in so far as these seek to explain delinquency in terms of factors associated with social category membership. It is quite clear that there are very substantial individual differences in degree of delinquent involvement within most of the social categories which have been the object of sociological theorizing, especially gender, ethnic, area-based and social class categories.

An interesting problem which has recently been raised by Hirschi and Gottfredson (1983) concerns the age distribution of delinquency. This has commonly been discussed in terms which imply a 'big dipper' model of delinquent involvement. At the beginning of adolescence young people are only just starting to ascend the incline. By the mid-teens they have reached its crest and are beginning to move down the other side. If this is so, then the individual differences in delinquent involvement reflect no more than differential progress along the big dipper curve. And this in turn should direct our attention to something which happens in adolescence, though with variations in timing, to all young people (like puberty or the growth spurt). Unfortunately for this interpretation, as Hirschi and Gottfredson (1983) meticulously document, individual differences – the rank order of persons in terms of delinquent involvement – remain rather stable across the same period in which age-related changes in rates of delinquent activity occur. In other words, if one boy is more delinquent than most of his peers at 11 years, he will still be more delinquent at 14, even though the delinquency of the group as a whole has increased, and more delinquent at 18 even though his delinquency has declined along with that of everyone else in the cohort. Hirschi and Gottfredson come to the startling conclusion that even theories which shed light on individual differences shed no light at all on age-related variation. Our own current view is that they may be correct in so far as extant explanations of delinquency are concerned.

Initially we considered another hypothesis: those who are more delin-quent are differentially sensitive to whatever produces the age-related changes. We therefore compared two groups of 11-year-olds, one relatively higher in delinquent involvement than the other. We expected that the sample as a whole would show an increase in delinquent involvement over the following 18 months, but that this would be due to an increase in the delinquent activity of those who were more delinquent at the outset rather than a general increase. If this were the case then individual differences (the rank order) would remain stable over the period but the increase would not be due to the independent and uniform effect of ageing on the entire sample. In the event our expectations were not confirmed. The delinquency of both groups increased over the period while the relative differences between them remained.

It seems, at least on the basis of this evidence, that Hirschi and Gottfredson's argument is supported; age operates in the manner of an independent 'situational' factor which affects levels of delinquent activity quite separately from any individual differences in inclination. And therefore quite different kinds of explanation might be required for each. If this is so, then adolescence may tell us something about the age function but nothing about individual differences.

4.7 Explaining Inter-individual and Age-related Variations: Unrealized Promises

In this section we will consider three possible psychological explanations of delinquency in the light of available evidence. These are explanations respectively in terms of neurotic extraversion, intelligence, and the sophistication of moral reasoning. The first promises to explain individual differences, while the latter two also offer some hope of accounting for the temporal pattern.

4.7.1 Neurotic extraverts

The idea that there is a disposition towards crime which reflects a disorder of personality remains popular, especially among clinical psychologists who continue to capture such behaviour within an impressive array of clinical terms (cf. Rutter & Giller, 1983). Young people who break the law are discovered to have conduct disorders, to be emotionally disturbed, to display negativism, behavioural disturbance, unmanageable behaviour, psycho-social disorder, troublesomeness, sociopathy, and even psychopathy. Setting aside the tone of this language, a serious problem for many clinical approaches is their assumption that there are different kinds of delinquency with different kinds of cause. We have already seen that the evidence for these differences is scant. This is not to say that there are not particular kinds of behaviour defined and treated as criminal, such as hard drug use or child molesting, which are relatively unrelated to involvement in common kinds of delinquency. But in so far as the aspiration is to explain the latter then typologies such as those proposed by Scott (1959) and by Rich (1956) are at variance with the current evidence.

Table 4.5 Correlations between self-reported delinquency and Eysenck personality dimensions

	E	N	P	L
A. 14–15-year-old males, n = 40[1]				
Delinquency sub-scale:				
Theft	0.26	0.19	0.63	0.62
Vandalism	0.07	0.26	0.78	0.62
Aggression	0.08	0.05	0.73	0.62
Drugs	0.20	0.05	0.38	0.28
Status	0.22	0.10	0.40	0.46
Minor/Nuisance	0.01	0.42	0.57	0.55
B. Male students, n = 54[2]				
Delinquency sub-scale				
Serious delinquencies (23 items)	0.55	0.12	0.46	0.31
Trivial delinquencies (17 items)	0.42	0.06	0.32	0.34
C. Female students, n = 51[2]				
Delinquency sub-scale				
Serious delinquencies	0.03	0.06	0.42	0.11
Trivial delinquencies	0.01	0.04	0.34	0.21

Source: [1] data from Emler, Reicher & Ross (1987); [2] data from Renwick & Emler (1984).
Note: E = extraversion; N = neuroticism; P = psychoticism; L = lie.

Eysenck's theory is a more plausible candidate because it assumes that crime is unitary and offers one kind of explanation for all common kinds of crime. Empirically it predicts that delinquency will be associated with higher scores on measures of the personality traits of extraversion and neuroticism. Tests of this prediction based on comparisons between offenders (usually incarcerated) and controls or test norms have been mixed at best (Cochrane, 1974). Given the problems comparisons of these kinds raise, self-reports of delinquency might provide a better test of the hypothesis. We conducted tests with two groups, 14-year-old boys (Emler, Reicher & Ross, 1987), and male and female college students. The findings are summarized in table 4.5. As can be seen, the prediction regarding neuroticism receives virtually no support, that regarding extraversion receives only mixed support. This is much in line with findings from other studies in which self-report measures have been used (Emler, 1984a). Extraversion emerges as a significant correlate of delinquency in some of the older male samples but virtually none of the younger ones and none of the female samples. From this we could reasonably conclude that Eysenck's theory is unsupported as an explanation for differential involvement in delinquency.

There remains perhaps an outside possibility that current measures of extraversion and neuroticism are poor operationalizations of Eysenck's theoretical constructs – cortical arousal and reactivity of the autonomic nervous system respectively – but until better come along we believe there is no case for keeping the file open on this explanation.

Two other possible explanations for a link between delinquency and extraversion – extraverts like hanging around in groups, and groups commit crimes, or extraverts, being more sociable, find themselves more often with obligations of sociability which conflict with the legal restrictions and regulations – are both simply extensions of a description of what it means to be an extravert. Neither make assumptions, genetic or otherwise, about the origins of extraversion.

4.7.2 Intelligence

There have been two phases in the argument about the role of intelligence in delinquency. The first phase was a dispute about whether there was any relation between delinquency and low intelligence at all. The second has been about the implication of such a relationship for the explanation of delinquency. The early attempts, by Goddard (1914), Burt (1925) and others to attribute delinquency to intellectual degeneracy were bound to be attacked from sociology as much for the unpalatable social policies which drew upon this thesis as for the scientific inadequacy of the evidence.

Some authorities insisted there was no relation between low intelligence and delinquency or at best only a circumstantial relation. If convicted offenders had lower measured intelligence than the population as a whole this was either (a) because their low intelligence had contributed to their incarceration, not to their criminality, or (b) because the same social conditions which had led them into crime had also bequeathed them a sub-standard education, or (c) because they were not unreasonably alienated from a testing procedure conducted by representatives of the establishment which had imprisoned them. Meanwhile, however, evidence for an association between delinquency and measured intelligence continued to accumulate (e.g. West & Farrington, 1977; Hirschi and Hindelang, 1977).

Currently one is more likely to find students of delinquency agreeing that a negative correlation between intelligence and delinquency exists, even if they disagree about what it means (Hirschi & Hindelang, 1977; Rutter & Giller, 1983). IQ might seem just the kind of variable needed to account for delinquency. Like delinquency, differences in IQ scores are relatively stable over time and, like delinquency, performance on intellectual tasks is age-related; on those tasks most commonly used in IQ measures it peaks or at least begins to level off at about 15 years. It is also related to gender; girls score higher on IQ tests than boys, before the scores are tampered with in the interests of 'standardisation', and boys are more delinquent than girls. However, it has yet to be shown that the sex difference in delinquent involvement is a function of intellectual differences.

But is there in fact a relationship between delinquency and intelligence, and if so what might it mean? Many published studies contain reports of an association. Riess and Rhodes (1961) identified an association between juvenile court records and IQ. West and Farrington (1973) found an association between convictions amongst 14-year-olds and scores on the Progressive Matrices Test. Hirschi (1969) similarly found an association between officially recorded offences and scores on the Differential Aptitude Test. Cymablisty, Schuck and Dubeck (1975) found that IQ scores correlated with incarceration. Wolfgang, Figlio and Sellin (1972) reported an association between a measure of criminality based on police records and a verbal ability test. Ouston (1984) found reading test and non-verbal intelligence test scores to be related to officially recorded delinquency among a sample of London secondary school children. And so on (see e.g. Reichtel, 1987).

Despite the consistency of these findings – they typically point to a negative though not a strong association between intellectual performance measures and delinquency – their interpretation is not straightforward. A measure of delinquency based on official records is potentially contaminated by other factors. Thus if offenders are incarcerated this can depress test scores. It is known that absences from formal education can have this effect, especially upon working-class children (e.g. Jencks, 1972), and incarceration of juveniles is likely to disrupt their education. If the findings are based on young offenders who are not and have not been incarcerated it remains possible that lower intelligence influences treatment by the police or the courts. In other words, with equivalent levels of offending, it is possible that police officers are more likely to charge and courts more likely to convict offenders with lower levels of intelligence.

Evidence of an association between delinquency and intelligence based on a more direct measure of the former would be more convincing. Until recently, there have been very few published studies of this kind. Hirschi's (1969) study provides one example; it confirms that there is such an association. It has been widely cited (Rutter & Giller, 1983; Hirschi & Hindelang, 1977; Hollin, 1989) and, perhaps because it replicates the pattern Hirschi found when he assessed delinquency in terms of official records, has been highly influential.

Curiously, although the article by Hirschi and Hindelang (1977) refers to IQ and Stanford–Binet Scores, the original study on which they draw (Hirschi, 1969) includes no reference to IQ or to Stanford–Binet test results. Hirschi (1969) instead reported Differential Aptitude Test (DAT) scores. He writes in a footnote, 'the test scores I use, although undoubtedly highly correlated with tests designed to measure intelligence, are not, strictly speaking, intelligence tests' (p. 111).

In another footnote Hirschi records that the DAT verbal scores correlated 0.08 with self-reported delinquency. This was statistically significant, but explained very little of the variance. The IQ data reported by Hirschi and Hindelang (1977) are said to be related to self-reported delinquency with Gamma values of 0.15 for whites and 0.07 for blacks. The other two self-report studies cited by Hirschi and Hindelang – West and Farrington (1973) and Weis (1973) – also supposedly indicate an association but no statistics are provided to indicate an effect size.

Menard and Morse (1984) obtained a correlation between IQ scores and a self-report measure of delinquency of –0.15. Stepwise regression, based on a causal model in which IQ was treated as an independent variable, indicated that IQ explained less than two per cent of the observed variance in self-reported delinquency. For some reason, perhaps because this finding contradicts the new orthodoxy that intelligence does influence delinquency, this well-designed analysis is seldom cited in the contemporary literature, except as the object of critical comment (e.g. Harry & Minor, 1986).

Emler, Heather and Winton (1978) used individually administered measures of self-reported delinquency, verbal intelligence, and level of cognitive functioning on Piagetian tasks. They thus reduced the risk that results would be contaminated by variations in literacy, a danger others have attributed to reliance on evidence from self-completed questionnaire measures (e.g. Erickson & Empey, 1963). The samples were small but there was no indication of any association between delinquency and either verbal intelligence or performance on the Piagetian measures of cognitive functioning.

In one of the best designed studies to date, Lynham, Moffitt and Stouthamer-Loeber (1993) examined links between IQ and scores on a self-report measure of delinquency among a sample of 12–13-year-old males. The IQ tests were individually administered and the individual test sessions videotaped so that each boy's effort and interest during the test could be assessed. These researchers found that performance measures of IQ were unrelated to delinquency but verbal measures were related. Moreover, the relationship remained statistically significant after controlling for the effects of observed level of test effort, and for effects of impulsivity as assessed by a composite measure. None the less, the relationship between IQ and delinquency was not strong, accounting for at most 6 per cent of the variance in self-reported delinquency scores.

We believe the best that can be concluded at present is that there may be a small negative relation between delinquency and IQ scores. Consider, however, how such a relationship might be interpreted. In so far as intelligence has been accorded a role in criminological theory it has been a causal role. This might seem natural and obvious. Individual differences in intellectual ability are assumed to emerge relatively early in life, having their origins in the quality of early childhood experience, differences in the pre-natal environment, differences inherited at conception and complex interactions of these. Intelligence then exerts an influence on conduct. For example, Farrington (1991) has argued that the causal link may be poor ability to manipulate abstract concepts, resulting in a limited ability to foresee the consequences of one's actions or to appreciate fully their effects on others.

There is, however, one serious obstacle to this kind of straightforward causal model. Involvement in delinquency increases up to a peak at around 14 to 15 years. IQ test scores reflect performance relative to an age group; the average score is, and is designed to be, 100 for every age level. However, in absolute terms intellectual skills increase with age, the rate of increase beginning to level off at about 15. Now it is difficult to see how delinquency could be causally linked to low intelligence given that delinquency also increases over precisely the same period that intellectual skills increase.

If we accept that it is implausible that low intelligence as such is a cause of delinquency – for if it was a simple cause, delinquency within the population should decline up to 15 years, not increase – there are none the less at least three other possible explanations for the association between IQ scores and delinquency. One is that low intelligence becomes a causal factor specifically when it is combined with opportunity. We will consider this possibility in more detail below when we look at the role of moral reasoning in social behaviour. A second is the explanation proposed by Hirschi (1969) in his Control Theory: intellectual ability influences the progress of learning in school. Poor progress has in its turn various repercussions – poor performance in tests and examinations, negative labelling by teachers and others, lowered self-esteem, loss of commitment to educational goals, loss of attachment to the school – which are themselves the more direct causes of delinquency. In this explanation it is not absolute intelligence that matters, but ability relative to age-equals, in other words precisely what is indicated by IQ scores.

The third and more radical explanation is that both delinquency and intelligence are dependent variables and any association between them reflects the influence on both of a common independent variable. We shall examine this and the previous possibility in chapter 6.

4.7.3 Moral reasoning

Kohlberg's theory also offers an explanation for the age pattern of delinquency, although this is not the feature for which he has tried to account (cf. Jennings, Kilkenny & Kohlberg, 1983). As we saw in the last chapter, Kohlberg predicted an inverse relationship between level of moral reasoning and delinquency. An inspection of the content of the stages suggests delinquency should be greatest at stage 2, declining thereafter and reaching its lowest level at stage 5 (though violation of the law in the service of moral obligations is assumed to be a possibility at this stage, cf. Kohlberg & Candee, 1984). Kohlberg and his associates (Jennings et al., 1983) talk of the higher stages (3 and beyond) as insulating the individual against the risk of delinquency. From this interpretation one would expect delinquency in any cohort to decline steadily through adolescence as an increasing proportion of the cohort pass beyond stage 2. An initial rise might be predicted at the beginning of adolescence when the proportion of youngsters entering this stage from stage 1 exceeds those moving on to stage 3 (this requires the additional assumption that delinquency is indeed less likely given a stage 1 moral perspective). So, on the face of it, Kohlberg's model could fit the temporal pattern for delinquency.

Unfortunately this promise begins to fade when one examines the age pattern for moral reasoning. Kohlberg's own data indicate that at 13–14 a majority are classified as 2/3. But the same data indicate the proportion of reasoning at stage 2 is already declining steadily from age 10 onwards, even in those groups whose rate of development is claimed to be the slowest (Colby et al., 1987, pp. 101–3). Yet over the same period involvement in delinquency is rising.

The theory can, however, still be rescued if an additional quite reasonable assumption is made. The development of moral reasoning endows the individual with increased internal control and autonomy of action. As an internalization theory, Kohlberg's belongs to a tradition which has assumed that in the course of growing up external controls are gradually removed so that ultimately they are so weak and intermittent that society depends on individuals to control themselves. A considerable degree of external control is still in place for most children at the start of adolescence; they are still extensively supervised by parents, teachers and other adults. Well-developed internal control is not yet much needed and its absence has few serious effects. But as they progress into adolescence the external controls over young people weaken. It is known that moral reasoning development proceeds at different rates in different individuals (Kohlberg, 1984). If so then some young people will begin to experience less external constraint on their actions when a moral appreciation which could insulate them against delinquent temptations is still unformed (a similar argument could be advanced for the role of low intelligence in delinquency). Are delinquents, then, young people in a hiatus between external and internal controls, after the police have left but before the conscience has arrived?

It is an attractive hypothesis but rather difficult to test. First, external control might well diminish at different rates and the well-founded measures of degree of external control which would be needed to test the hypothesis have yet to be developed. Second, delinquency is generally measured retrospectively, whether the measure is an official record or self-reported delinquency, while moral reasoning is assessed concurrently. A boy who displays a stage 3 understanding of moral questions today was not necessarily thinking in these terms when the offences on which his official records or self-reports are based were committed.

If we can set these difficulties aside for a moment, what does existing evidence show about the relationship between moral reasoning and delinquency? Jennings et al. (1983) reviewed the results from 13 studies in which this comparison has been made, seven of them published. All show the predicted negative relation between moral reasoning scores and the delinquency criterion used. The pattern is impressively consistent and the same relationship has been replicated since (Lee & Prentice, 1988), but its meaning is not entirely straightforward. The most common delinquency criterion used was associated with some form and degree of institutionalization following an offence (in at least nine of the studies). The difficulty is that the differences between delinquents and controls are seldom large in these studies and Kohlberg's own work has shown that institutionalization in itself can retard moral reasoning development. The one study which escapes these problems (Hains & Miller, 1980) did still produce a modest difference between the delinquents and the non-delinquents, though Hains was unable to replicate this difference in a later study (Hains & Ryan, 1983).

Given the problems of using official classifications, self-report measures of delinquency would be preferable. We undertook such a test in a study which also compared institutionalized offenders and controls (Emler, Heather & Winton, 1978); we obtained self-reports of delinquency from both groups. As in the studies Jennings et al. (1983) reviewed, we found that the institutionalized group obtained significantly lower moral reasoning scores than the controls. However, there was no relation whatsoever between moral reasoning and self-reported delinquency, either within the groups or across the sample as a whole. It therefore seemed to us more reasonable to conclude that the moral reasoning differences between the groups was a consequence of their institutional incarceration rather than a cause of their delinquency. This conclusion is supported by the other studies which have used self-report measures (Hains & Ryan, 1983; Renwick & Emler, 1984). In each case no negative relation was found between delinquency and moral reasoning; in the latter the relationship was if anything positive (though the sample is rather different – and a negative relation between stage 4 reasoning and delinquency was found).

In our view an adequate test of the applicability of Kohlberg's theory to delinquency has yet to be made. Such a test should have the following features. Moral reasoning level should be measured prior to the period to which the delinquency measure refers. Delinquency should be measured by self-report. Measures of external control over this period would also be desirable. The measure of moral reasoning should be dedicated to the stage 2/stage 3 difference, since this appears to be the most relevant division for delinquency. Several studies have used measures, such as Rest's (1979) DIT, which are particularly poor at differentiating around this point and also rather unsuited to the most appropriate age groups. Kohlberg's own measure is designed to assess moral reasoning over the full developmental range. Something analogous to Piagetian measures which pinpoint particular stage transitions would be preferable. Finally, a measure of attitudes to rules should be included to exclude the (very real) possibility that the difference between delinquents and non-delinquents is one of attitudes to which a moral reasoning measure might also be sensitive.

However, before embarking on such a difficult enterprise, one should seriously consider the prospects for success. Two matters in particular raise questions about such prospects. First, what light could this theory shed on the fact that females are less delinquent than males? There is no corresponding difference in moral reasoning sophistication (Walker, 1983). Second, how can the theory account for the content of delinquency? The unifying factor in conduct would have to be its moral coherence. Delinquency would consist of those activities which a stage 2 moral analysis allows but a stage 3 analysis does not.

If the theory has anything to offer to an understanding of delinquency, it is likely to be as a part explanation, perhaps accounting for something of the temporal pattern, but not for stable individual differences or sex differences. However, we will argue that even this prospect is limited because the theory is predicated on flawed assumptions it shares with most other developmental theories of socialization. Contrary to these assumptions sins are not solitary, sinners not secretive, good behaviour does not depend on self-control alone, and behavioural choices are as much the product of collective as of individual decision making.

4.8 Conclusions

In this chapter we have identified some of the features of delinquency which require to be understood. These include: relatively stable individual differences in degree of involvement in delinquent activities; the generalized nature of such involvement; the fact that delinquents are more distinctly differentiated from non-delinquents in terms of some activities than others; very marked sex differences in delinquent involvement; an age pattern that seems to be largely independent of individual differences. We have seen that these features pose difficulties for many sociological accounts of delinquency and for most psychological explanations.

In certain important respects these theories have been betrayed by the model of society from which they collectively stem, namely the mass society thesis of the late nineteenth century. The psychological analysis of social control has for most of the twentieth century proceeded on the assumption that behavioural control in a civilized society takes two forms, one external and one internal. First, individuals will not breach rules of conduct in the presence of others because they will express disapproval, which is inherently aversive, or punish the offender in more vigorous and painful ways. Given a fearsome array of threats against public misbehaviour only the most recalcitrant could remain undeterred. But this very power of external control all but deprived it of theoretical interest for psychology.

Instead attention concentrated on internal controls, and drew additional support for this emphasis from the assumption that modern social conditions provide too many opportunities for covert and solitary sin against which danger external controls provide no defence. Yet, as we have argued, the psychological theories developed from this analysis have not been conspicuously successful at accounting for some of the most salient aspects of the phenomenon of rule-breaking.

For us the conclusion is obvious: a reappraisal of the root social theory is required. In the next chapter we shall begin by offering an alternative analysis of social life. It is one in which social as opposed to purely individual and internalized control plays a major part in the regulation of conduct. However, this control is not invariably successful. We shall also develop an analysis of individual differences in behaviour in which these do not depend for their explanation upon some stable disposition of the person.

5

Social Control, Moral Behaviour and Reputation

5.1 Introduction

In this chapter we intend to establish that action is extensively controlled by considerations of reputation. But to reach this point there are a number of theoretical objections we must overcome. The argument will proceed as follows. First we will consider the conditions under which it is possible for people to have reputations, and those under which they can be aware of the reputations they have. We will then go on to show that reputations can and do typically refer to a person's conduct as a whole and not to some limited sub-set which is available for public scrutiny. Next we will consider the claim that people do not merely have reputations, they also seek to manage their reputations, and we will ask about the social and psychological conditions which make this management possible. We will then ask about the considerations that lead persons to care about their reputations and so want to manage them.

The objections this argument will face should by now be apparent. In a mass society few people can have reputations; reputation is a consequence not a cause of action; deviance is anyway hidden and so concern about reputation could not contain it. These will have to be faced, but we have a yet more difficult claim to establish.

It is that if this analysis makes sense of law-abiding behaviour it also makes sense of delinquency. That is, delinquency flows from a concern to promote and sustain a particular kind of reputation. In other words, there is not just one project – maintaining a good reputation – at which some succeed and others in varying degrees fail. There are alternative reputational projects, and delinquency arises directly from one of them.

To argue this successfully, we have to show that certain other hypotheses will not do, hypotheses about the origins of the delinquent's bad reputation: he (and it is usually a 'he') is the random victim of a reputation imposed by a society in need of villains – a victim of labelling; he fails to understand what the wider audience wants (because his own immediate audience has deviant values); he lacks the social skills to construct a good reputation or avoid a bad one; he lacks the self-esteem or positive self-concept needed to care; he lacks the social bonds that would lead him to strive for a good reputation. Later we will need to show what kinds of reputational project could be associated with delinquency, and how delinquent action could serve these (but we will save this for chapter 6).

5.2 How People Have Reputations

5.2.1 Social species

Chimpanzees are social animals; the economy of the species, its mode of adaptation, depends on group living (Humphreys, 1976). This is a distinction it shares with many other species from termites to humans (Wilson, 1975). However, one of the more striking differences between vertebrate and insect social species is that social structure in the former kind may be based upon the relationships between specific individual members. Among the latter it rests only upon category memberships. Termites and ants distinguish colony from non-colony members, and members of one caste from those of another, but no individual colony member has ever been found to show a distinct preference for, or even recognition of, any specific other individual colony mate. Among the social vertebrates, and particularly the higher forms such as primates, each member in the group may react to every other as an individual distinct from all other individual members; in other words, the members of social groups display individual-level recognition. Chimpanzees and other primates form social systems based on relationships between individuals (Dunbar, 1988). In effect, the social structure of the group is a system of related relationships (Hinde, 1979).

There is something else we must notice about these societies: they are small and they are face-to-face, two connected circumstances. If, for chimpanzees and other primates, knowledge of their societies is knowledge of individuals and their interrelationships, that knowledge is based on direct experience and observation. The social life of the group is carried out to all intents and purposes in the physical presence of the entire group.

5.2.2 *The human peculiarity*

Humans are categorically different and what makes them so is the capacity for individuals to become informed about the social environment without relying on their direct personal experience alone. This capacity reflects the unique power of language to exchange information about matters other than the immediate present (Hockett, 1958), and thus as a means for sharing social knowledge. Humans alone among the social vertebrates can know one another substantially by repute. People can inform themselves about events and exchanges at which they were not physically present from people who were, and so their knowledge of another individual can build on the experiences reported by third parties. In this respect what the members of human societies know about one another may be based on far larger and potentially more representative samples of each other's actions than could be provided by direct experience alone.

We are suggesting, however, that the members of human societies characteristically have reputations, and in this we are going a little beyond the idea that they are known to their fellows indirectly, on the basis of hearsay. There are factual details of a person's biography – in particular the history of their relationships with others – which acquaintances will piece together and which draw on reports from third parties. But reputations are also judgements – about vices and virtues, strengths and weaknesses – based on patterns of evidence which communities continually accumulate, process and reprocess about their members. The medium through which this social processing occurs is the conversational activity of group members, an activity in which observations about mutual acquaintances are continually exchanged (Emler & Fisher, 1981).

In order for people to have reputations, therefore, the minimal requirements are that they inhabit communities possessing some continuity of membership and in which the individual members continually converse about the deeds and qualities of other community members (Bailey, 1971). Individuals need to be linked to one another over time through a variety or 'network' (Mitchell, 1969) of indirect links provided by mutual acquaintances.

If this analysis explains how people have reputations, it does not yet tell us why. Why should reputations play any part in the affairs of human communities, why should human communities generate these phenomena, and why should their members put time and effort into acquainting themselves with the reputations of their fellows? We suggest that reputations have this kind of significance for the following general reasons. Human social existence leans substantially on patterns of cooperation which, as with other social vertebrates, involve contingent or reciprocal altruism: individuals exchange favours (Trivers, 1971). However, reciprocation is often long delayed, often indirect and often imperfect (Boissevain, 1974). Relations of credit and debt may endure for long periods. And debts may be both incurred and discharged through third parties; you help me and at some future date I help a close friend of yours or a member of your immediate family. For such an exchange system to work individuals must be identifiable to one another, they must have a capacity to recall favours given and received, and they must have some continuity of association. And individuals must be mutually and collectively dependent on this informal economy on more than a short-term basis.

As participants in these informal economies we can operate more effectively the more we know about potential exchange partners: are they reliable, do they return favours, can one count on their promises, is their advice sound? And what are their loyalties, where do their sympathies lie, against whom do they bear grudges, and what are their strengths and weaknesses? These kinds of details could be learned through direct experience and observation, but as already noted we are not limited to this source of information; we can learn much more, and perhaps learn more that is reliable, from third parties. In other words it is helpful to know as much as we can about the reputations of those people with whom we might conduct our business, where reputations refer both to general virtues as participants in the informal economy and virtues specific to the various roles they might perform in that system.

The system itself also benefits to the extent that reputations are accurately assessed. Biologists have observed that a central problem for cooperative systems in which the cooperators are also genetic competitors, as is the case with all vertebrates, is to limit cheating. If individual members of the group have too much scope to exploit its economy for their own advantage, in the sense of taking out far more than they put in, then ultimately the viability of that economy itself is threatened. In non-human vertebrates the solution is reciprocal altruism (Trivers, 1971); persistent cheats eventually run out of willing cooperators. The more complex economy of the human group requires that reputations be accurately assessed and acted upon to limit the damage this economy might otherwise suffer from greed, laziness, irresponsibility, or incompetence.

So far one can see that the members of a community would have an interest in acquainting themselves with the reputations of those around them. And one can see that the system as a whole benefits from this kind of interest. Indeed one fundamental principle to be derived from this analysis is that of social control through control of access to opportunities for interaction and exchange. Fools and scoundrels will do less damage and mischief to a social system to the extent that this system is so set up as to appraise their characters accurately and to control their access to opportunities accordingly.

But it is also apparent that the system is even more effectively defended if individuals modify their own behaviour out of concern for their own reputations. If people recognize that their prospects and fortunes depend on the moral credit they have within their communities then they could be expected to moderate those actions over which they have some control to ensure their reputations do not suffer. As self-conscious actors with some capacity to see themselves as others see them, to take the role of the other (cf. Cooley, 1902; Mead, 1937), humans might be expected to take an active interest in their own reputations. And in this sense the circulation of reputational information would play another kind of role in social control: it would encourage self-control.

So far, then, we have outlined conditions under which reputation might be expected to play a part in social life. We must next consider a major set of objections to this analysis, at least as concerns its applicability to social life in a contemporary society. That set of objections can conveniently be described as the mass society thesis and its basis is that very few of the conditions we have identified survived the industrial revolution.

5.2.3 Mass society reconsidered

The mass society thesis has implied that most individuals no longer dwell in the kinds of communities in which they could have personal reputations, or in which reputations could or would have any important consequences. The gist of the argument is that a mass society, simply by virtue of its scale, is of necessity organized and articulated in ways fundamentally different from those that can work in small-scale communities.

First, a society with millions of members is too large for any one member to know about and treat as unique all the other people he or she is likely to encounter (Milgram, 1970). There are simply too many potential and actual participants in exchanges for reputation to be a meaningful or practical basis for conducting social business. Under such circumstances there has to be some basis for distinguishing between people other than personal acquaintance. Twentieth-century social theory provides two such alternatives to reputation as organizing principles in social life, role and category.

Second, the anonymity and segmentation of social life in a mass society is anyway likely to render reputational judgements unreliable. Third, modern mass societies have devised economic systems, such as commercial or money-based exchange, in which there is far less need to make accurate reputational judgments or to rely on reputational concerns to keep trading partners honest. Fourth, and as we have already seen, it was assumed that the social control of action would be ineffective in a mass society because too much of the relevant action could be concealed. Thus internalized control would have to be substituted for social control. Finally, social life is less likely to be coordinated through informal face-to-face communication and is more likely to be administered through systems of formalized and mass communication.

Despite its enormous influence, the mass society thesis has never been convincingly proved. Studies from the Chicago school of sociology led by Park failed to find the anonymous society that Wirth (1938) and others postulated. In a classic investigation of the 1940 American presidential campaign, Lazarsfeld, Berelson and Gaudet (1948) failed to discover any evidence of widespread, direct media influence on a mass electorate, for example. But the thesis came under more serious and sustained attack in the late sixties and seventies as a result of more detailed studies of social life in cities (Boissevain, 1974; Fischer, 1981; Litwak & Szelenyi, 1969; Mitchell, 1969; Wellman, 1979; but see also Gans, 1962, Young & Wilmott, 1957, for earlier 'discoveries' of urban communities). The clear message of this research was that even in large cities people continue to inhabit social worlds populated by networks of mutually acquainted individuals. As the title of Fischer's (1981) book has it, we continue 'to dwell among friends' and, it should be said, potential enemies (cf. Bailey, 1971). The great majority of dealings we have with others in our daily lives are with people we know personally, and with people who know the other people we know. Thus at least some of the essential conditions for the existence of personal reputations still obtain for most people.

In our own research we have tried to estimate the range and frequency of regular contacts by asking different groups of people to keep a log, normally over seven days, of all their social contacts (e.g. Emler, 1984b; Emler & Grady, 1986; Emler, 1990). These and similar studies reveal that most contacts are informal; they involve friends, kin and acquaintances. Contrary to the mass society thesis, very few social interactions are purely formal or role-based and very few are with strangers. Even when higher proportions of formal contacts are reported, as they are for example by people in managerial occupations, it emerges that these contacts are not unknown as individuals to the people concerned (Emler, 1990).

These and other data strongly suggest, therefore, that it remains the normal rather than the exceptional condition of collective existence that the business of people's lives is primarily conducted with other people they know and identify as distinct individuals.

It is additionally the case that even with the advent of more universalistic, formalized and money-based exchange systems, informal economies remain important. People continue to achieve many of their social and economic goals through such informal systems (Boissevain, 1974; Granovetter, 1973; Kaplan, 1984). For example, Granovetter points to the key role of informal advice transmitted through personal networks in the process of job finding. Kaplan argues that managers can seldom accomplish their official business without the help informally provided by friends inside and outside their organizations. And Boissevain documents the numerous ways in which informal economies operate to supply individuals with material, technical, professional and other assistance.

Do people in practice seek to inform themselves about the people they know and deal with regularly? Does the kind of routine information exchange occur through which reputations could be constructed and disseminated? We have found that people do regularly exchange information about their mutual acquaintances (Emler & Fisher, 1981; Emler, 1989). In a series of small-scale exploratory surveys of the informal conversations of students and teachers, we discovered that people were more likely to talk about themselves than any other topic. However, the next most frequent topic of conversation was named acquaintances, rather than, for example, politics, religion or other impersonal topics. Within this topic the matters most often discussed were the doings of these acquaintances. Gossip of this kind does seem to be a pervasive human activity (Paine, 1967), and given the frequency of such conversations (Emler & Grady, 1986) it seems a reasonable inference that people do in fact engage in extensive information gathering about reputations.

If the social conditions necessary for the existence of reputations remain the norm, do people actually have reputations? There is in fact abundant evidence in the psychological literature that they do. For many years 'reputational measures' were popular in measurement psychology (e.g. Hartshorne, May & Shuttleworth, 1930; Havigurst & Taba, 1949). Critiques by Cronbach (1955) and others, the substance of which was that reputational measures revealed more about the perceiver than the perceived, caused their popularity to decline. Recently the method has been rehabilitated (e.g. Cheek, 1982; Moskowitz & Schwartz, 1982). Leaving aside the question of validity for the moment, these studies have consistently revealed the existence of a consensus among knowledgeable informants as to the attributes of targets. Though it is going a little further than the authors may have intended, we take 'knowledgeable' here to mean sharing community membership or having extensively overlapping personal networks. When researchers sample and aggregate judgements from knowledgeable informants, the result is an approximation to the community's collective judgement on the individual concerned.

If we accept that the conditions for the existence and impact of reputations remains, is there any evidence that people are actually aware of the reputations they may have, care about them, or try to do anything to protect them? In particular, can a concern with reputation limit people's tendency to break social rules, and thus operate as a significant source of social control?

5.3 The Significance of Reputation

5.3.1 *Impression management*

Let us begin with a simplification. Everyone may be thought of as standing in two kinds of relation to their social world. In one, each person is an observer and the social world the object of her or his observation; in the other each person is subject to observation by those others who make up this social world. Of these two relations psychology has traditionally had more to say about the former; the study of social perception in this sense has a long and distinguished history in the discipline (Tajfel, 1968; Ross & Fletcher, 1985). However, this emphasis fosters the idea that perception and interpretation are problems for the perceiver rather more than they are problems for the actor. A picture of action emerges in which individuals somehow unconsciously give off signs as they go about their daily business and these signs provide clues to others as to their feelings, motives, talents or character. Psychologically the interesting processes are not those which generate the signs or link them to underlying properties but the procedures perceivers use in attending to, organizing, and drawing inferences from this information.

There is another and in many ways radically different view, extending back through Goffman (1959), Mead (1937), and Cooley (1909) to William James (1890): interpretations are a problem for the person of whom they are made and not just for those who would make them. Our experience of the perceiver's role ensures self-consciousness in the actor's role. We cannot ignore the fact that others will draw inferences about our character from our actions and for this reason we will try to influence the conclusions they draw. In Goffman's (1959) terms a goal of all public action is self-presentation. Actions are managed in an attempt to induce others to credit us with particular qualities of character. As soon as others appear on the scene, says Goffman, whatever we are doing ceases to be merely behaviour and becomes instead a performance directed at creating a particular impression in the minds of the audience.

5.3.2 *From self-presentation to reputation management*

The idea of reputation management extends Goffman's (1959) analysis by taking into account the likely nature of the audience and the temporal dimension in behavioural strategies. Goffman recognized that audiences will sometimes have access to information about a performer prior to any particular performance, though he chose to emphasize the contingencies of self-contained face-to-face encounters, often between relative strangers. In terms of our foregoing argument, the audience will more often be one of acquaintances if not 'friends of friends'. And, because we and they are embedded in a network of linked relationships, each particular situationally-located bid at impression management is also a contribution to the longer-term enterprise of reputation management within our shared community. In this context, reputation management entails two contingencies which isolated acts of impression management before an audience of relative strangers lack. First, behaviour in specific encounters will have indirect and distant as well as immediate repercussions. Second, persons will be preceded by their existing reputation in any specific encounter.

Reputation is created out of the pattern of direct and indirect evidence accumulated within the social environment over time. It is shaped certainly by the person's doings but also by the constant reprocessing of this raw data which occurs through what that person and others say about what he or she has done as he or she and they interpret new evidence and try to fit it to the existing pattern. So, individuals must be sensitive to the long-term impact of actions which occur in the presence of those with whom they must deal again, but also the impact on those third parties whom they may encounter subsequently and who will hear versions of the events at second or even third hand.

But reputations are less easily managed than first impressions; they are assessments over which those to whom they refer have rather less than total control. Reputations are somewhat akin to what Moscovici (1984) has called social representations. They exist in no single head but in the conversations that circulate within communities, and they have to a degree a life and inertia of their own. Established reputations can be difficult to modify, but they are not beyond all control, and they may certainly suffer from neglect. These are the two great problems for all actors on the stage of everyday life; reputations can decay without constant attention but they can also persist to frustrate all efforts at personal change or betterment. Individuals can find themselves all too easily locked into patterns of transaction by reputations they cannot escape, like the ageing gunfighter of popular fable challenged over and over to display talents he would rather forget.

Reputation management, therefore, requires at least the following. The right public choices must be made. That is, one must as far as possible act in ways that are consistent with the reputation to which one lays claim. Additionally, however, one must attend to publicity; there is no guarantee one's achievements will be broadcast. Friends must be informed. But as Goffman observed, in all performances there can be problems of 'expressive control' caused by momentary lapses, slips and accidents which could convey impressions other than those intended. Therefore, one must also be prepared for reputation repair work, prepared to go out and 'put the record straight'.

At this point there is a problem our argument must face. We want to claim that people desist from sin out of fear for their good reputation. Yet there is an obvious objection to this: sins are deliberately concealed; how, therefore, could they have any repercussions for reputation?

5.4 The Myth of the Secret Sinner

The claim we wish to make here is psychologically, if not sociologically, somewhat controversial: sins are seldom entirely secret or anonymous. Transgressions are frequently and probably even typically overt and unconcealed, at least from certain audiences. Furthermore, it is difficult for sinners to keep their identities secret and in practice they make little attempt to do so. The claim is controversial because, as we saw in chapter 3, psychological theories have been predicated on the assumption that the principal problem of behavioural control is the inhibition of secretive offending.

Although no single piece of evidence by itself justifies our assertions, there are several indications which, taken together, form a convincing picture. Consider the following:

(1) *Transgressing the rules of interaction.* Many forms of transgression are by definition unconcealed, at least from the victim. For example, acts of aggression occur more often face to face between acquainted protagonists than from behind upon unsuspecting victims. Victim surveys reveal

that assailants are commonly known to those they attack (Hindelang, 1978). While recognizing that acts causing another discomfort, pain or injury can occur as elements of rule-governed activity (e.g. Fox, 1977; and even children have rules for fighting), physical violence in forms going beyond the rules could be regarded as extreme instances of a more general category of transgression, violations of the rules of social interaction.

Piaget (1932) has been virtually the only important contributor to moral psychology to have recognized the significance of this category of transgression. His is the only theory constructed quite explicitly on the assumption that the important violations of the rules are public, as is revealed in his decision to study the rules of children's games.

If total concealment is difficult in the case of certain kinds of behaviour, it is not impossible in others. So, the crucial question is whether there is any fundamental difference between the dynamics of those forms of anti-social behaviour which cannot easily be concealed and those which can. We shall argue that no such difference exists. But first, even if total concealment is theoretically possible, there is ample evidence that it is not successful.

(2) *The validity of reputational measures.* The clearest evidence against successful concealment is that reputational measures or observer ratings of conduct work (as we saw in chapter 4). Observers can provide reliable and valid assessments of an individual's habits of transgression, something that would not be possible if transgressions were routinely and successfully concealed. How are observers able to do this? It is possible partly for reasons we have already given. People do not dwell in an anonymous mass society. They continue to inhabit worlds populated by persons who are mutually acquainted and interconnected. Within such worlds, people are personally known and their doing known about. As the doers of deeds, anti-social or otherwise, they are constantly discussed among the people who know them. As might be anticipated therefore, the most reliable ratings of conduct are provided by knowledgeable informants (Funder & Colvin, 1988; Moskowitz & Schwartz, 1982), those acquainted with the targets and who in consequence share most directly in their social networks and who are able to draw most fully upon the corpus of community opinion regarding reputation.

One further and particularly important reason why individuals provide those who know them with consistent, reliable and unambiguous evidence of their degree of conformity or deviance is that their behaviour itself is reliably consistent. Because behavioural patterns in this area of conduct are stable and generalized it would be very difficult to conceal from one's acquaintances for long a habit of breaking the rules, even if one's responsibility for some individual acts remained hidden. Contrary to popular fiction, the identity of the villain in any particular piece of mayhem seldom comes as a surprise to those who know him (or her).

At this juncture we can look at another explanation for the delinquent's bad reputation. It is that delinquents are the more or less random victims – random in the sense that their sins make them intrinsically no more or less deserving than other candidates – of society's need for villains. Their reputation is entirely a consequence of a label imposed by the institutional system and not at all something they have earned by their exceptional behaviour.

Labelling theory, as developed by Becker (1963), Kituse (1962), Lemert (1967) and others, assumes there are watershed events, usually first convictions, which propel individuals from the occasional or 'primary' deviance which is the lot of most young people, into a deeper commitment to the deviant role, or 'secondary' deviance. These watershed events derive their force from the fact that individuals emerge from anonymity. Initially they are no different from their peers; afterwards they have acquired a public reputation, they have been singled out and formally identified as delinquent.

We believe the attention that labelling theory draws to the reactions of others to the actor and the effect these reactions have upon the actor is entirely appropriate; reputations are moral labels attached by communities to individuals. Moreover, actors can become trapped by labels. We differ from labelling theory, however, on three points. The first is that there is no dramatic discontinuity in identity or reputation created by watershed events such as arrests and convictions; individuals' behavioural inclinations are always relatively public and only become more so as evidence of their conduct accumulates within the social worlds of which they are a part. Research based on reputational measures reveals no sudden shifts into the limelight. Second, research also indicates that judgements of reputation reflect real behavioural differences. Third, labelling theory allows the labelee little agency in the process, a point also recognized by some labelling theorists (e.g. Kituse, 1980). A central plank in our argument is that young people are aware of the reputations or labels they may acquire through habits of obedience or mischief and their actions are directed towards influencing the outcome of the labelling process.

Up to this point the critic of our thesis could argue that whether or not concealment is successful in practice has little bearing on the issue of whether sinners are habitually inclined to attempt it. The tendency to lie and the absence of spontaneous confession could be attributes of sinners even if these stratagems are generally ineffective at concealing their delinquent character. But if this were true, and we dispute that it is, a vital conclusion would still remain: in practice there are few opportunities for entirely covert transgression, and few totally undiscovered persistent sinners. This being so, the claim that social order is utterly dependent upon internalized controls begins to lose some of its force.

(3) *Self-reports work.* There are also indications that concealment is not the natural reflex of sinners. One such is that a disposition to tell lies shows little relation to a disposition to break the law (Ekman, 1985). Another is that self-report measures of transgression also work. Contrary to the popular folklore of psychology, people who break the rules are not also habitual and compulsive liars any more than they are the sophisticated fabricators of a facade of unblemished virtue. As we saw in chapter 4, there is now ample evidence that self-report inventories of misdemeanours provide reliable and valid indications of an individual's degree of actual misconduct. People are apparently willing at least to make researchers privy to their past misconduct. More significantly, anonymity has very little impact on what is admitted; it affects reports only of more trivial forms of misconduct (Kulik, Stein & Sarbin, 1968b).

At this point we must say something further about the nature of self-reports. There are three relevant theories of item responses. Most familiar in psychology is that item responses are unproblematic indicators of underlying psychological characteristics. Their status is somewhat akin to 'symptoms' in medical diagnosis, signs given off by the patient that something internal is amiss. They are indirect or second-best indicators. Like a rash on the skin or a high pulse rate, the information they carry is unintentional. Their validity is established in actuarial fashion, on the basis of their correlation with the underlying condition. So, if self-report measures of delinquency predict actual delinquency, their capacity to do this has precisely the same basis as any set of responses quite unrelated in content to delinquency but which happen to be correlated with it.

The second theory of item responses is self-disclosure, reflecting what Hindelang et al. (1981) call the fundamental dictum of survey research: 'If you want to know something, ask'. This theory treats item responses as factual reports. That is, they are more or less accurate descriptions of what the person concerned has actually done or felt or believed. Thus if self-reports of delinquent behaviour are valid this is because people are both able and willing to report without undue error on their past behaviour.

The third theory is that item responses are self-presentations. They are communications to others (in this case the test-giver) as to how the person concerned wishes to be regarded. There are various indications that this is a more appropriate way to regard item responses. Johnson (1981), for example, shows that responses are more strongly associated with factors theoretically associated with self-presentational ability than with those associated with accuracy in factual reporting. In their extensive examination of the reliability and validity of self-report measures of crime, Hindelang et al. (1981) found that the most effective index they considered was one they called 'Ever variety'. Scores on the scale reflected the number of different delinquent activities individuals claimed they had ever been involved in. This worked better than a scale concerned only with activities occurring in the previous year, or one based on the frequency of involvement. Such a finding makes more sense in terms of a self-presentational than a self-disclosure theory. What makes a scale a successful vehicle for self-presentation is not the same as whatever might make it a comprehensive factual report.

But if item responses are self-presentations why should they accurately index actual criminal conduct? The first point to make is that their accuracy is as indicators of relative degree of involvement in criminal activities. The second is that self-presentations must have some basis in reality. Individuals not only claim to be particular kinds of people, they wish these claims to be accepted and those most likely to be accepted are those which bear some relation to the facts as others know them. Confidence tricksters and assassins (see Goffman, 1959) untypically engage in false presentations, at least during 'working hours', but they work outside the communities in which they are known.

In responding to self-report inventories, actual past conduct is thus the raw material out of which current self-presentations are constructed. And in this, strict accuracy of reporting is less important than the intentions which can be realized through the medium of the inventory. Hindelang et al.'s 'Ever variety' scale allows a more complete realization of the relevant intentions than their other scales.

The third point is that conduct is a product of the same self-presentational dynamics that lie behind item responses. Self-reports are valid in so far as they bring forth the same self-presentational aims. But this begs a question we have yet to answer: does conduct, including delinquent conduct, serve a self-presentational goal?

(4) *The immediate audience.* Finally, total concealment is apparently not even a consideration for most young offenders. If it were we could expect them at least to take the elementary precaution of committing their misdeeds alone. The evidence is again clear: they do not. As early as the 1920s criminologists had found from examinations of court records that the great majority of juveniles appearing before the courts had committed their offences in the company of others (Erickson, 1971).

The one suspicion concerning this evidence is that, like other observations about crime based on official records, it will be biased in various ways. For example, Hindelang (1971) argued that the police are more likely to arrest and institute proceedings against culprits seen to belong to groups, and courts are more likely to convict them, both dispositions which would introduce a systematic over-representation of group-based crime into official statistics.

Table 5.1 Degree of group involvement for different forms of delinquency

Area of delinquency	Group involvement[1]
Drug abuse	3.12
Theft	3.29
Aggression	3.24
Vandalism	3.16
Status offences	3.00
Minor/Nuisance behaviours	2.73

[1] Mean scores for sub-scales: 1 = always alone, 4 = always with others.
Source: data from Emler, Reicher & Ross (1987).

Research based on self-report methods appeared initially to confirm this suspicion. Lerman (1967) reported that over 50 per cent of a sample of working-class adolescents claimed most of their delinquencies were committed alone. Hindelang's (1971) own study of middle-class boys revealed few kinds of offence that were more likely to have been committed in the company of others than alone. But later findings reported by the same author (Hindelang, 1976) were more consistent with the majority of the recent evidence (e.g. Erickson, 1971; Erickson & Jensen, 1977; Klein, 1969; Shapland, 1978): group involvement in misdemeanours is the norm rather than the exception, at least for male juveniles.

Some of the apparently contradictory findings of this research may have arisen because the degree of group involvement in misbehaviour can vary substantially from one kind of activity to another (Shapland, 1978). Thus the particular behaviours sampled will affect the group involvement rate obtained and any estimate of the general level based on a small sample runs the risk of distorting the true figure. In one of our own studies (Emler, Reicher & Ross, 1987) we tried to increase the accuracy of this estimate by sampling a much larger range of activities than has been typical in earlier research. This also allowed us to examine the possibility that there are general categories of transgression that are characteristically solitary (see table 5.1).

Although there were specific forms of misconduct, all trivial, which were more likely to have been committed alone, there was no broad category of this kind. Activities which could be more readily concealed, such as theft, vandalism or drug abuse were as likely to occur in the company of others as those such as aggression which cannot be totally concealed. In a further study we found that offending in the company of others was even more characteristic of girls than of boys (Emler, Reicher & Ross, 1987).

Conclusions based on evidence of this kind face two obvious objections. The first is that solitary offences are as numerous as their group-based counterparts but that their perpetrators are simply lying to maintain their facade of innocence. The same boy may deny the things he has done alone but still admit to those committed with others in the belief that he personally bears less of the responsibility in these latter cases. This particular argument would seem to be contradicted by the fact that condemnation is actually more severe and sanctions more likely when offences are seen to have been committed in groups (Hindelang, 1971, 1976). The basic point, however, seems to be consistent with the finding (Powell, 1977) that 'lie scale' scores correlate negatively with admissions on self-report inventories.

The surface issue here is the interpretation of lie scales, the deeper issue yet again whether habitual liars and habitual sinners are one and the same. Lie scales are intended to detect individuals who are disposed to conceal any socially undesirable behaviour and to present themselves in a more favourable light than their conduct merits. If we accept that lie scales are successful in this then it suggests that those who admit to few transgressions on self-report inventories are lying. But consider the logic of lie scale construction. Questions describe misdemeanours which are both very trivial and very common. It is assumed to be improbable that anyone could honestly deny having ever been involved in a high proportion of these activities, and so a high proportion of denials would indicate lying. But it is not clear what justifies the assumption that genuine conformity to trivial rules is so rare.

In addition, the lie scale format is identical to that of self-report measures of misconduct. Indeed, one of the first self-report scales was actually constructed, by Hartshorne and May (1928), as a measure of lying. The convoluted rationale underpinning the lie scale is essentially that of a 'psychological indicators' theory of item responses. Psychologists could not accept the possibility that people might try to tell the truth about their own misbehaviour, or present themselves as they really were. Freudian logic dictated that the most moral people would admit the most sins. Hartshorne and May apparently did not notice the flaw in this logic when children known to be more badly behaved actually obtained the lower 'lie' scores. If people are willing to be candid about their more serious transgressions – and the evidence is that self-report measures are more appropriately represented in terms of the self-disclosure and self-presentational theories of item responses – then why should they not be as honest about trivialities? In other words, it is more plausible to assume that the high scorers on lie scales are simply exceptionally good or conforming.

The second objection to evidence on group-based offending is that it all refers to adolescents and we cannot say with certainty that solitary and covert anti-social behaviour is equally uncommon amongst adults. But we would make two points. One argument for a shift toward more solitary crime with advancing age is that there is also a shift in the nature of crime. Loeber (1982), for example, has claimed that misbehaviour becomes more covert from childhood to adolescence because it shifts from aggression to theft and vandalism. But there is no evidence that the latter are more solitary than the former among adolescents (see table 5.1). The second point is that anti-social behaviour does peak in adolescence. Whatever is the case for adults it is essential to recognize the conditions under which the age group most involved in proscribed activities habitually commit their misdeeds.

If the case for the mythical status of the secret sinner in delinquency was not yet solid enough, the young sinners concerned will tell you the same story. Their misdeeds are done when and because there is an audience, not when there is none.

5.5 The Visibility of Deviance: Theoretical Consequences

The evidence reviewed so far points to two related but distinct conclusions. The first is that anti-social behaviour is not typically covert or secret. The second is that such behaviour is also seldom solitary. Anti-social behaviour is social in two senses. It is a socially visible activity and it is also frequently a group activity. If these conclusions are correct they require a substantial reconsideration of psychology's theories of deviance. More than that, they compel us to the position that the entire enterprise represented by psychological accounts of socialization and socialization failure has been betrayed by a flaw in its most basic assumption: there is no great potential for secretive misbehaviour which requires internalized controls to contain it.

Perhaps it has been psychology's traditional taste for individualism that caused theories to be aimed in the direction of solitary action, but it is largely an empty space; there is very little of significance that people do, good or bad, legal or illegal, which is not done in the company or with the knowledge, direct or indirect, of those who know them. The secret sinner, the Raskolnikov figure, tormented by guilt and confessing only to his priest (or his psychiatrist) is largely a fictional character.

Hence, like the British guns defending Singapore against Japanese invasion in 1941, pointing out to sea to the south, psychology's theoretical armament has likewise been pointing almost entirely the wrong way. The domain of covert and solitary misconduct is an almost empty space. Meanwhile, much as the Japanese invaded overland from the north, a direction that was supposed to have been impossible, anti-social behaviour was already in the supposedly impregnable backyard, the domain of overt and publicly identifiable action. Consequently, there is no need to postulate an internal gyroscope, an autonomous moral sense, that prevents covert badness. But there are now other questions to be answered.

First, why was the domain of overt and publicly identifiable action not impregnable to anti-social behaviour after all? The simple answer is: because sanctions are neither certain nor in an absolute sense severe. What hurts is relative to the person. People may be like other animals in their absolute aversion to physical pain, but sensitivity to the disapproval of others, the shame of public exposure, rejection, criticism, or other social and emotional hurts is more uncertain. Differential sensitivity to sanctions as an explanation for delinquency is a possibility which deserves more consideration than it has hitherto received.

Second, what then is it that normally contains – and in some cases fails to contain – public violation of the rules of conduct? All manner of plausible external controls can be imagined but the problem in each case is to explain why certain young people should be less sensitive to these than their peers. The devotee of internal psychological determinants might want to argue that self-control driven by an autonomous conscience still provides the key. For example, the autonomous conscience could still be rescued as equipment vital to civilized existence by showing that it is all that immunizes people against the immoral influence of the group (see chapter 7).

An alternative argument is that moral conduct remains basically a problem of self-control, whether we are talking about private or public behaviour. When people make spectacles of themselves, when they disgrace themselves in front of others, it seems natural to say 'they should control themselves.' But are delinquents to be bracketed with public drunks and others chronically or temporarily unable to sustain the normal requirements of public conduct? We believe this is an inappropriate characterization and hope that our reasons will emerge as the chapter progresses. However, the more general issue as to where the determinants of conduct should properly be located, whether within the psyche of individuals or within the conditions of their environments, is unlikely to be resolved by any arguments mounted in this volume, partly because it is a matter of philosophical as much as scientific choice. Our preferred answer is that conduct reflects both self- and social control; but we have in mind self-control as a socially supported and socially sensitive process.

Perhaps the single most important consequence of the visibility of conduct is that conduct can be cause and not merely consequence. It has been the habit in psychology, though somewhat less in sociology, to treat conduct, whether delinquent or law-abiding, as the matter to be accounted for. So long as one assumes misconduct is concealed it is difficult to regard it as having social goals or social consequences. Consequences can be conceded if we can show that concealment is not generally successful. But the possibility that it has also social goals must be considered if we can also show that total concealment is not even attempted. The goals for which we wish to argue are related to reputation.

In the second half of this chapter we will explore, and in most cases reject, a variety of other possibilities: that many of the social consequences of identifiability are unforeseen, unnoticed or unintended, or else that they have no importance to the offender. First, however, there are two other issues to consider.

5.5.1 *Pockets of anonymity*

It will now be clear that we have deprived ourselves of an obvious alternative to explanations of crimes as conscience failures. If most people are restrained most of the time by the difficulties of concealing offences, by the chronic visibility of action, perhaps those who commit them are individuals who, either temporarily or more permanently, have slipped through the network of surveillance. Perhaps the mass society thesis is still appropriate, but on a more limited scale: it defines the social environment only of a minority.

For example, could delinquency not reflect a different kind of hiatus, between policing of one kind – by parents and teachers – and policing of another which arrives with the accoutrements of adult status, jobs, marital and parental responsibilities, in-laws, and simply becoming more widely known within one's neighbourhood and community? And could not more persistent crime result when individuals remain on the margin of any community, not incorporated into any social roles, relative social isolates, known to hardly anyone? Then again, could not inner cities have higher rates of crime for precisely the reasons mass society theory proposed – in so far as they afford a degree of anonymity (cf. Freudenberg, 1986; Freudenberg & Jones, 1991)? Let us consider why this alternative solution will not do.

(1) *Delinquency stems from the social isolation of individuals.* We have already said that delinquency is not a solitary activity. Delinquents are also not solitary people. They are, for example, no less likely to have friends than more law-abiding teenagers, nor are their friendships any less stable or more superficial, or their contacts with friends any less frequent (e.g. Giordano, Cernovich & Pugh, 1986; see also chapter 7).

(2) *Delinquency stems from the social isolation of the age group.* Again there is no evidence that adolescents as a category temporarily slip into anonymity between 12 and 18, or that boys do so more completely than girls. If this were so, it would be hard to see how reputational measures could work. On the other hand, there are indications that the social worlds of adolescents, and of adolescent boys in particular, are more segmented and that adolescent boys are less closely supervised by parents than girls, and these may be enabling conditions for the pursuit of delinquent activities.

(3) *Delinquency stems from opportunities for anonymity afforded by the environment of the city.* It is important to distinguish here between social or environmental conditions which render individuals anonymous and conditions which allow certain kinds of delinquency to be carried off successfully. There can be little doubt that the latter is often an important part of opportunity, but it does not help us to understand why some seize the opportunity when others do not. We might also add that visibility is relative; teachers may well see things happening that remain hidden from parents. This raises an issue, to be considered in a later chapter, of who the primary or intended audiences are.

5.5.2 *Residual problems of concealment*

The Freudian image of the sinner, one driven to transgress as a bio-logical compulsion and equally driven by shame to do so privately and secretively, may fit the middle-class boy masturbating in guilty solitude, but it is not relevant to delinquency. However, this image does tell us both who might be left in the category of secretive offenders, namely those who lead double lives, and why they should not be confused with delinquents.

The remaining members of the category are people committed or attached to an activity by virtue of qualities intrinsic to the activity, but who must pursue their practice covertly because they know more powerful voices in society condemn it, would see it punished, and have the means to do so. In different times and different societies these have included adherents to minority religions, prostitutes, homosexuals, women seeking abortions, illicit lovers, people with sexually deviant com-pulsions, and smokers of marijuana, to name a few. It therefore includes two groups, those emotionally attached or economically committed to the activity but who may none the less accept on another level that it is wrong and worthy of punishment, and those who are in disagreement about what is wrong but lack the means to make their judgement stick on a more public level.

There is nothing absolute about this division, and there are many examples of the movement of activities from the first to the second group, a transformation Moscovici (1976) describes as from deviance to active minority. This reflects the history of homosexuality and abortion, and is beginning to describe that of soft drug use. But once a proscribed activity changes from a private matter to one recognized by its adherents to be shared, then something else frequently happens. The minority seeks to bring about public acceptance, to produce a change in majority moral opinion (cf. Moscovici, 1976; Paicheler, 1988). In this, campaigns for the liberalization of laws on homosexuality, abortion and soft-drug use are quite unlike the activities of delinquents.

The essence of the difference is in attitudes to moral boundaries. The former are attempts to move the boundaries, the latter are movements across a recognized boundary. This signals another important step in our argument, and we shall need to say in more detail what allows the step to be taken: delinquents are not simply young people confused about where the moral boundaries lie any more than they are, as some labelling theorists would have it, the losers in a struggle to decide where those boundaries should be drawn. Labelling theory works best for activities which contain some inherent moral ambiguity such as drug use or other 'victimless' crimes. But there is not the same kind of ambiguity over crimes with victims.

5.6 The Requirements for Reputation

It seems obvious enough that if misbehaviour is likely to become public knowledge, people would avoid such behaviour to protect their reputations. What is more puzzling is why some individuals would consistently act in ways that will give them a bad reputation. There would seem to be two kinds of explanation for those who embark on this course. The first is that individuals differ in their ability or skill at managing their reputations. The second is that some individuals lack the reasons to want or care about having a good reputation. Neither proves to be entirely satisfactory. While we are saying why they are not, we can also look at two perspectives on delinquency that have recently become popular, social skills theory (Spence, 1981; Henderson & Hollin, 1986), and social control theory (Hirschi, 1969).

5.6.1 Delinquency as a consequence of skill deficits

There are at least three components to the successful management of moral reputation. First, one must appreciate that one has a reputation to manage. Second, one needs some knowledge of the social and psychological processes through which reputation is generated. And third, one must be sufficiently adept at influencing these processes.

(1) *Awareness of reputation.* It would be anticipated that consciousness of one's own reputation would grow with the development of role-taking skills and expanded social participation. You discover your reputation in the opinions of others. Anticipating that other people will have such opinions is a part of developing the capacity to take the perspective of others (cf. Flavell et al., 1968). Learning what those opinions are requires the kinds of social contacts in which they can be expressed. Teachers and parents may not hesitate to express them but outside of these power relations matters are more delicate, and even within them it is not clear that opinions are taken as anything other than personal judgements. Many opinions, and perhaps most of those which matter, come to us through hearsay: one friend tells us another thinks we are unreliable or selfish, a new acquaintance says they have heard we are aggressive or rude.

Kenny and DePaulo (1993), from a review of studies of metaperception – people's perceptions of the way they are perceived by others – concluded that people are substantially correct in their views about how others generally see them. But these authors also concluded that people overestimate the consistency of the impressions they make on others, and more interestingly that their views about others' perceptions are not based on feedback received from others but on their own self-perceptions. In other words, they guess – correctly in general – that others will see them as they see themselves. The interesting question here is whether individuals differ in the accuracy of these kinds of guesses.

Do delinquents have less capacity to foresee how others might regard them? Chandler (1973) has reported a link between delinquency and deficits in perspective-taking skills, so it seems that delinquents could simply fail to anticipate the impact of their deeds on others' opinions. On the other hand, this study has yet to be replicated and is so much at variance with other evidence that its implications remain unclear. This other evidence includes clear indications that delinquent adolescents are quite conscious of the poor opinions that others have of them (e.g. Thompson, 1974), but this is to anticipate another issue, a capacity to appreciate how delinquent conduct is regarded. Appreciation or anticipation of one's own reputation is a more complex matter.

(2) *Knowledge about reputational processes*: (a) *Temporal and spatial perspectives*. One possibility we cannot dismiss is that perceptions can vary about the reach of reputation, both in social and temporal space. If reputation is founded on a pattern of evidence which accumulates over time, its effective control by the individual requires recognition of the wider and longer-term repercussions of particular actions: persons must ask 'how far through a social world which matters to me will this action reverberate, and how long will its effects linger?' There are two sides to this, of course. Actions can fail to have the reach or endurance one would like – Shakespeare's problem of 'keeping honour bright' – or rather more than one expects. Is the latter the kind of error delinquents make? Stein, Sarbin and Kulik (1968) reported that juvenile offenders have shorter future time perspectives than their more law-abiding peers, but whether this reveals an inability to visualize their futures or indifference is not so clear. And whether there are differences in the anticipated social reach of actions no one yet knows.

(b) *Perceived seriousness*. The crucial question is whether delinquents appreciate that what they do will be regarded as wrong by most people, or at least by respectable, law-abiding society. In other words, have they simply failed to notice that certain forms of behaviour are commonly condemned as wrong, wicked, irresponsible, undesirable, or anti-social?

If so, they should be rather puzzled about the disapproval their activities seem to excite.

Some versions of cultural diversity theory are based on the idea that delinquency and non-delinquency arise from different kinds of values. Delinquent activity reflects a range of social experience which has brought certain adolescents more frequently into contact with values supporting delinquency than with values which do not (e.g. Miller, 1958; Sutherland & Cressey, 1970). They may therefore simply fail to appreciate what the wider and more powerful audience approves and disapproves, perhaps until it is too late.

In absolute terms this just is not plausible. Early in the twentieth century psychologists tried to show that delinquents were young people ignorant of the rules. Their attempts were utter failures (Pittel & Mendelsohn, 1966). Everyone, irrespective of their own compliance with the rules, seemed to know what the rules required. More recently, Turiel (1983) has shown that even young children are uniformly convinced of the unalterable wrongness of, for example, stealing or physical attacks on people. Some years earlier, Matza (1964) had come to a similar conclusion; the idea that delinquents are marching to a different drum because they have not heard the louder beat of conventional middle-class morality is not likely.

Is there something else delinquents may fail to understand about moral judgements? Kohlberg argued they fail to understand obligations to rules in conventional terms, seeing these obligations as merely pragmatically advisable given the punishment associated with breaking them. But we have seen that this case has yet to be made to stand empirically.

A more promising possibility is that delinquents underestimate the relative seriousness of their activities. Offending is not a continual activity. Perhaps they merely fail to appreciate that their occasional misdemeanours – the normal pattern – will be regarded so seriously or do such damage to their reputations.

The perceived seriousness of most common criminal activities is known to decline over the same period of adolescence in which delinquency increases (e.g. Turiel, 1973). Several investigations demonstrate that perceptions of the relative seriousness of different offences are related to the relative likelihood of their commission (Erickson et al., 1977; Silberman, 1976). There is also, however, a strong empirical association between perceived moral disapproval of activities and perceived certainty and severity of punishment (Jensen et al., 1978; Silberman, 1976). This must raise some question as to whether the moral disapproval or the legal sanction is the more relevant deterrent (Grasmick & Bryjack, 1980). Nevertheless, both Hindelang (1973) and Jensen (1972) have shown a direct connection between delinquency and perception of crime seriousness: young people who regard crime less seriously are more likely to be delinquent. Hindelang (1970) has also shown that the probability of a specific offence being admitted on a self-report inventory is inversely related to its perceived seriousness; individuals regarding any particular offence as less serious are more likely than others to admit to it.

So perhaps delinquents do miscalculate the degree of damage to reputation their actions can produce. This in turn may reflect a generally imprudent or reckless approach to life. But it is also possible that they disagree, and know they disagree, with common opinion. To choose between the two one would have to show that delinquents underestimate the seriousness with which others regard their actions.

Finally, it is perhaps possible that delinquents are just incautious people. Hogan and Jones (1983) have shown, and we have been able to confirm, that young people who describe themselves as imprudent are also more inclined to be delinquent.

(3) *Reputation management ability*: (a) *Knowledge of accounting conventions.* Following Goffman (1959), Scott and Lyman (1968) developed the idea of 'accounts' to refer to those means, usually verbal, by which people attempt to control or modify the meanings their actions have for others. Scott and Lyman, like Goffman, assumed actions can sometimes convey an unwanted negative impression of the actor. Later Blumstein (1974) demonstrated that the perceived appropriateness of the accounts people provide for their actions can have a greater impact on the audience's moral evaluations of actors than the deeds themselves. These 'accounts' can be explanations, expressions of regret, apologies, or any other means by which persons suggest that they did not deliberately intend to transgress. Experimental studies of mock juries have confirmed the value to defendants of giving appropriate accounts: culprits are judged less harshly if they show remorse (Harrell, 1979; Rumsey, 1976). Similarly, Darby and Schlenker (1982) have shown children judge culprits more leniently when they apologize. Clearly, therefore, no well-equipped social actor should be without a repertoire of accounting devices. The question for us is whether some young people are insufficiently practised in accounting routines to avoid trouble with authority or peers.

Failures to provide acceptable accounts in confrontations with authority can be consequential. Piliavin and Briar (1964) found that a young person's demeanour when apprehended by a police officer strongly influenced likelihood of arrest. Hindelang (1976) also discovered from police officers themselves that they were more inclined to arrest a young person for an offence if that person was also verbally abusive.

Other indications of differences in accounting habits related to crime include Hogan and Jones's (1983) demonstration that a sample of violent criminals were less likely than non-violent and apparently less serious offenders to claim they were under stress at the time of the offence, that the act was due to some compulsion or impulse, or that they felt shame or guilt. In other words, contrary to Matza's (1964) expectation, those found to have been involved in criminal behaviour are not particularly inclined towards self-exculpatory accounts. When we learn that psychopaths display no remorse for their misdeeds (cf. Cleckley, 1976), or that delinquents are low in guilt (Hogan & Jones, 1983), should we therefore conclude that this reveals a lack of internalized control? It is equally plausible that they simply fail to use the various verbal and non-verbal forms of accounting which we are used to calling 'expressions of guilt'. The difficulty yet again is that this and other accounting failures could arise from disinclination rather than a shortage of skill, and we need more direct evidence that delinquents do not even know their position could be improved by giving appropriate accounts. We need next to consider if they also do not know how to provide these.

(b) *Social skill deficits.* Accounting can be regarded as an aspect of social skill (cf. Trower, Bryant & Argyle, 1978), that is, a set of routines which require to be learned and rehearsed if they are to form an effective contribution to social performances. As yet there has been no research into accounting skills as such but several theoretical statements have included claims for an association between weaknesses in social skills and delinquency. Moreover, programmes of offender rehabilitation which include social skill training have become increasingly popular (Gross et al., 1980; Hollin & Henderson, 1981; Ollendick & Herson, 1979; Spence & Marziller, 1979), and earlier programmes based on modelling (Sarason, 1968; Sarason & Ganzer, 1973) have been interpreted as providing delinquents with socially skilled role models. One might have supposed these efforts to have stemmed from solid evidence that social skills deficits contribute to delinquent involvement or that increments in social skills reduce the likelihood of further offending. In fact evidence for the social skills–delinquency link is rather modest.

Freedman et al. (1978) and Rosenthal-Gaffney and McFall (1981), using a role-play technique, compared the response strategies selected by institutionalized offenders and controls across a variety of interpersonal situations. The strategies selected by the offenders were rated as significantly less socially skilled. Interestingly, however, Rosenthal-Gaffney and McFall (1981) found that the differences occurred mostly for situations involving confrontations with authority, and did so far less for peer exchanges. Furnham (1984) examined the relationship between self-reported delinquency and social skill deficits operationalized as social difficulty (after a measure developed by Bryant and Trower, 1974). In this case no relationship was found.

Spence (1981) made a more direct examination of social skill elements, such as gestures, smiling and head movements, and found that young offenders differed from controls on 5 of the 13 elements assessed. They showed more fiddling and gross body movements and less head movements, eye contact, and total amount spoken. Ratings of video tapes also produced differences in global assessments of social skills, social anxiety and employability, but not friendliness. Spence (1981, p. 170) observed that 'it may be plausible that the results reflect the tendency for juveniles lacking in social skills to receive less favourable dispositions from the police and the courts'. Perhaps, but it would also be precisely the kind of reason why accounting disability would be related to delinquency.

Spence's comment does point to a general problem of interpretation; the studies, apart from Furnham's, compare officially identified offenders and controls, raising the possibility that skill deficits are contaminated by institutionalization effects. Furthermore, particularly in the case of the Freedman et al. (1978) and Rosenthal-Gaffney and McFall (1981) findings, one cannot rule out a motivational explanation; offenders use the 'less skilled' strategies because they choose to, not because they are incapable of doing otherwise. A recent study clearly indicated that, given appropriate role-playing instructions, delinquents had no difficulty in reproducing a 'socially desirable' performance (Renwick et al., 1993).

Renwick has made one of the most thorough examinations of the link between skills deficits and delinquency to date (Renwick, 1987; see also Renwick & Emler, 1991). He used a variety of indices of social skills, including those employed by Spence, by Furnham and by Freedman and his colleagues. Delinquency was defined both by self-report and official designation. Renwick could find no consistent link between delinquency and any indicator of skill deficit. He also found that different skill indices related poorly to one another, while the best validated of them seemed to be measures of social introversion. And introversion is unrelated to delinquency.

There is, however, a view that the crucial social skills have a cognitive basis. Dodge (1986), for example, proposes that skilled interpersonal behaviour, particularly in situations involving a degree of conflict, requires appropriate processing of various kinds of social information. His argument was developed to explain aggressive behaviour among children but could be applied as readily to delinquent behaviour in general. Slaby and Guerra (1988) have taken a step in this direction, using a version of Dodge's argument to explain aggression in adolescent offenders.

They looked at six possible information processing biases relating respectively to information search, problem definition, goal search, generation of alternative solutions, anticipation of consequences and prioritization of responses. They found significant differences in all of these areas between incarcerated young offenders and a sample matched for age but rated low on aggression by physical education teachers, but also differences between this latter group and high school pupils rated high on aggression.

The results of the Slaby and Guerra study are impressive but again a motivational interpretation is not entirely excluded. Why, for example, does preference for a hostile rather than a non-hostile solution reflect a cognitive deficit and not a choice consistent with a conscious desire to sustain a reputation for toughness and aggression? The ideal test would be to ask, as with Freedman et al.'s (1978) task, whether aggressive adolescents can reproduce the 'social information processing style' of non-aggressive adolescents under appropriate role-playing instructions.

To draw this discussion together, even if skill or knowledge deficits could be shown, there would still be a question as to their causal significance. One scenario is that young people who discover they lack the skills to sustain a good impression of themselves gradually cease to care and give up trying. But causality could be working in the opposite direction. After all, social skills are not natural endowments but the products of practice and one needs a reason to want to persevere with the necessary practice. But before it is worth trying to distinguish between these, it needs to be shown that skill differences exist. Thus far there is little solid evidence that they do.

Delinquents are not unaware they have reputations – though they may not think about how far these reach. Delinquents do not use the normal accounting conventions – but this may be out of choice. Delinquents do not lack basic social skills – and it is not clear why this kind of deficiency would itself produce deviance, though it could exacerbate the consequences in ways unwanted by the deviant. In those cases where delinquency is associated with using 'ineffective' strategies, these are only ineffective if you want to appear good. Delinquents know how to do this (Rosenthal-Gaffney & McFall, 1981; Renwick et al., 1993) but apparently choose not to. Why? One possible argument centres on the quality of the self-concept. Another approach, suggested by Social Control theory (Hirschi, 1969), is to ask why anyone wants to be good in the first place; what makes people care about having a good reputation?

5.7 Having Reasons to be 'Good'

5.7.1 Self-esteem

Various writers have proposed that delinquency stems from a poor self-concept (e.g. Kaplan, 1980; Reckless, 1967; Rosenberg & Rosenberg, 1978). Reckless proposed that a positive self-concept insulates against delinquency. In our terms, persons with positive self-concepts are concerned that other people should think well of them because they value themselves. Something they treasure, their self-image, would be damaged by any public judgement that they had behaved badly.

Kaplan (1980) puts a different argument. Low self-esteem is distressing. Children whose self-esteem has been lowered, perhaps by constant negative feedback from others, turn to delinquency as a means of regaining their esteem. It is not entirely clear, though, why vandalism, fighting or theft should have such beneficial effects for self-respect.

For other reasons, however, we confess ourselves not a little puzzled at the persisting popularity of hypotheses linking delinquency to self-esteem. Our puzzlement stems from the number of questionable assumptions and difficulties they contain. For example, why should people with a robustly positive self-image be more concerned that others share a good opinion of them? The opposite conclusion seems equally likely, and has the merit of some empirical support (e.g. Jones, Knurek & Regan, 1973); people with high self-esteem are less concerned with the good opinion of others than people with low self-esteem. Similarly, why should adolescents with low self-esteem willingly incur further negative judgements by misbehaving? It would only seem to worsen their plight.

Beside these objections there is the greater difficulty that empirically hardly any relationship between delinquency and self-esteem appears to exist (e.g. Bynner, O'Malley & Bachman, 1981; Wells & Rankin, 1983). In one of the most comprehensive studies of this relationship to date, McCarthy and Hoge (1984) explored the direction of effect in a three-wave panel study of adolescents. They found no effect of esteem on delinquency, but a slight effect of delinquency on esteem. However, most of this was attributable to a tendency for those adolescents who had been more delinquent over the previous year to describe themselves as less truthful and honest, less good at school or less well thought of by adults. Such self-descriptions hardly amount to low self-esteem. In the event, McCarthy and Hoge's conclusions seems entirely reasonable: 'The weakness of the results suggests that researchers should look elsewhere than self-esteem for a fuller understanding of delinquency' (p. 398).

5.7.2 *Commitments and attachments*

Our argument about reputation so far has been that people want to sustain good reputations because they expect negative consequences will follow if they do not. Loss of moral credit will begin to shut them out from the benefits of many kinds of social exchange. The other members of their social worlds will be disinclined to give them material or financial assistance, share strategic information, loan property to them, pull strings or exert influence on their behalf, give them emotional support or their time or company. More direct punishment may follow and include anything from excommunication, through deprivation of the means of earning a livelihood, to informal or formal deprivations of property, liberty or the protection of the law.

Hirschi's (1969) point was that these consequences are not inevitably motivating. Before you can care whether other people help you, you need to be in a position where their help is important to you. Before you can be concerned about the loss of emotional support or affection, you need to have attachments which provide these. To this we can add that legal and other sanctions for crime are, even in the case of recordable offences – recordable by virtue of their social visibility – neither certain nor intrinsically aversive. So now we are in a position to answer another question. The domain of publicly identifiable action was never entirely immune to offence because the supposed guarantee of its immunity, the certainty and aversiveness of sanction, cannot be assumed. In this context it is interesting to note that some research in the field of early childhood socialization reveals that the first problem for parents is to secure obedience, not after their backs are turned, but while they are still looking (e.g. Minton, Kagan & Levine, 1971). School teachers at all levels also know this well enough.

Hirschi (1969) starts from the position, which has many parallels with Freud's, that all humans have a natural capacity for crime. Special conditions have to occur to make them not want to indulge this capacity. One of these is that a person should acquire and retain commitments which would be put at risk by non-conformity. The most common source of a stake in conformity for adolescents will be provided by investment in an educational career, an investment made in the hope of a return in the form of employment prospects. To break the rules and risk a reputation for delinquency would also put the entire educational investment at risk. We look at this in some detail in the next chapter.

The idea of commitments could be developed in other directions. For example, it is possible that adolescence as a whole involves a gradual dawning of the extent of one's dependence on one's reputation and, for certain purposes, on one's possession of a good reputation. Adolescents, not yet having to come to terms with the informal economy of life, can be casual with their reputations. As they grow older, and acquire other needs, they are increasingly confronted with this dependence. The attractiveness of this idea is that it offers an explanation for the age function and particularly the decline of delinquency beyond mid-adolescence. We find some support for this in evidence discussed in the next chapter.

Hirschi's second condition for wanting to limit one's natural inclination to transgress is the possession of strong emotional ties to others, particularly parents, teachers and friends. Young people who are strongly attached to their parents will not wish to upset them and endanger the relationship by breaking the law or by exposing their parents to the kind of reputation within their community that delinquency would give them. In the absence of such attachments, or if parents do not figure prominently as an audience, then another reason for avoiding delinquency is absent. At root this is the same idea as that of commitments; if one depends on others for any valued resource then one will not put at risk their good opinion and one's access to such resources. In the case of attachments, the resources at stake are more psychological or symbolic – respect, esteem, affection.

The simple association required by this argument is well established. For example, numerous studies demonstrate a relation between delinquency and lack of attachment to parents (Dentler & Munroe, 1961; Farrington et al., 1982; Hirschi, 1969; Jensen, 1972; Johnson, 1979; Piliavin et al., 1969; Poole & Rigoli, 1979; Slocum & Stone, 1963). It is more difficult to say whether weakening attachments frees young people for delinquency or whether their delinquency fractures their attachments. Liska and Reed's (1985) analysis suggests in this case that parental attachment is predictive of non-delinquency more than it is predicted by it. But they also conclude that delinquency could adversely affect the parental bond through its impact on the young person's reputation with the school.

The traditional, post-Freudian view of parent–child relations, as we saw (chapter 3), is that strong attachment to parents favours the child's development of strong internalized controls (cf. Bowlby, 1946, 1969;

Hoffman, 1977). There are certainly indications that parents who culti-
vate such attachments have children who are less inclined to break the
law subsequently (Farrington & West, 1981; Glueck & Glueck, 1968).
But we need not accept that parental influence is therefore acting at a
distance, through the medium of internal controls. Hirschi's argument
draws our attention to the possibility that children who had good
relations with their parents when they were young are the ones most
likely to have relatively good relations in their adolescence and that it
is the quality of the relationship currently which shapes their conduct.
Likewise, those with poor relations in early childhood are those most
likely to have poor relations in adolescence.

Taking the overall question of why people should want a reputation
as 'good', we would argue that much of the substance of social control
theory, unlike that of esteem theories, appears both plausible and consistent with the facts. It points to the conditions which lead some people
to want to avoid a bad reputation. But as a theory of delinquency, it
depends on the idea that the absence of these reasons is sufficient to
produce delinquency. Young people are delinquent only because they
lack reasons to be good. We believe that the absence of reasons to be
good allows delinquency but does not ensure it. Delinquency requires its
own conditions. We could go further and say that when these conditions
are met, they will in turn weaken the 'reasons to be good'. What are
these conditions? Before trying to answer this, we need to examine
another questions. Why should delinquency be considered as flowing
from a reputational project in its own right?

5.8 Delinquent Action as Self-presentation

Our analysis requires that behavioural choices and in particular
choices between breaking certain rules and not breaking them are
self-presentations, that is, public and recognizable claims to different
kinds of identity. There is evidence that physical aggression, a rather
public and visible form of anti-social behaviour, serves self-presentational
goals (Felson, 1978, 1981, 1982). There is also some evidence that
aggressive adolescents believe in the self-presentational efficacy of
aggression (e.g., Slaby & Guerra, 1988). But we have assumed that
a principal objection to the extension of this analysis to other forms
of delinquency would be the invisibility of non-compliance and we have
spent some time showing that delinquency is normally sufficiently visible
to serve as self-presentation.

We have also shown that certain kinds of action are more typical or representative of delinquent inclination as a whole. But if delinquency occurs as part of a reputational project then these typical delinquencies should derive their representativeness from their particular effectiveness as vehicles of self-presentation. This suggests they should possess two qualities in greater measure than less typical or representative forms; they should be more visible, and they should be more readily interpretable.

Some evidence for the first prediction is provided by comparing the factor loadings of self-report delinquency items with the extent to which the activities these items describe are claimed to be committed in the company of others. Two assumptions are required here, both of which we believe can be defended. The first is that factor loading is a satisfactory index of prototypicality. Items with the highest factor loading are those which most clearly distinguish between those young people who claim extensive involvement in delinquency and those who claim very little. Whether a boy admits or denies having written on walls with a can of spray paint is predictive (i.e., typical) of his conduct more generally. Whether he admits or denies having truanted is far less so.

The second is that the most common immediate audience, and therefore the basis of social visibility, for all the behavioural choices young people make, whether these involve breaking the rules or not, are their peers. The first source of visibility for delinquent conduct is the group of accomplices in whose company it occurs.

We were able to compare the factor loadings of 33 items from an index completed by one sample with group involvement data provided by a second. The correlation was 0.63 ($p < 0.001$), supporting the prediction. That is, those activities which were most typical were also those most likely to occur in groups.

The second prediction requires a demonstration that the behavioural choices involved with respect to 'typical' delinquencies have clear and shared meanings for all the relevant audiences. Consider what this could imply. One possibility is that writing on walls with a spray can is an unmistakable message to anyone who receives it that the actor is delinquent (that he or she has deliberately chosen to cross the boundary marking the limits of what is acceptable behaviour). Another is that doing this is the more informative choice. In other words, 'doing' and 'not doing' do not necessarily have equal clarity as messages.

What makes something a distinctive message is the fact that the choice is highly definitive of membership of the category, by common consent. This common consent is probably influenced by two judgements, first that the choice involved is relatively free of situational constraint or restriction (i.e., it is unambiguously deliberate), and second that it is unusual for members of the contrasting category to make this choice. In these terms, not having engaged in robbery using or threatening violence is not particularly definitive of the category 'non-delinquent' since the situational pressures against robbery with violence are rather strong. Consequently most boys who are otherwise delinquent will not have engaged in the activity. On the other hand, those who do claim it are especially likely to be delinquent. Riding a bicycle after dark without lights or smoking under the legal age are not particularly definitive of the category 'delinquent' because so many young people in the relevant population, both those who are generally delinquent and those who are not, do these things. Yet other activities are largely uninformative about delinquent inclinations because a variety of reasons for the action can readily be called to mind. If boys break into stores, the one thing they are likely to have in common is a willingness to break the law. If they truant from school they could do so for many different reasons, apart from any willingness to violate regulations requiring school attendance. The point is not that a social scientist could think of such reasons but that a lay audience could do so.

It would be interesting to test this argument directly by asking young people; we undertook a slightly different test of the argument. We reasoned that claims about typical forms of delinquency should convey clear messages about the choosers to young people, and that the messages would be clear to non-delinquents and delinquents alike. We expected that the messages conveyed by choices with respect to less typical forms would be less clear.

The research, conducted with one of our students, Bridget Ronson, was based on a sample of secondary school pupils, 86 in all, 43 girls and 43 boys. Each participant completed a self-report measure of their own degree of delinquent involvement and this allowed us to divide each sex into those with relatively high levels of reported involvement and those with relatively low.

The procedure for the study was as follows. Each participant was presented with a set of descriptions of boys of their own age, four descriptions in all. One boy was described as claiming to have been involved in four illegal activities which we had identified as highly representative, a second as claiming not to have been involved in any of these. A third was described as claiming to have been involved in four illegal activities rather less typical of delinquency as a whole (and generally more trivial), and a fourth not to have been involved in any of them. Each description was followed by a set of dimensions referring to personal characteristics – reliable/unreliable, friendly/unfriendly, and so on. Each pair defined the respective end points of a seven-point scale. We

Table 5.2 Perceived personal attributes of characters varying in delinquent involvement

Attribute	Admits serious	Admits trivial	Denies serious	Denies trivial
Exciting (=1) – Boring (=7)	4.04	3.65	4.34	4.37
Dirty (=1) – Clean (=7)	3.51	3.57	4.87	5.73
Strong (=1) – Weak (=7)	3.02	3.90	4.36	4.27
Good at school work (=1) – Bad at . . . (=7)	5.93	5.55	2.63	1.80
Lazy (=1) – Hard working (=7)	2.71	2.64	4.66	5.80
Honest(=1) – Dishonest (=7)	6.22	6.02	2.65	1.73
Clever (=1) – Stupid (=7)	5.62	5.58	2.79	2.16
Cowardly (=1) – Brave (=7)	5.03	4.74	4.02	3.89
Unreliable (=1) – Reliable (=7)	2.55	2.52	4.92	5.66
Likeable (=1) – Not likeable (=7)	5.25	4.70	4.33	3.11
Selfish (=1) – Generous (=7)	2.58	2.61	4.65	4.98
Cruel (=1) – Kind (=7)	2.60	2.90	5.06	5.40
Fair (=1) – Unfair (=7)	5.67	5.55	2.79	2.38
Lonely (=1) – Not lonely (=2)	3.84	3.91	4.21	4.36
Tough (=1) – Not tough (=7)	2.95	3.22	4.52	4.78
Emotional (=1) – Unemotional (=7)	5.36	5.20	3.38	2.96

Table 5.2 Continued

Attribute	Admits serious	Admits trivial	Denies serious	Denies trivial
Stands up for rights (=1) – Does not . . . (=1)	3.57	3.63	3.42	3.57
Immature (=1) – Mature (=7)	2.75	3.26	4.96	5.08
Popular (=1) – Unpopular (=7)	4.50	4.25	3.78	3.68
Responsible (=1) – Irresponsible (=7)	6.06	5.72	2.75	2.23

Source: data from Emler, Reicher & Ronson (1987).

asked our participants to make a judgement, given the description, about the likely characteristics of the boy so described. Table 5.2 presents the average estimates by the sample as a whole of the characteristics of the four boys.

As will be seen from this table, the results failed to confirm our expectation that the judgements would be much further from the scale mid-point of four when made of boys admitting or denying typical activities than for boys admitting or denying less typical misdemeanours. In retrospect it was probably a mistake to describe a boy admitting several untypical (and trivial) delinquencies. Doing one of them may say little; doing several, even if relatively trivial, begins to convey something more distinctive. On the other hand, denying having done several trivial things conveys a clearer message that one is good than denying having done several less trivial things.

What table 5.2 does not show but should also be noted is that boys on the whole agreed with girls, but more significantly, the more delinquent agreed with the less delinquent. This provides further confirmation, if such were needed, that delinquents are not to any significant degree failing to understand the way that delinquent action is regarded. Nor, contrary to some claims, do they believe it to mean something different.

There are also some interesting indications in the data concerning the kinds of personal quality conveyed by the behavioural choices described. Some of these indications have been replicated in a study of 96 14–16-year-olds. In this study (Haswell, 1991) a description was provided of one of three characters. The description included details of academic record, home life, and behaviour. The behavioural descriptions varied in

Table 5.3 Evaluations of targets of varying levels of delinquent involvement

Attribute		Non-delinquent delinquent	Target Moderately delinquent	Highly delinquent
Tough (=1)	M	2.81	2.37	2.00
– Weak (=5)	F	3.48	2.21	2.00
Emotional (=1)	M	2.62	3.50	3.54
– Unemotional (=5)	F	2.19	2.90	3.04
Mature (=1)	M	2.00	3.81	3.69
– Immature (=5)	F	2.17	3.65	3.83
Dependent (=1)	M	2.65	2.90	3.00
– Independent (=5)	F	2.83	3.29	3.19
Reliable (=1)	M	3.83	2.10	2.46
– Unreliable (=5)	F	4.02	3.35	2.12
Happy (=1)	M	2.98	2.75	3.19
– Sad (=5)	F	3.04	3.04	3.10
Honest (=1)	M	1.77	4.29	4.12
– Dishonest (=5)	F	1.52	3.90	4.23
Friendly (=1)	M	1.96	2.96	3.75
– Unfriendly (=5)	F	1.94	3.17	2.56
Stands up for self (=1)	M	2.56	2.02	1.87
– Does not . . . (=5)	F	2.79	1.98	1.56
Fun to be with (=1)	M	2.75	2.92	3.42
– Not fun . . . (=5)	F	2.77	2.79	3.54
Lazy (=1)	M	4.02	2.60	2.81
– Active (=5)	F	4.35	2.56	2.90
Rude (=1)	M	3.81	1.87	1.56
– Polite (=5)	F	4.23	2.12	2.06
Boring (=1)	M	3.19	3.44	3.13
– Exciting (=5)	F	2.85	3.35	3.17
Fashionable (=1)	M	3.06	2.85	2.89
– Unfashionable (=5)	F	3.15	2.67	2.54
Popular with opposite sex (=1)	M	3.15	3.10	2.92
– Not popular . . . (=5)	F	3.21	2.60	1.96

Note: n = 16 per cell. *Source*: data from Haswell (1991).

terms of the amount of delinquency depicted, either none, relative minor delinquencies, or more serious offences. In this study boys were asked to make judgements about male characters, girls about female characters.

The more delinquent male characters were seen by boys to be neither more nor less dependent or happy, exciting or fashionable, and no more or less popular with the opposite sex. The more delinquent female characters were slightly more likely to be seen by girls as more exciting, fashionable and popular with the opposite sex. Boys and girls agreed that the less delinquent characters were more likely to be active and friendly, and that the more delinquent characters were more likely to be dishonest, unreliable, rude, and immature. However, they also agreed they were more likely to be tough and unemotional, and to stand up for themselves (see table 5.3). Moreover, subjects' own relative level of involvement in delinquency had no significant effects on perceptions.

By itself this study cannot support any strong conclusions. The sample was drawn from a rural high school and the absolute levels of delinquency in the group were relatively low. It would be desirable to see such results replicated with other samples and with stronger contrasts between high and low delinquency youngsters. However, taken together with the results of the previous study, certain themes do emerge. First, there is a clear moral dimension to the impressions conveyed – unreliable, dishonest – and delinquents and non-delinquents agree. Second, there is a dimension relating to education. Third, there is a dimension relating to toughness. This last is consistent with the beliefs aggressive teenagers hold about the advantages of aggression (Slaby & Guerra, 1988).

We can now begin to see that not only is delinquency a coherent choice which communicates an unambiguous and well-understood message; we also begin to detect some of the attractions of this particular choice, a point we will develop in the next chapter.

For the present there is one final feature of the pattern illustrated in table 5.3 to which we would like to draw attention. Choosing to do is, on the whole, more informative than choosing not to. What is interesting about this is that saying something clear and distinctive about yourself is more easily done by breaking the rules than by keeping to them. The implications can perhaps be better understood by turning the issue around and asking how can particular personal qualities be communicated or, in Goffman's terms, 'dramatized'? Rothbart and Park (1986) have demonstrated that some traits are more readily deniable than others, which is to say the ease with which an actor can provide an audience with evidence that he or she does not possess a trait varies with the nature of the trait. Skowronski and Carlston (1989) have argued that individuals' claims about their moral traits present particular difficulties because negative evidence is more informative or 'diagnostic' than positive evidence. The reason they give for this is that morally desirable behaviour is so strongly encouraged and rewarded that even immoral individuals are likely to behave morally much of the time; this behaviour does not distinguish them from moral individuals. On the other hand, moral individuals are very unlikely to behave immorally. There is now a body of evidence supporting the asymmetry in the informativeness or diagnostic value of honest and dishonest conduct, though this asymmetry may have sources other than that proposed by Skowronski and Carlston. Whatever the case, however, its consequences are of particular interest. On the one hand it is more difficult to develop a reputation for exceptional virtue than it is to acquire a bad reputation. On the other, a bad reputation once acquired is particularly difficult to shed (cf. Skowronski & Carlston, 1992).

5.9 Conclusions

In this chapter we have shown that the social conditions under which people can have reputations are also the normal conditions of most people's lives. The social environments people inhabit, even those who live in large cities, bear very little resemblance to the image of a 'mass society'. We have also argued that reputations, including bad reputations, are neither the products of faulty perceptions by others nor accidental and unintended by-products of behaviour. In particular there is as yet no convincing evidence that young people who acquire bad reputations do so because they lack the basic tools of reputation management. If a degree of choice lies behind the reputations young people have, the next question to consider is the nature of the choices involved. This chapter has ended with some indications of the kinds of choices involved and their relative attractions. In the next the nature of the choices is considered in more detail.

6

Young People and the Institutional Order

6.1 Introduction

In this and the next chapter we consider the different kinds of reputation projects that might be pursued by young people. We argue that in order to understand the actions of young people it is necessary to appreciate the social framework within which their actions occur. Two features of this framework are considered in particular; each assumes a special importance in adolescence. One is the institutional framework of society, experienced most directly by adolescents through their formal education and through contacts with various agencies of the state. The other is the informal social group, and in particular the peer group.

The latter is examined in more detail in the following chapter. Here we argue that adolescent delinquency can be interpreted in terms of the kinds of accommodation teenagers make to the demands of the institutional system. Young people negotiate and construct public identities in terms of a set of choices determined both by the institutional structures in which they participate and the various social relationships in which they are embedded. A delinquent reputation is no more an incidental and unsought by-product of action than is a reputation for honesty, reliability or diligence.

6.2 The Young Person's Relationship to the Institutional Order

Social theorists are generally agreed that a qualitative change occurred in European societies sometime around the end of the eighteenth century. One analysis of this transformation locates its origins in the progressive rationalization of productive labour and so labels it the Industrial Revolution. Whatever the origins, this period in European social history was characterized by several roughly concurrent trends which included industrialization, urbanization, mass literacy, and secularization. Furthermore it saw the emergence in recognizably modern form of what is now the dominant kind of political unit, the nation state.

As we have argued, there is now considerable doubt as to whether the transformation in social relationships wrought by the industrialization of Western societies was either so discontinuous with the past or precisely of the kind envisaged by social theorists in the nineteenth and early twentieth centuries. However, these early analyses did have the merit of drawing attention to a pervasive feature of contemporary life, the prevalence of formal, large-scale institutions and organizations, or what Weber (1947) called 'bureaucracies'.

There are two things to notice here. The first is that much of the public, and indeed private, business of our lives is conducted within frameworks provided by bureaucracies. Weber applied his thesis about the rationalization of social relationships primarily to productive labour. He foresaw that economic enterprises organized around wage-labour relations would be progressively bureaucratized. But he saw that this process also applied to the apparatus of government, and to the whole range of institutions which deliver public services.

The second thing to notice is the special character of bureaucratic relations. Weber argued that the bureaucracy differs from other kinds of social organization, notably those based on ties of personal loyalty and those based on respect for custom and tradition, in a number of crucial respects. It rationalizes the relation between the individual and the system: individuals are formally clients, customers or members, with formally defined rights, entitlements and obligations which depend on status. It also rationalizes membership status, awarding positions on the basis of technical qualifications rather than, for example, on the basis of personal preferences or family connections. Finally, it rationalizes norms and authority relations.

If the social revolution which accompanied the industrial revolution hastened the spread of bureaucracy it did not so much create distinct spheres of social relations as introduce new principles into the regulation of all social relationships. The state seeks to rationalize all relationships by formally defining the rights and obligations of all citizens, rights which are backed up by formal guarantees of protection, and obligations which are to be enforced by formally defined sanctions. This pattern is then reproduced in the various institutions within the state; individuals will also have formal rights, entitlements and obligations in their institutional roles as patients and doctors, employees and employers, pupils and teachers, and even as parents and children.

6.2.1 Institutions in the social worlds of adolescents

The purpose of this preamble, of course, is to make a point about the social worlds of adolescents – a point that will provide a theme for the remainder of this chapter: relations with the institutional order assume a particular significance in adolescence. There are various reasons for this.

At the beginning of adolescence the typical child's life will revolve around the family, friends and school. The institutional or structural order will, with one very important exception, impinge on life in only a relatively limited way. By the end of adolescence, most of the formal entitlements and obligations of the adult citizen will have been acquired. Many individuals will have entered the labour market, if they are not undergoing more intensive and advanced preparation in the form of higher education. And the labour market in the contemporary nation state is dominated by highly bureaucratized employment relations. Over the course of adolescence individuals will have made various transitions towards adult status and towards placements within the social order which will owe much to the kinds of accommodations they have made to the institutional system and its peculiar requirements.

Consider first of all the kinds of experience adolescents will have of formal organizations and formally ordered relationships. One will be experience of commercial organizations, encountered through the purchase of goods and services. Certainly during childhood there will have been extensive if episodic and vicarious experience of relatively impersonal commercial transactions. Consequently by age ten or eleven children already have a well-developed understanding of the institutions of buying and selling (Berti & Bombi, 1988). But much of their experience will have been as onlookers, making sense of the activities of their parents and other adults. In adolescence they increasingly make these transactions themselves, and increasingly on their own behalf; adolescence sees a change in the individual's role as commercial customer and consumer.

For most individuals adolescence brings more extensive recognition of the degree to which activities are subject to legal regulation. In this period of life there are typically increasing opportunities to be in public places and to participate in activities beyond the direct supervision of parents or other adults. Young people are increasingly expected to exercise control over their own behaviour and are increasingly held legally responsible for their actions. Whereas earlier in childhood parents stood between the child and the law, in adolescence this relationship becomes more direct. And indeed many young people will, over the course of their adolescence, have direct personal contact with the law-enforcing agencies and agents of the state.

Finally, all adolescents will have one institutional experience in common; they will all have, for several years, directly experienced formally ordered relations in the shape of their schooling. In this respect, there is continuity between childhood and adolescent experience, though there may be some differences associated with adolescence; the schools may be larger units than those of the childhood years and they may be characterized by greater formality. Also, at some point, continued participation in full-time education becomes voluntary. The decision made at this point – whether to continue or to leave – is fundamental for its repercussions upon almost every detail of the individual's subsequent life course (Banks et al., 1992). How young people adapt to formal education is central to their relations with the institutional order of society generally.

At this juncture we may note that adolescence represents a significant new phase in the individual's relations with the institutional order. To begin with this is not so much because of changes in educational experiences but because of a combination of physical changes and increased independence. In a sense a crisis or decision point arises early in adolescence, a crisis in relations with the wider community in which the choice is: will I allow the state to mediate in and stipulate the terms of my relations with others or will I seek to conduct these relations directly?

The thesis we wish to develop is as follows. First, at the heart of young people's relation to the institutional order is their orientation to formal authority. Second, the most important context for the development of their relationships with the institutional order and the formal authority it embodies is formal education. Third and finally, the kind of accommodation young people make to formal authority is expressed in the degree to which they engage in or avoid delinquent activities.

The remainder of this chapter will develop this thesis and its implications, and will set out the empirical and theoretical basis for these various claims and the ways in which they are related to one another.

6.2.2 *The institutional regulation of conduct*

The link we are proposing between juvenile delinquency and orientation to institutional authority can be understood by first considering the nature of such authority. This, we have argued, may be regarded as a system for organizing and regulating relations between individuals. It provides means for coordinating activities, allocating resources and duties, resolving conflicts of interest, and settling grievances. Consequently each individual stands in two kinds of relation to this system. One is a relation of constraint; the individual is required to abide by regulations, to observe formally defined proscriptions and prescriptions and to obey the instructions and directives of those who are formally authorized to issue them. The other relation is one of protection and promotion. The system offers individuals protection of their rights, their person and their property, and provides them with means of redress when these are violated. It also offers social advancement. There is here an implicit contract: in exchange for obedience and support of the system the individual is offered protection and the prospect of social mobility.

But if the institutional order is, among other things, a system for managing relations between people, is there an alternative? The answer is 'yes'; what Mitchell (1969) called the 'personal order' provides a parallel system for the regulation of social relations. The personal order consists of the network of informal and personalized links between the individual members of communities. It represents a range of informal means for achieving the same objectives as the structural or institutional order. People can coordinate and organize informally, making informal arrangements and deals. And they can also cope with the hazards of social living by informal action. They can seek mutual protection, defend themselves directly, take direct retaliatory action when offended or attacked, and seek mobility or social advancement through alliances.

We suggest, therefore, that these are two broad ways of managing relations with others, two kinds of strategy which individuals and communities can adopt to cope with the requirements and hazards of social life. These two approaches are not entirely incompatible and young people will embrace a mixture of both. Delinquency can be regarded as expressing a greater commitment to the informal solution and rejection of the formal solution, while non-delinquency expresses a greater commitment to the institutional solution.

It would be inappropriate, however, to exaggerate the contrast between formal and informal solutions – delinquency is one variant of informal solution, a variant which does actually emphasize a contrast – others involve reputations which make the solutions complementary. On the one hand, the formal solution is imperfect and for this reason if no other everyone also makes some use of informal methods. On the other hand delinquency is by no means an entirely successful solution, even without the punitive response of the institutional system; it provides only limited and sometimes temporary gains in security or status. None the less, it may still appear to the young people who adopt it to be the only viable option.

Is there any evidence to support this interpretation of delinquency? Three kinds of evidence will be discussed, relating respectively to the content of delinquency, to the relation between delinquency and beliefs about formal authority, and to the relation of both to educational career.

6.3 Delinquent Action as the Conduct of Social Relations by Extra-legal Means

Consider again those activities the admission or denial of which most clearly differentiate between those extensively and those minimally involved in delinquency. They are not merely ways of having fun; many other things are fun which are not delinquent. Neither do these activities represent a choice between accepting and rejecting illicit means of material gain. Cohen's (1955) objection to Merton's strain theory remains valid; delinquency is not particularly about pursuing material goals by illegitimate means.

What the most representative forms of delinquent action do have in common is that they are illegal. So are we saying that delinquencies are committed primarily because they are delinquencies, and not for instance, because they provide intrinsic satisfactions? Not entirely. Our working hypothesis is that what is most significant about these activities, or rather about claims made in respect of them, is that they are clear statements about where one stands in relation to the institutional order of society. At the heart of delinquency is the expression of a particular relationship with formal authority. Delinquent acts are announcements that one is unwilling to accept the claims the law wishes to make upon one's self, or one's relations with others; they are expressions of a breach in relations with the institutional order and its demands.

This rejection is expressed first in continuing to pursue grievance methods which lie beyond the law – direct physical attacks on enemies and opponents. Likewise it is expressed in routine preparedness for aggression – carrying weapons in case they are needed in a fight, for example. Black (1983) has argued that many crimes can be understood as forms of self-help justice; that is, they are motivated by a desire to rectify what the actor sees to be unjustified injuries to the self. Black instances cases of theft arising from disputes over ownership, of vandalism directed against the property of enemies, and assaults arising from perceived provocations.

There is also ample evidence that members of delinquent groups refuse the help of authorities in dealing with adversaries and rivals. Patrick (1973), in his study of Glasgow gangs, gives a dramatic illustration of this. He tells of one boy, who needed 59 stitches after a knife attack, refusing to identify his assailants. Another, stabbed in the side by a peer, declined to prefer charges. We encountered similar albeit less dramatic examples. One boy we interviewed at the end of school hours was unwilling to leave the premises when the interview finished. A rival gang member was waiting outside with a spiked club. Nervous as he was, he refused to ask teachers to remove this outsider.

We can begin to see in these examples that teenage delinquency can be part of an informal strategy in another sense. It provides a public demonstration that one has no need of formal protection because one is both willing and able to defend one's interests by direct retaliation. Felson's (1978, 1981) analyses of aggression support a similar conclusion. Felson argued that acts of aggression normally reflect attempts at impression management – managing the impression that one cannot be insulted or victimized with impunity. His own and other data confirm that aggressive retaliation is more likely when both initiating insult and the aggressive reply have an audience. Dodge (1986) has likewise argued that aggression is typically a reaction to a perceived insult, though Dodge also argues that aggressive boys chronically misperceive others' intentions towards them.

Rejection of the formal solution is expressed second in actions which challenge the capacity of the institutional order to defend those values it most conspicuously supports, particularly property – thefts from shops, cars, slot machines. Third, it is expressed in direct attacks on concrete symbols of the institutional order itself – writing graffiti on walls or otherwise vandalizing public property – and direct defiance of its representatives, teachers and policemen. A confrontational style with respect to officials is not an incidental feature of misbehaviour but an intrinsic element in the delinquent pattern. Interestingly, police records reveal fewer attacks on police officers by juveniles than adolescents themselves claim to make. This particular form of behaviour may therefore be exaggerated in self-reports but the point of interest is that young offenders should wish to make such claims at all.

So why are status offences not more prototypical, for they would surely express a rejection of those demands which might seem to have the most precarious legitimacy? One reason perhaps is that status offences are not highly distinctive; most young people violate some of these requirements anyway. Another is that commission is more ambiguous; it could be a matter of taste or opportunity. There are always opportunities for theft, vandalism and fighting, but those for under-age drinking, drug taking, gambling, or seeing X-rated films can be more arbitrarily distributed.

6.3.1 *Attitudes and beliefs about institutional authority*

If delinquency really is centrally a statement about relations with formal authority, then it should be associated with other even more explicit statements of the same relationship. For example, it should be associated with an adolescent's expressed beliefs and opinions about institutional authority as such. Evidence pointing to such a link is to be found in several places. Thus there are numerous reports of a relationship between delinquency and measures of attitudes to law (Brown, 1974b; Clark & Wenninger, 1964; Waldo & Hall, 1970; West & Farrington, 1973), to the police (Gibson, 1967) and to authority generally (Rigby & Rump, 1979).

Unfortunately, in some of these cases the relationship between delinquency and attitudes to authority is confounded with age. Samples have spanned age ranges as wide as 11 to 17 years, and it is known from other research that attitudes of the kind sampled change over this period. Attitudes to law, for example, become less positive (Brown, 1974a; Gallatin & Adelson, 1971; Hess & Torney, 1967; Mussen, Sullivan & Eisenberg-Berg, 1977). During the same period general levels of involvement in delinquency increase. It thus remains possible that we are simply observing the effects of another age-related variable on both attitudes and conduct. For this reason it is desirable to study the relationship between attitudes and delinquency independently of the relationship of both to age.

The other limitation of this research for our purposes is that it does not sample attitudes within the domain of formal authority as such. Attitudes to law, to the police, to parental authority, to crime, to school rules, and to teachers have all been sampled, either separately or in various combinations, but in no case was there a systematic attempt to test the hypothesis that attitudes to institutional or formal authority constitute a distinctive and coherent domain, or that attitudes so defined are related to delinquency.

We undertook such an attempt. We assumed first, following Weber's analysis of legal-rational or bureaucratic authority (1947), that institutional authority involves obedience to a legally established impersonal order and to its formally designated representatives when operating in terms of their formally defined powers and spheres of jurisdiction. Such authority is theoretically entirely impartial, does not depend for its legitimacy on any personal relation between the official who exercises it and those over whom it is exercised nor on any personal quality of this official, and is enacted according to specified and recorded rules and statutes. It is thus, for example, different from any authority parents may have over their charges by virtue of any personal bond between them or of the superior power of the parent, though not different from the parent's authority as legally responsible guardian. It is also different from authority claimed by custom, tradition or convention.

Table 6.1 Attitude–behaviour correlations by age and sex

	Males	*Females*
12 Years	0.735	0.521
13 Years	0.692	0.755
14 Years	0.673	0.575
15 Years	0.535	0.693

Using these guidelines, we collected together a set of attitude statements which seemed to sample the domain so defined. We then asked 95 secondary school children, age 12–14 years, to indicate their opinions of 57 such statements. The item–whole correlations ranged from 0.03 to 0.75. On the basis of these results, we selected 24 of the statements and asked a further group of 107 secondary school pupils, all 13-year-olds, to express opinions on this more limited set. Item–whole correlations were all significant. Principal components analysis revealed a first factor which accounted for 28.7 per cent of the variance. All others accounted for less than 10 per cent. It therefore seems reasonable to conclude that there is a general factor underlying attitudes to institutional authority, whether these are attitudes to the police, to the law, to school rules or to teachers. We have since collected data from a further 435 secondary school pupils, aged 12–15. The findings from these studies are consistent in confirming that attitudes to institutional authority do constitute a distinct and coherent domain.

The next question is, are these attitudes related to delinquency? In the first study, positive attitudes to authority were significantly, strongly and negatively correlated with self-reported delinquency (–0.60 for boys and –0.68 for girls). The relationship was also of an equivalent order whether for public or for school-related authority (0.65 for the former, 0.68 for the latter).

In the second study a similar pattern of relations between delinquency and attitudes was found, 0.68 for males and 0.76 for females. The correlations for the third and larger study are given in table 6.1.

Table 6.2 Attitudes to authority and self-reported delinquency as a function of high school year and sex

	Males		Females	
Year	Attitudes[1]	Behaviour[2]	Attitudes	Behaviour
One	2.47	5.27	2.19	2.17
Two	2.78	9.70	2.23	3.61
Three	2.76	7.49	2.44	3.51
Four	2.87	8.75	2.66	3.66

[1] On a scale from 1 (= favourable) to 5 (= unfavourable).
[2] Maximum possible score = 24.

We can safely conclude therefore that the activities young adolescents claim to have been involved in are strongly related to their expressed attitudes to institutional authority. But does not this evidence simply show what both social control and cultural diversity theorists have argued all along, namely that behaviour is a function of beliefs, attitudes and values? For example, in Hirschi's (1969) rendering of social control theory, young people who believe in the legitimacy of the legal order do not break its rules, whereas those who lack such beliefs are free to do so. Sutherland (Sutherland & Cressey, 1970) proposed that compliance with the law follows from exposure to definitions or values favourable to the criminal law, whereas delinquency follows from assimilation of values unfavourable to the law.

Certainly, it is common in the social sciences to suppose that behaviour will be a function of attitudes, but we believe this is an inappropriate interpretation of our results. This kind of interpretation is based on a distinction between, on the one hand, attitudes as internal mental states sampled by 'attitude measures', and, on the other, overt behaviour sampled here by self-reports. It is more consistent with our self-presentational interpretation to regard delinquency, self-reports of delinquency, and responses to attitude statements as similar kinds of events, namely communicative acts. Delinquency and attitudes to authority are both forms of action which express, in different ways, the same relationship. It is not therefore appropriate to regard one as the cause of the other (which is not to say that the content of expressed beliefs is uninformative). Our research provides two kinds of support for this argument.

The first is from cross-sectional comparisons. Differences in behaviour across age groups directly parallel differences in attitudes (table 6.2). If increasingly negative attitudes were producing increasingly serious and regular delinquency then one would expect changes in attitude to precede changes in behaviour. This is not apparent in the data.

The second is a more direct test. We re-interviewed 150 of the 435 pupils questioned in the third study 18 months later. This allowed us to look directly at the capacity of attitudes to predict subsequent behaviour. Behaviour over the preceding year, or over a 12-month period 18 months earlier, was as likely to predict attitudes as attitudes were to predict subsequent behaviour (figure 6.1). Moreover, initial attitudes did not predict behaviour change.

There are two final observations to make at this point about the attitude–conduct relationship. First, the very close similarity of the age-relation in each case supports the view that not only is relatively greater involvement in delinquency at any age an expression of a more negative relationship to authority, but also increases in delinquent involvement over age reflect an increasingly negative relation with authority. Second, if delinquency and attitudes to authority are appropriately regarded as facets of the same relationship, then gender differences in attitudes should directly parallel gender differences in conduct. We found this to be the case (Reicher & Emler, 1985a; Emler & Reicher, 1987). Boys expressed more negative attitudes to authority than girls and a covariance analysis confirmed that this difference was correlated with the observed gender difference in self-reported offending; controlling for attitude virtually eliminated the effect of gender on offending.

The content of young people's attitudes to authority provides further clues about preference for informal solutions that are consistent with the argument advanced here. As might be expected, typical attitudes are those which endorse rule-breaking and defiance of authority. But another significant theme concerns the impartiality of authority. Young people differ sharply in the degree to which they believe that police officers are honest, that they are not unnecessarily brutal, that they are impartial in the protection they provide and so on. Thus, if an adolescent believes that the police and other legal authorities are unlikely to provide protection for his interests or redress for his grievances then direct action might seem like a more realistic personal solution. Of course it is difficult to decide what is cause and what is effect here; adolescents may be reporting perceptions that their own actions have helped to confirm.

This problem of cause and effect is even more evident with respect to another strong theme in adolescent attitudes to authority. Adolescent opinions are sharply divided as to whether the authorities are themselves

Sample 1 (n = 25; 12 years old at T1)

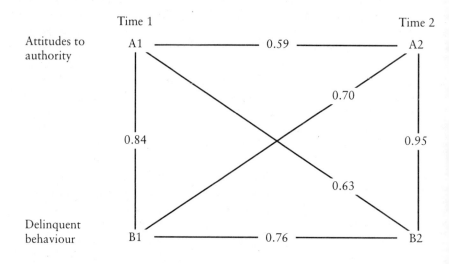

Sample 2 (n = 31; 14 years old at T1)

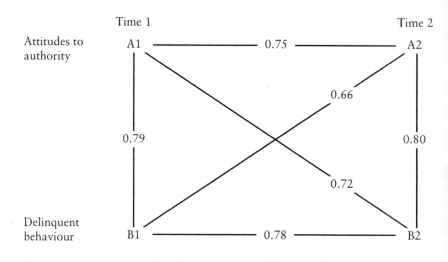

Figure 6.1 Attitude–behaviour relations over time among male adolescents:
interval T1 to T2 = 18 months

sources of victimization. If some young people feel that they or the social categories to which they belong are unduly persecuted by the institutional system, then it might seem reasonable to them not only to reject the institutional solution but retaliate against the institutional order as well, to attack policemen or vandalize public property, for example. But again the treatment they experience and report at the hands of institutional authorities could itself be a response to their own criminal habits.

Whether the institutional system somehow alienates a particular section of the adolescent population and so pushes it towards both informal solutions and retaliation, or whether some young people are unwilling or unable to accept the demands and requirements of the institutional system in the first place is the fundamental theoretical question. Some answers to this question will be examined below. Before that, let us briefly consider other aspects of young people's orientations to informal solutions.

There is rather less research which can answer questions about the attitudes of young people toward direct retaliation and other informal responses to the risk or experience of victimization. Piaget (1932) found that boys were more likely than girls to favour direct retaliation but also suggested that belief in the legitimacy of retaliation would give way with increasing age to attitudes favouring other solutions such as forgiveness or attempts at reconciliation. Other researchers have generally endorsed these conclusions (e.g. Durkin, 1961). The implication is that by adolescence only a small minority of immature individuals will still cling to the view that retaliation is a legitimate strategy in the conduct of interpersonal relations.

Some more recent work (Emler & Ohana, 1992) reveals a different picture. It produced no evidence of any developmental trend in opinions about appropriate responses to victimization. Children's views fell into three broad categories, unrelated to age. One category involved suggestions that adults should be persuaded to intervene. This might be regarded as the childhood equivalent of the institutional solution: look to the appropriate authorities for protection and redress. A second category involved suggestions about persuading the culprit to recompense the victim. The third category included recommendations for various forms of direct action, such as taking back stolen property, by force if necessary, and physically attacking the culprit. Though the categories of response were unrelated to either age or sex, they were related to the child's social background; working-class children were more likely to favour direct action.

It still remains to be determined whether these various preferences can also be found amongst adolescents and whether a preference for direct action is associated with delinquency. However, in a study referred to earlier, we found that delinquent and non-delinquent adolescents disagreed about whether delinquents and non-delinquents respectively are people inclined to stand up for their rights. Those who were themselves more delinquent believed that delinquents are more likely to stand up for their rights, whereas those who were themselves less delinquent believed that it is the non-delinquents who are more likely to do so (Emler, Reicher & Ronson, 1987). This is at least consistent with the suggestion that delinquency and non-delinquency reflect alternative strategies of self-protection. However, in the follow-up study (Haswell, 1991) delinquents were seen as more likely to be people who stood up for themselves by more and less delinquent 14–16-year-olds alike.

Finally, if a pattern of informal solutions to social organization involves informal deals, alliances, agreements and obligations, as well as informal retribution, this also implies a certain quality of participation in a network of informal social relationships. Some writers have argued that juvenile delinquents are typically young people who have rather impoverished social relationships. Hartup (1983) has written that 'delinquency among adolescents and young adults can be predicted mainly from one dimension of early peer relations . . . not getting on with others' (p. 165). The expectation that not only will delinquents be unpopular with their peers but that this unpopularity is a product of their own delinquency has received some support (e.g. Vuchinich, Bank & Patterson, 1992).

However, other work has shown that it is important to distinguish unpopularity from social isolation. Cairns and colleagues (1988) found that, although aggressive 13-year-olds were indeed more frequently disliked by the members of their peer group as a whole, they were equally as likely as non-aggressive teenagers to be integrated into friendship groups. Giordano, Cernovich and Pugh (1986) found that in some respects the strength and significance of personal ties may be even greater for delinquent adolescents than for their more law-abiding peers. This is more consistent with what would be expected if the informal and institutional solutions in some degree operate as alternatives for teenagers.

6.4 Education and Orientations to the Institutional Order

Formal education provides most children with their first direct and extended experience of a formal organization and institutional authority. It seems likely, therefore, that this experience will be the basis on which children construct a preliminary understanding of formal authority and the principles according to which it operates. It appears that by 10–12 years children do have quite a well-developed understanding of many of those features that are definitive of formal or legal-rational authority as defined by Weber (Emler, Ohana & Moscovici, 1987). Certainly, within the context of the school their insight into formal authority is more advanced than research by Adelson (1971), Furth (1980) and Kohlberg (1976) had previously seemed to suggest.

Does experience of formal education also shape attitudes to institutional authority? Given the prominence of school in the lives of young people, one would expect that their attitudes to authority generally would be related to their attitudes to formal authority as encountered in the school. In fact, adolescents' attitudes to school rules and regulations and to the authority of teachers are closely related to their attitudes to the law and to other forms of institutional authority (Reicher & Emler, 1985a; Rigby & Rump, 1979).

The next question is whether these attitudes and the associated patterns of behaviour are related to particular patterns of experience in education. Again the answer is in the affirmative. More precisely, adolescents who are more delinquent than their peers are less likely to enter public examinations (West & Farrington, 1977), more likely to drop out of school (Hathaway, Reynolds & Monachesi, 1969), more likely to have records of low academic attainment, and more likely to leave school with poor academic records and examination results (Hargreaves, 1967; Hindelang et al., 1981; Hirschi, 1969; Jensen, 1976; Kelly, 1975; Rhodes & Reiss, 1970; Slocum & Stone, 1963). Academic career shows the same pattern of association with attitudes. Thus, for example, in the United Kingdom attitudes to formal authority are strongly related both to level of academic attainment and to school leaving age (Emler, 1988a; Emler & St James, 1990).

What is to be made of these associations? Hypotheses about the role of positive self-esteem provide one interpretation, control theory another. As we have seen there is little clear support for the mediating role of self-esteem.

What of control theory? Hirschi (1969) writes:

The academically competent boy is more likely to do well in school and more likely as a result to like school. The boy who likes school is less likely to be delinquent. Thus by hypothesis, academic competence is linked to delinquency by way of success in and attachment to school. (p. 115)

Consider the sequence of events social control theory envisages. Early in their educational careers, children are not particularly conscious of the possibilities of failure. A promise of future reward ensures they desist from misbehaviour and work towards this end. By the early teens the relation between present efforts and future success has been irredeemably disconfirmed for some of the school population. They have lost their stake in continuing conformity and now feel more freedom to transgress. They no longer have this reason to care about their reputations. Others still entertain hopes of success, and for so long as these hopes and their consequent stake in conformity remain they will continue to avoid the risk of a bad reputation.

This sounds reasonable, but why should we rule out the following: the pupil who likes school is more likely as a result to be a diligent and attentive student, and in consequence is more likely to increase his or her academic competence and so do well in school. Hirschi considered the possibility of delinquent behaviour influencing academic performance (as indicated by marks in English and Mathematics) but rejected this as well as the possibility that conduct could influence academic career through its impact on the reactions of teachers. None the less, there are grounds for supposing that conduct will not be purely a dependent variable in its relations with educational career, academic attainment or even intellectual ability. At the same time, there is no overwhelming evidence that conduct is the dependent variable. So let us see whether a reversal of this causal sequence is really so implausible.

A possible argument would run as follows. When children begin their formal education they encounter a new way of ordering social relationships and coordinating activities, a bureaucracy. They must develop ways of responding to its requirements, but they will differ in their capacity and willingness to make a positive accommodation. Such differences may be a function of a host of factors including temperament, role relations in the family, attachment to parents, the degree of interest parents take in their children's education, and any prior experiences with formally ordered relations. But they will not necessarily be related to any differences in intellectual ability that are present before formal education begins.

Some children will find the regime of the school congenial or at least not irksome. They will happily accept the way it structures time and activities; they will readily follow the various regulations which govern life in school; they will persevere at the tasks they are given; they will willingly accept instructions and advice from their teachers. And this kind of accommodation will contribute to success in school, independently of ability. It is as well to remember that measurable differences in intellectual ability by no means explain all the variance in educational attainment (Jencks, 1972). Moreover, relative ability is not fixed from the beginning of formal schooling. Children who find it easy to work with the system might be expected to improve their intellectual skills during their first eight to ten years in school rather more than those who do not so readily make this accommodation.

Children who find the bureaucratic regime uncongenial will adapt less positively to the demands of timetables, regulations, classroom interaction rules and teacher authority. Within this kind of structure they are liable as a result to work less effectively. Moreover, their conduct in school will be visibly different. It would be surprising if teachers did not react to such differences in conduct and attitude.

According to this interpretation, educational career, and the resulting attainments or lack of them, will be a function of both ability and orientation to institutional authority. This is not an entirely novel idea. Both Danziger (1971) and Jencks (1972) have argued that the school acts as an extended test of the child's capacity and inclination to accommodate to the requirements of a bureaucratic system. Jencks (1972) has further argued that employers consider educational credentials when selecting employees not so much because of the particular technical or cognitive skills to which these attest but because they are reliable markers of an individual's success in accepting bureaucratic regulation. In so far as educational credentials signal a positive orientation to formal authority then they suggest the holder of these credentials will also adapt well to bureaucratic authority and control in the workplace.

Liska and Reed (1985) have used panel data to examine the competing claims of control theory and this alternative interpretation and conclude that the direction of causality implied in the latter has more support. It is also consistent with the empirical links between delinquency on the one hand and intelligence on the other. If educational failure produced delinquency then, because educational failure is related to low intelligence, delinquency should also be clearly related to low intelligence. In fact, as we have seen, the relation between delinquency and intelligence is weak at best. On the other hand, this is precisely what would be expected if the orientation to institutional authority that lies behind delinquency also influences educational career.

All the other observed associations between delinquency and educational variables are equally explicable in these terms. If orientation to authority influences both delinquency and educational attainments then delinquency should be negatively correlated with academic performance, liking for school, school leaving age, and number and level of examinations entered, and it is.

6.4.1 *The occupational culture of the school and its impact on the shape of adolescent delinquency*

It should be emphasized that we are not ruling out any influence of schooling on delinquency. On the contrary it plays an important part in at least three ways. First, it does impose the institutional order upon children and forces them into making some kind of response to its requirements. Second, it provides a particular kind of interpersonal environment within which that response will be made, an environment dominated by age-equals and at secondary or high school level also increasingly structured in terms of their orientations to education and authority: schools group together children with similar levels of attainment. There are several indications that preferences for informal and delinquent versus institutional solutions are consolidated at a collective level. That is, these are not preferences which individual adolescents pursue by themselves. Rather they pursue one kind of solution in preference to the other to the extent that they have consistent social support for this preference. This issue will be examined in chapter 7.

Finally, schools, like other organizations, seek to control and coordinate the actions of those who work within them. To this end they implement certain patterns of social control the result of which is to induce a characteristic pattern of reaction by those subjected to these controls. In other words, the secondary school is not just an institution or social organization but a particular kind of organization, and commonplace misbehaviours among teenagers are partly to be understood in terms of the kind of organization school is.

Mars (1981) has argued that occupations provide characteristic forms of culture. Occupational cultures can be described in terms of two principal dimensions, an approach which Mars borrows from the work of Mary Douglas. One dimension is 'group' or the extent to which tasks involve teams of people working together as integrated units. The 'group' dimension can be defined in terms of frequency of interaction on tasks, the extent to which individuals are linked by mutually interconnecting networks, the range of areas of social life which fall under the aegis of the group, and the number of opportunities to assemble together as a group. In some forms of work this group quality is highly developed as for example among refuse collection crews. In others it is almost completely absent.

The second dimension is 'grid' or the extent to which a culture imposes its social categories on its members and therefore fixes their appropriate behaviour and that of others towards them. In occupational cultures it refers to the extent to which working procedures are defined or standardized by rules and regulations. Some work allows considerable individual autonomy and initiative whereas other work is tightly defined in terms of the manner in which it is performed. Where, when and precisely how tasks are performed may be subject to detailed specification and close supervision. The grid dimension is also defined by the degree to which individuals are insulated from one another by lack of reciprocity and by lack of opportunity for competition. These two dimensions, group and grid, provide a fourfold classification of types of work or occupational cultures. The point of Mars's analysis is that the occupational cultures so defined each represent a distinctive form of control over the individual and each generate their characteristic reactions, which involve the taking of unofficial and illegitimate rewards, or 'workplace crimes'.

Formal schooling can be thought of as equivalent to an occupational culture. In terms of Mars's fourfold classification the role of pupil would appear to correspond most closely to what he called a 'donkey' job, high on grid and low on group. However, the precise extent to which this is true will vary between levels of the education system, between state and private education, and even between individual schools. In boarding schools, for example, the group dimension is likely to be stronger, particularly with respect to scope. In traditional grammar schools individuality and autonomy was occasionally more highly valued and this can also be true in higher education. But if a school inclines towards specifying appropriate behaviour in terms of fixed categories such as age, sex, ability or social background, if it imposes a ranking system based, for example, on age and ability, if it imposes a single standard of evaluation – academic attainment – and recognizes no innovation or creativity in evaluative dimensions or competition on other dimensions, if it insists on evaluating only individual efforts and discourages cooperation on tasks, then it moves the pupil role more decisively into the high-grid category.

The low-group character of this culture is less obvious. School children, particularly in secondary schools, do seem to be immersed in a strong group environment. None the less, school work has traditionally been organized, and especially at the secondary level, to de-emphasize the group. Pupils are normally expected to work alone, they may be discouraged from interacting during working periods, and their efforts are assessed as if they were individual efforts. The group life is there, as it is in many high-grid/low-group occupations, but it is incidental to the work, not intrinsic to it.

The value of this analogy is in its capacity to make sense of certain features of adolescent delinquency. High-grid/low-group occupations are typically low status occupations – characterized by isolated subordination; incumbents have little power. The reactions of people in this kind of occupational culture have, according to Mars, two motivational sources. One is resentment at the impositions of the system and a desire to hit back. The other is a desire to regain some autonomy and control over one's time and one's behaviour. Activities experienced as repetitive and meaningless can be reinvested with challenge and interest by systematically breaking the rules. Thus elaborate cheating and cribbing schemes can inject enjoyment into otherwise pointless classroom exercises, at the same time regaining some control for the pupil. Similarly pupils, like their counterparts in other donkey jobs involving endlessly repeated cycles of activity, can be expected to fiddle time. As the rules and controls tighten and further limit autonomy then resentment in donkey jobs shifts towards withdrawal from the system and sabotage. The equivalents for school children would in the first case be increasingly frequent absences, either through sickness or straightforward truanting. In the second case, defacing textbooks and carving initials into furniture are relatively mild forms of sabotage. Setting fire to school premises is rather more extreme and uncommon, but not unknown. Classroom teachers will be familiar with various stratagems to disrupt or sabotage lessons.

It is characteristic of donkey jobs that there is little effective informal control, little collaboration in mischief, and little mutual defence against the system. Consequently donkey fiddles tend towards excess, are relatively easily detected, and tend to result in expulsion of the culprit who benefits from no solidarity on the part of his or her peers. Again there are parallels with the school. Cheating, classroom disturbance, unsanctioned absences and destruction of school property will all tend to increase in the absence of any control by peers (private schools and particularly boarding schools, by encouraging the group dimension and therefore informal controls, may be less vulnerable). The culprits are easily identified, probably having made little or no attempt at concealment anyway. And if the school chooses to exclude or expel the culprit it will face no organized resistance from the student body as a whole.

There are two final points to make in this section. The first concerns the nature of the school as a bureaucracy. One might suppose that bureaucratic institutions are all the same and will therefore generate essentially the same 'occupational culture' for their members. The point Mars makes is that they are not the same, and the point is reinforced by several other organizational theorists. Many different mechanisms of coordination and control are to be found in social organizations (see Mintzberg, 1973). The traditional school with its emphasis on standardized working procedures and extensive direct supervision corresponds to a highly 'mechanical' bureaucracy. Mars shows that other kinds of occupational culture are not immune to all mischief; rather, it takes quite different forms and elicits quite different reactions from the organization itself. It could be a useful exercise to ponder the consequences of transforming the 'occupational culture' of secondary schools, but it is not one we can indulge here.

The second point, which Mars does not address, is that individuals can react in different ways to the occupational cultures in which they find themselves. In fact, there is likely to be a degree of self-selection with respect to the alternatives available. With respect to education, however, there are no alternatives and the same culture is inhabited by individuals who find it entirely congenial as well as by those who are extremely uncomfortable with its requirements. In the next section, we look at some further consequences of these differences, drawing upon our own research.

6.5 Future Expectations

We have considered and rejected the idea that delinquency arises from a weakening of investments in educational goals. Instead we have proposed that delinquency is in effect part of an orientation to the institutional system and by implication therefore to the goals which can be reached through it. Hence we would expect that teenagers who take different approaches to the demands made upon them by institutional authority will also take a different approach to those future opportunities that are linked to educational career.

The issue of what young people consider to be their likely fate in the future and the effects this has on their commitments in the present was a central theme of interviews we conducted with 120 of the 435 teenagers included in our survey of attitudes and behaviour. Both boys and girls from each of the first four years of secondary school were selected, an age range from 12 to 15. This sub-sample was also selected so as to include those with relatively high and those with relatively low levels of self-reported delinquency. For convenience they will be referred to respectively as the delinquents and the non-delinquents though it should be borne in mind that these classifications are relative. The questions we asked were open-ended and allowed respondents the option of declining to answer. This, together with the absence of clear answers to some questions, accounts for the varying number of responses to the different questions. Where appropriate we have presented results in terms of response categories.

We have already seen how those youngsters who have committed more delinquent acts also show greater hostility to the system of school authority. It is hardly surprising therefore that they should show a correspondingly greater desire to leave school at the earliest opportunity (see table 6.3). In our interviews, 34 out of 54 (63 per cent) of the delinquents expressed such a desire, compared to 20 out of 48 (42 per cent) of non-delinquents (chi square: 3.81, p < 0.06). Conversely while 24 out of 48 (50 per cent) of the non-delinquents indicated a wish to stay on at school past 16, only 11 out of the 54 (20 per cent) in the delinquents concurred (chi square: 9.61, p < 0.01). These differences are consistent with questionnaire evidence indicating that attitude to formal authority is a strong predictor of school leaving age (Emler & St James, 1994).

Table 6.3 Preferred age to leave school for 'high' and 'low' delinquents

	As soon as possible	At 16	Stay on after 16
'High delinquent'	34	9	11
'Low delinquent'	20	4	24

This desire of the delinquents was not based on any romanticism about what lies beyond. When asked 'what do you think you are most likely to be doing when you leave school?', of the 48 who expressed some expectation, 30 (63 per cent) thought they would be unemployed or on government job creation schemes, while only 9 out of 34 (26 per cent) non-delinquents voiced a similar expectation (chi square: 11.82, p < 0.001). An identical number of non-delinquents expected to go on to higher education but only one of the delinquents envisaged such a future (table 6.4).

Table 6.4 Expected occupation after leaving school for 'high' and 'low' delinquents

	Don't know	Unemployed/ job creation scheme	Employed	Higher education
'High delinquent'	6	30	17	1
'Low delinquent'	14	9	16	9

Although the numbers were low, the pattern among the 12- and 13-year-olds seemed to match this general finding. The fact that two-thirds of our more delinquent group – even those only beginning in the secondary school system – see a future with no clear prospect of employment may seem somewhat depressing. However, it is hardly unrealistic. It should be borne in mind that at the time our research was carried out, local unemployment was around 15 per cent, though on some of the estates where the participating schools were located, estimates for youth unemployment were as high as 70 or even 80 per cent. The chances of entering directly into employment at 16 were low; probably no better than 25 per cent. It could therefore be argued that the delinquents were the realists while the non-delinquents had based their commitments on an illusion.

Also, however, the labour market is highly stratified. It is important, therefore, to consider the kinds of jobs teenagers expect to get. In some cases our respondents gave ambiguous or imprecise responses, simply saying for instance that they expected to get some sort of job. Nevertheless, 15 of the delinquents and 11 of the non-delinquents specified particular jobs or careers.

Of the delinquents, five mentioned the armed services and six mentioned getting some kind of job through a relative or acquaintance. Of the remaining four, three mentioned trades and one being a policemen, with more than a hint of irony in his voice. Thus the majority identify jobs which are minimally dependent upon academic criteria and in which character references matter little. If you wish to join the forces, being 'hard' is unlikely to disqualify you and, if a relative can vouch for you, a teacher's report becomes irrelevant. To quote one of our respondents, who was getting a job through his 'sister's lad', 'if you know you are getting a job you don't need to work hard'.

The non-delinquents provided a very different picture. Of the eleven, one gave as his options joining the Navy or getting a job through his father. The others all mentioned occupations in which character and qualifications are important requirements. Of the four boys, one mentioned the police and two talked of apprenticeships. In the words of one of these boys:

> I've had application forms for apprenticeships and I filled one in and on the back the head teacher had to fill it in and say what she thought of you. I got a reply so I must have got a good report from the teacher.

Of the seven girls, all mentioned 'responsible jobs', with nurse or nursery nurse accounting for four of them. They were aware, to select one quote, that this requires giving the impression 'that you take good care of children and are reliable'.

In summary, then, the majority of our delinquent sample see their most likely future in terms that make the positive pursuit of official recognition and approval quite irrelevant. Yet for a sizable proportion of the non-delinquents such approval is necessary if they are to get to where they want to go.

If we turn from expectations to aspirations a somewhat different contrast emerges (table 6.5). When we asked not, 'what are you most likely to be doing?' but rather 'what would you like to be doing when you leave school?' then, of those who had a view, the majority of the delinquents (40 out of 50) and the non-delinquents alike (30 out of 39) mentioned having a job. Of the remaining few, eight of the delinquents wanted to do nothing and two wanted to go into further education. One of the non-delinquents wanted nothing and eight wanted to go to college. Using the Fisher Exact Probability Test, this difference is highly significant ($p < 0.0002$).

Table 6.5 Ideal occupation after leaving school for 'high' and 'low' delinquents

	Don't know	Do nothing	Go to college	Have a job
'High delinquent'	4	8	2	40
'Low' delinquent'	9	1	8	30

When we examine the type of job desired further differences emerge. Of the 28 delinquents who were specific about their aspirations, six mentioned the armed forces and two wanted to be lorry drivers. Fifteen referred to skilled trades requiring apprenticeships, such as joiner, welder and carpenter. The remainder varied from 'game-keeper' to 'working with computers'. In the majority of cases, therefore, these aspirations have two characteristics. First, they are focused on skilled working-class jobs. Second, they are jobs in which a reputation for reliability is important. To put it slightly differently, these young people may have wished to be 'labour aristocracy' but they did not wish to be beyond labour.

Of the 29 low delinquents who mentioned specific types of jobs, only two mentioned the armed services and only four mentioned traditional working-class jobs or trades. Their choices were much more heterogeneous and fanciful, ranging from professional sports through airline pilot and artist to journalist. In other words, the choices were not limited to the world of employment occupied by their parents.

The contrast between the low and the high groups is particularly marked if we consider only the younger age group and here only the boys, since no girls under 14 in our interview sample reported high levels of delinquency. Consider the following lists:

Jobs mentioned by delinquents	Jobs mentioned by non-delinquents
Merchant Navy	Work with computers
Army	Airplane pilot
Lorry driver	Car salesman
Joiner	Reporter
Carpenter	Football player
Work at local marine engineering company	Policeman
	Professional snooker

Although the number of respondents is low, there is almost no overlap, even at 12–13 years, between delinquents whose horizons are bounded by class barriers and non-delinquents whose aspirations reach beyond these horizons.

Putting all these responses together, we are presented with a rather complex picture. It is not wholly true to say that delinquent youth are detached from the conventional world of achievement, for they do hope for and desire traditionally valued employment. Nor is it accurate to represent delinquency as flowing from a discrepancy between aspirations and the means of achieving them. Amongst both high and low delinquents there were discrepancies between what was regarded as desirable and what was believed to be likely. Rather we see two different ranges of ambivalence. For at least a proportion of the non-delinquents social mobility was thinkable even if in the end they might not move very far. For the delinquents almost without exception the horizon is fixed no matter what. They aspired to skilled labour at best but their expectations were more likely to be that they would find no work at all.

If this interpretation is correct it suggests a corresponding difference in young people's practical orientation toward authority. On the one hand, some of the non-delinquents believe that submission to authority will bring rewards whereas the delinquents regard the inducements of authority as a con since their structural position is determined. We have already seen this reflected in differences in attitudes to authority. On the other hand, whatever their attitudes, both groups know that their aspirations can be destroyed if they are too far on the wrong side of these authorities. For high delinquents, as for low delinquents, a bad record can leave you without even the hope of a job. Even if you have contempt for the system you do not want to burn your boats completely. To put it more formally, whereas low delinquents have both an attachment to and a dependence on authority, the high delinquents have only a dependence.

This is confirmed by responses to the question, 'Would having a good or bad school report make any difference to you?' Of the delinquents, 57 per cent thought it would, compared with 90 per cent of the non-delinquents. Although the difference is statistically significant (chi square 5.66, $p < 0.05$) it is more interesting that a majority of both groups believed the nature of their school reports made a difference. The reason is clear. One of the young people who reported high delinquent activity and who expected to be unemployed on leaving school simply replied, 'You have more chance of getting a job than people who didn't have a good record.'

The pattern is even more exaggerated when we ask 'would having a police record make it difficult to achieve what you want?' Of those who gave a clear response, namely 40 of the delinquents, 35 thought it would, and all but one of 32 non-delinquents concurred. Once again, it is not hard to find a reason for this general agreement. There is broad recognition that employment opportunities and a police record do not go together. Perhaps this is best expressed by one of the delinquent group who wanted to go into the army. After saying he would not be bothered if people thought of him as delinquent and that a police record would make no difference, he then paused and said, 'well, it would in a way because you have not to get in trouble with the police to get in the army'.

There is another dimension which should be added to this picture. A number of our respondents spontaneously introduced the matter of age. That is to say, you can get into trouble with the authorities, you can even get a police record, but if you are young enough it will be discounted when you are older. There is, however, some uncertainty about the matter. One 14-year-old boy says:

> Some folk say if you have a police record it gets scrubbed when you are sixteen and some folk say it doesn't. Some folk bother about it and some folk don't. Yes, it would matter to me. If you are joining the army, if they see you have a police record, you stole a car or something, they wouldn't want you.

or, to quote a 15-year-old:

> Some records – I do have one but it was accidental and it gets destroyed when you are sixteen as long as you have got one chance.

This suggests a qualification to the argument we presented above. If it is true that delinquency at a young age can be discounted later ('I was only a child then, I am different now') then it is less likely to impinge on future prospects. Thus the negative sanction of authority is relatively less strong for early adolescents. Where there is no positive attachment either, we might expect an age effect. Whereas younger age groups can express their hostility towards an unequal society without too great a cost, as they get older the cost rises and therefore delinquent activity should decrease.

Our interviews give some support to this deduction. Looking through the transcripts of interviews with the delinquents, we found that 17 out of 26 of the 15–16-year-olds claimed that their delinquency was located in the past and that they had since changed their behaviour. Only one out of ten 12–13-year-olds made a similar claim (Fischer Exact Test for this difference, $p < 0.003$).

Of those who indicated a change, several stressed the fact that they 'knew better now', that they had offended a long time ago when they were 'small'. One respondent drew a particularly strong distinction between younger adolescents who generally glorify trouble-making and those like himself who are older. Talking of involvement in fights, he said:

> Most of the younger ones would think you were a hero . . . The older ones would think you were childish.

It might be objected that these protestations of reform do not reflect reality, that these respondents are just trying to appear good. Our data do not allow us to decide whether this is so, but the objection in any case misses the point. What is significant is that the older adolescents should wish to appear good whereas the younger ones do not. Once we acknowledge that one's reputation with institutional officials becomes more consequential or important as delinquent teenagers approach school leaving age, it is fair to assume that this will have some impact on those behaviours which could affect this reputation. Indeed, as we shall argue in chapter 8, perhaps by combining the lowered commitment to formal authority upon entry to secondary school with the sharpened appreciation of the negative sanctions of authority as the world of work looms, we can explain the age profile of delinquent action.

6.6 Conclusions

It has been argued in this chapter that the orientations adolescents take towards the institutional system of society are reflected in their willingness to comply with laws and regulations and in their views about formal authority. It has been proposed that the institutional order is a system for regulating social relationships and that in so far as they reject this system, young people are opting for an alternative and more informal system of social regulation.

It would be wrong to conclude that adolescents are completely polarized on this issue. We have discovered that when we examine answers to questions about attitudes, in practice most responses range from highly positive to ambivalent. And the conduct of most adolescents is somewhere between consistent compliance with law and authority and occasional serious violation of laws. In other words, the common pattern would seem to be a mixture of solutions.

Considered from the point of view of societies as a whole, the institutional system has many apparent advantages over the informal alternative. Its capacity to rationalize productive labour has generated considerable material wealth. It has permitted the development and effective administration of large-scale organizations for the provision of welfare and security. And, in principle at least, it offers rational procedures for delivering justice.

So why are some teenagers less than enthusiastic about this system and more attached to informal alternatives? It cannot be claimed that the informal solution, represented by delinquency, is an objectively more successful alternative for those young people who adopt it. First, they are actually more likely to be victims of crime than any other group in society; their own delinquency has apparently offered them little reliable protection. Second, they are more likely to be among the economic and social losers in society to the extent that their poorer educational qualifications and earlier departure from full-time education exclude them from good jobs, good marriages and political influence (e.g. Banks et al., 1992). And as we have seen, young people are not entirely insensitive to such longer-term repercussions of a bad reputation.

None the less, there are several factors which can favour unofficial, informal and delinquent solutions to some degree. Here we will mention only the following. The institutional solution is inherently imperfect; it cannot, for example, deal with every little slight and injury that a person may suffer, yet even when the injury is small the sense of grievance is real. For such matters, informal reparations in the form of apologies and expressions of regret are common. The problems arise when culprits are unrepentant. We can only expect police or courts to intervene when some threshold of seriousness is passed. For some matters, for example family violence, that threshold might be rather high. And it may be perceived, rightly or wrongly, as much higher by particular groups of individuals because of the categories to which they belong, for example, male, working-class adolescents.

There is finally the perception that the institutional system will not deliver on its implied promise of social advancement in exchange for obedience. Whether young people withdraw their commitment to the contract only after they find the system has not honoured its side, as Cloward and Ohlin (1960) claimed, is less clear. The evidence available to date is, we think, more consistent with the conclusion that young people differ in their inclinations to accept the contract in the first place.

Some of the other factors which we believe to be significant, both in making adolescents as a whole more receptive to informal solutions and in underpinning the greater delinquency of some adolescents, are best understood in terms of the informal society of teenagers. This informal society forms the focus of the next chapter.

7

The Collective Character of Adolescent Conduct

7.1 Introduction

The social historian Walzer has argued that 'disobedience, when it is not criminally but morally, religiously or politically motivated is always a collective act and it is justified by the values of the collectivity and the mutual engagement of its members' (1970, p. 4). We would concur with everything in Walzer's assertion except his qualification. Criminal disobedience, especially when perpetrated by adolescents, is also more often than not a collective act. In chapter 5 we challenged the mass society tradition both in its representation of society as an agglomeration of strangers and in its view that lawful behaviour depends on individual moral autonomy. We have also argued that action in relation to laws and regulations has an expressive as well as an instrumental function. It is a means by which individuals communicate about themselves to others who know them. For adolescents it provides information about a key issue of their social world, how one should relate to institutional authority.

Yet something needs to be added to this picture; as it stands it remains only half a departure from psychology's traditional view. Even if action is placed in the context of overt social interaction it can still be represented as the social expression of an autonomous individual stance.

Young people spend their time in the company of people who know them – other family members, adults outside of the family, friends of their own age and also a variety of more casual acquaintances. In this they are no different from any other age group, and like other age groups they work out their views and make their choices within the personal relationships their social lives provide. Thus a more complete picture requires some consideration of the informal social life of adolescents, the origins and consequences of their patterns of mutual affiliation, and the role these play in their social conduct. In this chapter we shall explore these issues, and in the process we shall challenge a third major strand of mass society theorizing: a view of the group as generically pernicious.

7.2 Groups in Adolescence

As we showed in earlier chapters there has been a long association, in the minds of criminologists and others, between delinquency and the phenomena of groups. In the 1920s the British Board of Education reported that 63 per cent of delinquent boys were gang members (quoted in Mays, 1972). In the 1930s Shaw found that 81 per cent of offenders brought before the Juvenile Court of Chicago had committed delinquencies in the company of others (Lerman, 1967). Lerman observed that the terms 'gang' and 'delinquency' had become virtual synonyms. As he noted, this was exacerbated by a methodological habit of selecting samples of gangs from 'cases known on complaint to the police; adjudicated delinquents; institutionalised boys; or groups of concern to social agencies and demonstration projects' (1967, p. 64). Morash (1983) reinforces the point, citing as an example the work of Tracy and Piper (1982). Their conclusion that gang membership leads to delinquency was based on the Philadelphia Police Department's categories for defining a gang.

We would not dispute that adolescent delinquencies are typically committed in the company of others. Almost all available research points to this conclusion (see chapter 5). Nor would we disagree that this fact alone makes an analysis of group processes essential to an understanding of delinquency. As the Sherifs put it:

> The statistical fact that the overwhelming majority of unacceptable behaviours of a serious nature committed during (adolescence) are attributable to members of adolescent groups makes it imperative for the psychologist interested in explaining social behaviour, as well as the social scientist interested in the social problem, to study the formation and inner working of such groups. (1964, p. 47)

Our argument is only with the proposition that group membership in and by itself produces delinquency. It is logically fallacious to conclude that because delinquency occurs in groups then group activity will necessarily be delinquent. The fallacy has been sustained by a tendency, theoretically driven and methodologically supported, to sample only delinquency in groups and sample only groups that are delinquent. A broadening of perspectives reveals a very different picture.

In the first place, even groups of the most habitual delinquents spend only a minute proportion of their time together in proscribed activities. The Sherifs (1964) concluded from their study of American juveniles that 'much of the time in every group was spent just hanging around together – talking and joking'. The same conclusion emerges in a study of British youth: 'much of the most common and intensive activity engaged in by the majority of working class kids is the simple but absorbing activity of "passing time"' (Introductory note to Corrigan, 1979).

Thus, the notion of a delinquent group is misleading if it is taken to suggest that individuals will offend as soon as they gather. Of course, over time their occasional delinquencies may add up in a way that constitutes a problem for agencies of social control. Yet, on the psychological level, any attempt to depict the group as a setting which automatically causes all moral standards to evaporate cannot account for the relative rarity of delinquent acts.

Moreover, if one holds that group behaviour is necessarily anti-social it becomes impossible to explain the conditions under which such actions occur and conversely the conditions under which they are absent. In other words, a crude assertion of the existence of delinquency is substituted for an understanding of its pattern. However, delinquent action is not merely patterned within groups; it is also patterned between groups. If it is a fact that teenagers who commit delinquent acts generally do so in groups, it is also the case that the many young people who rarely do anything criminal spend just as much time in the company of others, in groups.

This fact, hidden by the tendency to select groups for study on the basis of their delinquency, is obvious to those who have studied adolescent groups in general (e.g., Morash, 1983; Palmonari et al., 1991; Sherif & Sherif, 1964). Even Thrasher (1927), in his seminal study, 'The gang', had to concede that not all gang members were delinquent (though he did maintain that all lacked 'wholesome direction').

Our own data confirm this picture. The interviews described in the previous chapter also explored the social relations of the interviewees. Each interviewee was asked whether they had a group of friends with whom they spent time and did things. All of the boys and all but one of the girls in the 'high' delinquency category reported this was the case, but so also did 80 per cent of those in the 'low' delinquency category.

We sought to develop the detail in this picture and get a little closer to the everyday reality of adolescent social life by gathering some more direct data on patterns of social contact. For this purpose we selected 25 'low' and 25 'high' delinquent boys in the age range 13–15 from the original larger sample. Each was asked to keep a diary over a two-week interval covering all the periods when they were not involved in classroom activities. The first week served as a practice period for the participants, allowing them to familiarize themselves with the diary procedure. Data analysis was confined to records of interactions in the second week. For each interactive episode an 'activity sheet' was completed. On this was recorded details of who else was present, what they did and ratings of the quality of the interaction on various dimensions. Forty-two of those who began the study provided completed diaries.

First we examined the data in terms of the principal activity for each evening of the week, dividing activities into five distinct types. Table 7.1 presents the mean number of evenings during the week on which each of these five was the main activity. What clearly emerges is that both 'high' and 'low' groups spend more evenings a week with friends than in any of the other circumstances.

Table 7.1 Mean number of evenings per week spent in various contexts for 'high' and 'low' delinquents

	Organized activities	*With family*	*With friends*	*Alone*	*Family and friends*
'High delinquent'	1.0	1.0	3.9	1.0	0.1
'Low delinquent'	1.3	1.8	2.8	0.9	0.4

There are two kinds of objection to the relevance of this evidence. One is the position of crowd psychology: commitment to moral standards evaporates not in friendship groups but in the presence of strangers. According to this view some teenagers would end up involved in more criminal or anti-social mayhem than their peers only because chance or circumstance had more often put them in the company of a group of strangers. It would be irrelevant that much of the rest of their time was spent in the company of friends. The second is the subcultural theorist's objection: the delinquent gang has a qualitatively different structure to the friendship groups of non-delinquents. In effect, the gang is more group-like; it has greater solidarity, a stronger internal structure, more definite boundaries, greater intensity, and greater durability.

7.2.1 Anonymous crowds and friendship groups

One of the most reliable correlates of deviance, a finding to have emerged in study after study, is having friends who are similarly deviant.

Short (1957) and then Voss (1964) found that degree of self-reported delinquency was correlated with reported frequency and extensiveness of association with others who were also delinquent. In other studies the questions have been about numbers of delinquent associates, or friends ever picked up by the police (Elliott & Voss, 1974; Hindelang, 1973; Hindelang et al., 1981; Hirschi, 1969; Jensen, 1972; Johnson, 1979; Voss, 1969). Akers and colleagues (1979) and Meier and Johnson (1977) found that, of a number of possible factors predicting young people's alcohol and marijuana use, the most powerful was proportion of friends as users. Kandel (1978) found that adolescent friendship pairs were characterized by a high degree of similarity in marijuana use. Of more direct relevance to delinquency, Silberman (1976) found that self-reported criminal activity was correlated with perceived peer criminal involvement. In both Johnson's (1979) test of a multifactor explanation of delinquency and Menard and Morse's (1984) re-analysis of data collected by Elliott and Voss, 'delinquent associates' was the strongest single correlate of delinquent conduct. Finally, Dishion and colleagues (1991) found that the anti-social behaviour of 10- and 12-year-old boys was related to having friends who also engaged in anti-social behaviour. What are we to make of this pattern?

It is possible that young people are systematically wrong about the habits and conduct of their friends. If you are up to no good now and then you might after all prefer to believe that the people you know and like do things just as bad. But it is unlikely that teenagers could be so misinformed about the conduct of people with whom they spend so much time, and it has to be said that this fancy hardly bears scrutiny by the evidence; reputations are rarely so wildly off the mark. The principal reason these perceptions of friends are accurate is that, in so far as delinquent acts occur at all, these friends are the individual teenager's most regular partners in crime. In other words, they know what kinds of things their friends do or do not get up to because they do precisely these things with their friends.

The rather implausible alternative is that young people who get up to mischief or get into trouble know they have friends with similar habits but only ever succumb to such temptations in company other than that of their friends and associates. Any lingering appeal this convoluted proposition has should evaporate as we describe in more detail what young people actually do in the company of their friends.

7.2.2 The quality of group structure

If group delinquency is the delinquency of groups of friends, are these particular friendship groups none the less different in structure from those of non-delinquents? In particular, are 'non-delinquent' groups weaker social formations? Do they lack the kind of cohesiveness that will cause the 'submergence' and consequent loss of moral standards which some have associated with group behaviour? Certainly there is a tradition which associates delinquent groups with this kind of structure. For Thrasher the delinquent gang was characterized by 'the development of tradition, unreflective internal structure, esprit de corps, solidarity, morale, group awareness and attachment to a local territory' (1927, p. 46). Yablonsky (1962) represented the delinquent gang as a 'near group', which is to say that it has a certain level of structure but not a formal hierarchy. However, these authors along with others (e.g. Scott, 1956) seemed to agree that structure at some level is necessary. So when adolescents say they spend time with groups of friends are they simply referring to a loose association of acquaintances or a tight-knit group of friends? Again our diary data shed some light on this issue. With respect to each recorded activity we asked about the extent to which participation was out of choice rather than compelled, how close the participants felt to any others who were involved, and how much they enjoyed the interaction. Each of these qualities was rated on a ten-point scale.

Table 7.2 Quality of interactions with family and friends for 'high' and 'low' delinquents (10-point scale)

Interactions with:	Family			Friends		
	Choice	Closeness	Enjoyment	Choice	Closeness	Enjoyment
'High delinquent'	7.1	7.7	7.9	8.3	7.0	8.2
'Low delinquent'	7.8	7.7	7.3	8.3	6.8	7.8

The results of these ratings are summarized in table 7.2 and they clearly fail to support the notion that delinquent and non-delinquent teenagers differ in these qualities of their interactions. When those in the 'low' delinquency category interacted with their peers they did so every bit as freely, and with as much intimacy and enjoyment as did the 'high' delinquency boys.

Morash (1983) comes to very similar conclusions about the relationship between group structure and delinquency on the basis of work which also included data on girls. She found that gang-like structure in groups, using Thrasher's criteria of territorial basis, well-defined leadership, age structuring and regular interaction, was only very weakly related to delinquency (the index of 'gang-likeness' was correlated only 0.13 with delinquency). She found, moreover, no relationship between group solidarity and delinquent activity. However, 'peers' delinquency, combined with solidarity and peers' delinquency combined with gang-likeness were both strongly related to individuals' delinquency, regardless of sex' (p. 322). In other words, tighter structure may amplify the behavioural inclinations of group members; it does not of itself produce those inclinations. We would again echo the Sherifs when they say that:

> To call groups in low rank areas 'gangs' and those in higher rank areas by nicer names does not change the finding that they are all groups, with distinctive properties as social units. These properties have unmistakable consequences for individual members, whether group activities are directed toward socially desirable activities, towards sexual satisfactions, experimentation with forbidden drinks and drugs, social distinction, stealing or establishing a territory. (1964, p. 238)

7.2.3 The importance of groups

It is now also hard to see how the psychoanalytic argument can be sustained that peer groups provide psychological refuge for those with problems. There is certainly little evidence that the peer group is a refuge for adolescents when family or other relationships are in crisis. To the contrary, the clearer message from research is that those who get on well with their parents also have good peer relations and are more likely to identify strongly with peer groups (e.g. Palmonari et al., 1991). When we asked in interviews whose opinion was most important to them, similar percentages in the 'high' as well as 'low' categories (80 per cent and 85 per cent respectively) mentioned their parents.

The peer group, then, is not a substitute for the family. But if the peer group is of importance in the social worlds of adolescents as a whole, why should this be? Consider the complexity of the tasks that face individual teenagers. In the transition from child to adult they must make some sense of and work out an accommodation with the complex political, institutional and economic structures which dominate adult society. Not only is this a formidable intellectual task, it also requires each adolescent to weigh issues of which he or she has no direct experience. For instance, upon entering secondary education how can one know whether a commitment to its expectations will lead to a decent job?

The tasks of adolescence require a cultural understanding that is beyond the reach of the isolated individual. As Willis (1977) argued, it is only through group membership that one can build a map of social reality: 'It give the bits and pieces of information for the individual to work out himself what makes things tick.'

Willis then goes on to make clear that the group provides something more than cognitive resources. As he puts it, 'it is impossible to form a distinctive culture by yourself. You cannot generate fun, atmosphere and a social identity by yourself.' In other words, culture is practical as well as intellectual. It involves doing things and that depends on the support of others. The argument involves two stages. First it would be impossible to view oneself as rebellious if one constantly conformed in practice. For those who tried, the legitimacy of their claims would be denied by others. Moreover, while oppositional identities require oppositional action, this action cannot be accomplished successfully alone. Corrigan (1979) deals with this issue at length. He shows that, for example, individual adolescents resisting their teachers on their own are readily isolated and their actions repressed. It is an entirely different picture for groups of individuals supporting one another's resistance or defiance of authority.

What is more, as Corrigan makes clear, group support in the classroom depends on a prior knowledge of how and when support will be elicited. It depends, in other words, on common experience and a common culture, built up around shared activities outside the classroom. Corrigan says of such activities as going down to one's 'favourite end' together at a football match that 'without experiences such as these the boys would be much "easier" for the teachers'.

Our interview data allowed us to expand upon this point. The support of the group is important not only in the classroom but with respect to authority in general:

Int.: Why did you (break windows) with others but not alone?
Resp.: (13-year-old boy): You are with others when you are getting chased.
Int.: For the security?
Resp.: Yes.
Int.: Does being in a group make you more or less likely to do the sort of things that get you into trouble?
Resp. (12-year-old boy): More likely. If I was on my own I'd probably not go around smashing windows and that. When there is a gang of you there is a better chance of not being seen.
Resp. (16-year-old boy answering the same question): When you

are on your own and you do something, if someone sees you you are the one person to get caught. But if there is ten or fifteen and you throw a stone at a window – there is going to be one of that fifteen and maybe not you.

The advantages of anonymity within the group, decreasing the chances of being singled out for punishment, do not by themselves produce anti-social behaviour. Anonymity only enhances behaviours which are already normative for the ingroup and only when these are liable to sanction by outgroups. In the present case, anonymity in the sense of not being readily identifiable to anyone in authority may well encourage the delinquent activities of 'oppositional' groups, but it will not cause the members of 'conventional' groups to turn to crime.

In other contexts, anonymity may be important to conventional adolescents. Though their actions arouse no official disapproval their very conformity to conventional standards of good behaviour brings them into conflict with their 'oppositional' peers. For example, most studies of working-class youth make clear that there is a tension between those who accept and those who reject the institutional order of the school. The terms may vary between 'rebels' versus 'middle class' (Wilmott, 1966), 'lads' versus 'ear 'oles' (Willis, 1977) and 'lads' versus 'citizens' (Jenkins, 1983) but the basic division is the same. Conventional youth are derided by the others for showing interest in lessons and respect for teachers, but anonymity within a group reduces the identifiability of particular individuals as targets of ridicule or abuse. Just as anonymity facilitates delinquency in the intergroup antagonism between 'oppositional' groups and authority so it may facilitate conventional commitments in the intergroup antagonism between conventional and oppositional groups.

There is a more general point implicit in this argument. In making the case for the importance of group support, most of our points have concerned the situation of delinquent youth. Indeed some of the literature and notably Willis's (1977) seminal study virtually represents the world through 'oppositional', or in his terms, 'lads' eyes. Thus the conformist 'ear 'oles' are portrayed as having no life except as teachers' lapdogs. This is clearly unsatisfactory. Willis's own suggestion that the 'lads' reflect working class values, echoing Miller's (1958) subcultural view of delinquency, implies that 'ear 'oles' are ideologically at odds with their own community and therefore if anything more in need of group support for their own inclinations.

We do not, however, need to accept that delinquency is simply the expression of working class cultural values to recognize that conventional youth can also find their position under challenge.

Under certain circumstances they will find themselves a target for the rebels. They may be the victims of no more than ragging and insult but matters can go as far as physical attacks and even extortion (Willis, 1977). We would predict, therefore, that whatever a young person's own inclinations, the more these make the individual a target for attack the more important solidarity with like-minded peers becomes.

There is one more way in which group support is important, and one which further underlines its general significance. It concerns the simple but fundamental issue of how to fill time. We should not allow our labels to give a one-dimensional portrait of complex lives. As already noted, even the most committed of delinquents spend only a tiny proportion of their time in criminal activities. And even the most committed of conformists have a great deal of time which is not filled with school work. Mostly, young people's leisure time is spent in findings things to do which are cheap and accessible. Staying at home is not much of an option if you have to compete with brothers and sisters for private space and parents as well if you want to watch TV or videos. When we categorized our diary returns for the number of evenings spent at home or out, the 'high' delinquents spent on average 5.8 evenings out during the week, the figure for the low delinquency category being 4.2.

Outside the home the options are still limited, however. Commercial entertainments cost money and public facilities may be few. One estate on which our research was conducted, with a population of 10,000, boasted a single youth club. Young people are often left, in Corrigan's (1976) graphic phrase, with 'the dialectics of doing nothing'. So, when it comes to whiling away the time the company of others is a vital prop. As one of Willis's 'lads' put it, 'I don't know what I would do if I didn't have the gang.' Both Willis and Corrigan discuss in some detail how their rebellious youth seek to generate interest and excitement together but this need to have others around to find something entertaining to do is shared by all youth. Only the most introverted can find sufficient diversion in solitary pursuits.

The general conclusion supported by these various observations is that the group is central to the manner in which adolescents find their way in the world. It both allows them to understand their predicament and provides them with the means to act accordingly. In the words of Sherif and Sherif (1964), groups give 'effective support and vehicles for carrying out the business of living'. However close teenagers are to parents or other adults, these relationships are not by themselves sufficient to negotiate and support a path through a social environment dominated by age-homogenous contacts. From this vantage point it becomes clear that most delinquencies are committed in the company of others not because their presence subverts morality but more simply because most of the things adolescents do they do with others.

7.2.4 *Conduct and interaction process*

What can adolescents do in the company of friends that they could or would not do alone? We have suggested that relationships with a peer group support the process of developing an understanding of the social environment. The company of peers engaged in similar activities provides a degree of security and support in sustaining a particular attitude in the face of opposition. The peer group also provides sympathetic companionship to share in the business of finding diverting ways to spend time. There are two further ways in which the company of others is significant. It provides a particularly effective means for reputation management, and it allows for the generation of coherent action.

We have already proposed that delinquent acts are as much bids by the actor to shape his or her reputation as are more conventionally virtuous actions. We have noted the kinds of reputation that can be at stake in each case. And we have also pointed out that actions of any kind have no consequences for reputation unless the actor can be identified by others and the actions appropriately interpreted. People can of course tell tales of their daring deeds and hope that their audiences will be suitably impressed. A very few people do get all the way to adulthood and beyond still harbouring the illusion that this will suffice and for an even smaller minority it may indeed be sufficient to sustain a reputation of sorts. But the majority will be forced to abandon this illusion in childhood; they will discover that there is no substitute for witnesses, and equally no point in wasted efforts. Certainly our interviewees had learned these lessons. Few of those in the high delinquency category were willing to waste their efforts on stealing or vandalizing on their own.

It is not, however, quite as simple as having witnesses around when those opportunities arise to perform. There is always a degree of ambiguity about the choices available in real situations. Reputations may be represented in abstract categories – courage, loyalty, reliability, honesty – but they are earned through concrete deeds. There is no simple and direct connection between particular deeds and the virtues (or vices) they might exemplify. The abstract categories must be continually defined by reference to particular instances, a task beyond the means of single individuals. And the meaning of particular choices and actions must be agreed. The social comparisons that a face-to-face group affords (cf. Festinger, 1954; Myers, 1982) allow individuals to fine-tune, for example, the levels of risk they take so that they can be just as daring or cautious as they wish to be seen.

7.3 Delinquency and Group Norms: The Centrality of Delinquent Action

Adolescents may in the main be group members but this does not mean that all adolescent groups are the same. Indeed, ever since the 1920s, initially under the influence of the Chicago school of 'social ecologists' it has been recognized that different groups espouse very different values and manifest very different behaviours (e.g. Shaw & MacKay, 1931; Thrasher, 1927). What is more, studies of adolescent groups, whether sociological or psychological, whether carried out in the United States or elsewhere, have one general point of agreement: these groups can be divided into those which accept conventional mores and those which reject them (Brake, 1985; Cloward & Ohlin, 1960; Cohen, 1955; Corrigan, 1979; Jenkins, 1983; Sherif & Sherif, 1964; Short & Strodtbeck, 1965).

The division is both ideological and practical. For some it is normative to voice cynicism about systems of authority and to flout the rules. Others trust such systems and observe the rules. The division we noted in the last chapter between those who accept formal authority and those who do not is a matter of collective orientations and not just individual attitudes. Moreover, in so far as delinquency is the clearest expression of how one relates to authority, so it follows that levels of delinquent action should be matters of central concern in the normative structure of adolescent groups. Responses given in our interviews provide strong support for this idea.

First, different groups have different effects on the incidence of delinquent acts. This is indicated in answers to the question 'do you think that having friends around makes you more or less likely to do the sort of things that could get you into trouble?' Of the 33 'high delinquents' who gave a response, 26 (79 per cent) answered 'more', whereas only 18 (39 per cent) out of 44 'low delinquents' answered likewise (chi square = 13.91, p < 0.001). If anything however, these figures underestimate the difference between groups. Many of the low delinquents interpreted the question as being about the likely behaviour of people in general rather than their own behaviour in particular. Several indicated that they thought being in a group led to more delinquency even when they had never personally committed such an act. Thus when we asked whether there were things they would do with others although they might never do these by themselves, the differences were even clearer (see table 7.3).

Table 7.3 Answers to the question: 'Are there things like vandalism or fighting or stealing that you would do with others but that you would never do alone?', according to gender and level of delinquency

	Yes	*No*
Male 'High delinquent'	23	5
Female 'High delinquent'	7	3
Total 'High delinquent'	30	8
Male 'Low delinquent'	5	13
Female 'Low delinquent'	3	9
Total 'Low delinquent'	8	22

These data rebut the notion that the group in itself predisposes people to behave anti-socially. It is true that some groups make delinquent activity more likely but equally true that others inhibit it. The division between groups in which delinquency is normative and those in which it is counter-normative emerged in other ways in the interviews:

Int.:   What would your group of friends do if you got involved in a fight?
Resp.:   Try and stop me.
Int.:   Would it change the relationship at all?
Resp.:   If you went about fighting all the time nobody would want to be friends with you.
Int.:   What if you stole?
Resp.:   They wouldn't go about with me.
Int.:   And vandalizing?
Resp.:   Try and stop me.
Int.:   How would that affect the relationship?
Resp.:   If I was spraying on walls and that it would affect them as other people would think they were like that too.
Int.:   What would happen?
Resp.:   They would leave me.

These kinds of answers were found repeatedly amongst those who reported low levels of delinquent action. In the 'high' delinquency group of interviewees we found almost the mirror image.

Int.:   What would happen if there was a fight going on and you refused to take part? How would your friends react?
Resp.:   They don't bother – just call you a coward and that is it, finished.
Int.:   Would you lose your position in the group?
Resp.:   Yes.
Int.:   What if, in the past, people had been smashing windows and again you refused to take part – what would they do then?
Resp.:   Just say that it is up to you and you don't get to come with me then.

However, these answers do more than indicate that delinquency is a matter about which groups have norms. They show that if one displays normatively inappropriate behaviour, one risks exclusion from the group. Delinquency appears to be a criterion of group membership. Two things follow from this. In the first place, should an individual change between two groups in which the norms differ, there should be a corresponding change in behaviour. The following comes from an interview with a 13-year-old girl:

Int.:   Did you used to fight on your own or in a group?
Resp.:   With somebody. People were annoying me, they kept annoying me.
Int.:   Do you still go around with these people you knew then?
Resp.:   I still see them but I'm in a different school now.
Int.:   Why don't you fight now?
Resp.:   There is nobody to fight with. I don't get in that much trouble.

Or, in the case of a 14-year-old girl:

Int.:   Why do you think you have stopped (being a nuisance) now?
Resp.:   I moved and got different pals. Moved from Whitfield to Pitkerro Road.

In the second place, when individuals seek to alter their level of delinquency, a change of group will also be necessary. Again our data confirm this is so. Of those who indicated that they no longer committed delinquent acts, all reported a change in the friends they spent time with, although the transition was rarely an easy matter. This is illustrated in the account of a 15-year-old boy.

> What happened was there was a fight and I didn't go back. I spent quite a while just staying in the house at nights and I didn't go back. I got with the other friends. He invited me across to his house.

Another boy got into trouble with the police after throwing a petrol bomb at a derelict building. As a result:

> I got kept in for six months so I'd rather not go about with the same boys and I changed the friends.

We can conclude that group membership and levels of delinquent action are interdependent. Being in a group requires adherence to group norms concerning delinquency and conversely a given level of delinquent activity depends on membership of a group with appropriate norms.

7.3.1 From delinquent norms to delinquent action

In previous sections we have argued that groups are important in the social lives of adolescents – the great majority of young people claim some kind of group affiliation – and that delinquency is of central importance in groups – either group members define their group in terms of willingness to commit acts of delinquency or they define the group in terms of its rejection of delinquency. Putting these observations together suggests that decisions to offend or not are taken in the context of the group. To understand delinquency it is therefore also necessary to include an analysis of group processes. In the words of Short and Strodtbeck (1965), 'between position in the social order, including detailed knowledge of the subculture which this implies, and behaviour there intervene processes of interaction between individuals in groups.'

Sherif and Sherif (1964) regarded delinquency as essentially instrumental, stemming from the fact that all youth desire the same things. Thus groups cooperate to get what they want, for example to steal cars if they cannot come by them legally. Short and Strodtbeck, in their own analysis of group processes, argued against this kind of instrumentality. Instead they proposed that 'selectivity for failure' leads to groups that are qualitatively distinct. Where group members have no prospects of achievement there will be little instrumental basis for cohesion. Unlike more privileged groups whose mutual activities develop those skills necessary for further success, they will lay stress on activities which lead to dependence between members in and of themselves. The group will indulge in exciting, dangerous and illicit activities which encourage members to stick together. Moreover, given the precarious nature of group membership there will be particular emphasis on the symbols and signs of inclusion; style, reputation and status will be particularly important.

Despite these differences both sets of authors start from a common conception of the relationship between individual and social structure. Both assume that their subjects (all males) have a clearly defined place in society. Some have prospects of conventional success. Others realize such success is out of reach and their reaction is delinquency. This assumption is in part a reflection of the age range of their samples. The Sherifs state that their sample is between 13 and 18 without giving any further breakdown. However, judging by the associated details (boys who are leaving school, getting jobs, getting married, buying and driving cars), most would appear to be towards the upper end of this range. Short and Strodtbeck's males had a mean age of 17, and some were well into their twenties. In these cases it is difficult to decide to what extent delinquency is the result of these young males' social status and to what extent it is the source.

We have been concerned with a younger group. The 11–16-year-olds we have studied may have been from disadvantaged backgrounds. They may have witnessed failure in their families and among their neighbours. But their own fate has not yet finally been decided. Their behaviour cannot therefore be explained by this fate though it might be influenced by their perceptions of what that fate is likely to be. Thus our conception of the relationship between the individual and society differs from that of these earlier studies. For us there is no single direction of causality from objective social position to action. We have proposed that levels of delinquent action are means by which individuals define their place in the social world as well as being means of coping with this assumed place. For instance, settling one's scores through fighting rather than appeals to authority demonstrates a belief that the world is tough and one has to look out for oneself. It also says quite clearly ' . . . and don't mess with me.' Both the definitional and the coping aspects of delinquency have implications for collective processes which we shall deal with in turn.

7.3.2 Delinquency and intra-group processes

The stress we are placing upon 'definitional' factors rests upon the assumption that even if external factors frame the options open to an individual the decision whether to undertake or desist from a delinquent act still represents an active choice. We are therefore open to the objection that volition is irrelevant. Groups may simply compel individuals to act in particular ways. However, we found very little evidence of collective coercion. When we asked those who reported high levels of delinquent activity 'do (other group members) pressure you into doing things?', only 9 out of 42 indicated this was the case. Moreover, out of those nine, only three mentioned the use of direct pressure compelling them to act. Others indicated a different form of pressure.

> Int.:   Do they pressure you into doing things?
> Resp. (16-year-old male):   Certain amount of pressure. Started off with one person having the idea and it spread like a cancer.

When we asked, during the interviews, how they became involved in particular delinquent acts one theme emerged repeatedly.

> Int.:   Can you tell me about the last time you got involved (in vandalism)?
> Resp. (13-year-old male):   We were down at a building site a couple of years ago and everyone was jumping on the panes of glass that were lying on the ground and they were all saying 'come on, come on', so I just started doing it. Somebody started it and everybody just kept joining in.

> Int.:   Would you mind telling me about the petrol bomb incident.
> Resp. (15-year-old male):   Well the linoleum works in Linlathen. There was a lot of old factories and derelict properties and there was petrol. Somebody suggested making petrol bombs so we got a cloth and that and just threw them. The police came along.

> Int.:   Describe what would happen (when you caused damage).
> Resp. (16-year-old male):   Somebody would kick something over and we'd all just start kicking it along the road.

> Resp. (15-year-old female):   When I broke windows, that was in the industrial estate.
> Int.:   You were with a group of friends?
> Resp.:   Yes.
> Int.:   What happened?
> Resp.:   Nobody suggested it. We were just throwing pebbles and started hitting the windows and somebody broke one.

> Int.:   How did you get involved in vandalizing things?
> Resp. (13-year-old female):   Just because my pals did it and I'd

join them. If one person did it then the rest of them did it as well and I didn't want to be left out so I'd do it as well.

The key feature of these responses is the self-evident and unquestioned nature of the action – 'one person did it, and everybody joined in'. As the penultimate example makes clear, it is not even necessary to have an explicit suggestion. There is another way in which the acts are presented as 'self-evident'. They are presented as the only available options.

Int.: Did you go around throwing stones at people?
Resp. (16-year-old male): Yes.
Int.: Why did you do that?
Resp.: There was never anything to do. Always with other people. Other people started it and I was walking about and joined in.

Int.: Why do you think you vandalized things?
Resp. (16-year-old male): Just something to do.

Int.: Why did you spray on walls?
Resp. (15-year-old female): I was just bored and fed up with nothing to do.

A similar assertion is that delinquency is the only enjoyable option available.

Int.: I see you have vandalized things. Why do you think you do it?
Resp. (16-year-old male): Enjoyment.

Int.: Why did you used to (vandalize)?
Resp. (15-year-old male): For a laugh.

Int.: When you get into trouble, is that alone or with others?
Resp. (15-year-old boy): With others. They just did it for a laugh.

This is reminiscent of Willis's observations about the importance of 'having a laff' – an inherently social activity. As one 15-year-old boy put it, 'I wouldn't do that stuff (things that get you into trouble) on my own. You wouldn't get a laugh at it on your own.' However, it is clear in one sense that claims about there being no other options but delinquency are false. There are other things to do; one can stay in and do homework, write computer programs, read books, play music. Obviously our respondents were aware of this. Thus these extracts reveal an unspoken premise: forms of misbehaviour are the only ones possible or enjoyable once others clearly unacceptable to group members have been ruled out, and school-related or intellectual pursuits fall into this latter category. Indeed these do not even count as options.

> **Int.:**   In the class were there two lots of folk – one lot snobs and the other lot – there was just a straight choice between them?
> **Resp.** (16-year-old male):   Yes.
> **Int.:**   What were the snobs like?
> **Resp.:**   Boring. They don't do nothing. Just stay in and everything. Don't do anything.

Once this premise is made explicit it is clear that although group members will spontaneously follow certain actions they will not blindly follow anything. Certain acts are 'self-evidently' the thing to do because they are in tune with taking an oppositional stance. Acts which express 'the sort of people we are' are liable to be taken up by other group members. In contrast, being studious or obedient are rejected as forms of action since they would mark 'us' out as 'soft'. They would place 'us' in support of the system; they would define 'us' as 'conventional' rather than 'oppositional'.

What is happening here can be seen as a specific instance of a more general process: group members will only act in ways which are consonant with their collective definition of self. This analysis directly parallels our interpretation of crowd behaviour (e.g. Reicher, 1982, 1984); even in riots there are clear limits to what rioters will do and these limits derive from the identity which unites crowd members.

According to the 'self-categorization theory' (Turner, Hogg, Oakes, Reicher & Wetherell, 1987) from which this interpretation derives, the individual's sense of self is constituted by the social categories (Catholic, socialist, Scottish, etc.) to which he or she belongs as well as by more idiosyncratic attributes. With respect to any particular category or group membership, individuals partake in a process of self-stereotyping. They learn first of all what it means to be a member of that particular category or group and they then conform to this consensual definition. Thus while the process may be common to all groups it does not follow that all groups will be the same. Consider our 'oppositional' and 'conventional' groups. We have shown that delinquent acts are supported in the former because they accord with collective identity while more conventional ways of using time are not even considered. For those in the conventional groups, by contrast, it is delinquent acts that contradict identity, and so their occurrence meets with a very different reception, as the following extracts make clear.

> **Resp.** (13-year-old female):   My friend stole chewing gum and I said to her if you had no money how did you get that and she said she stole it. I said you'd better put it back and she refused and walked away.

> **Int.:**   If you were inclined (to commit delinquent acts) do you think your friends would stop you?
> **Resp.:**   (14-year-old female):   They'd try to discourage me but wouldn't do it themselves. They'd just walk away.

> **Resp.** (12-year-old make):   If you were going to do something bad – they'd just say 'don't do that – if you get caught you will get into trouble and it will be bad for your school record.'

It is important not only to eschew such behaviour oneself but also to dissociate oneself from those who commit them. Our respondents were keenly aware that they could be judged by the actions of their peers. The following quotation, from a 14-year-old boy, is typical: 'If (your friends) go round school and do things that are wrong and bad they associate you with being wrong and bad as well.' Thus, where delinquent acts are consonant with identity they are pursued with little hesitation. When they would negate identity they are actively avoided.

It is not enough, however, to characterize delinquent activity as a straightforward reflection of an already adopted identity. Such action is also a communication of identity, a means of showing others what kind of person one is. Patrick (1973) shows how delinquency can result, particularly when one's identity is in question. One boy, who had a Polish father, reported how he 'had tae go screwin tae live doon yon name'. Another who had revealed ineptitude at football responded by increased violence. Short and Strodtbeck report a number of similar instances. In one case a boy was told that he was cowardly for beating up others; his response was to 'drink excessively and then get into fights that demonstrated how tough he was'. Another concerned 'Commando', a boy reputed for his flamboyant troublemaking:

> The worker decided to 'put down' Commando in front of the rest of the group by telling him that he really was not tough or brave. He concluded

by saying 'you ain't nothin'.' Commando reacted by being even more reckless in his actions, particularly when members of the rival group were on the scene. He continued to demonstrate to the group that he was not chicken and that he was somebody until the worker ceased his public ridicule. (1965 p. 191)

Being seen as tough and hard by fellow group members is clearly important for these boys. However, these examples should not be taken to imply that threats to identity inevitably incite an aggressive response. Short and Strodtbeck provide another example concerning a drug-using group who were urged to get involved in group conflict on Chicago's beaches with insinuations that anyone who did not was 'chicken'. Their reaction was to get high on pills, to go to the other end of the beach and play cards.

> Their reaction to this threat was withdrawal from the larger group and participation in an activity expressive of the norms that distinguished them from the conflict-oriented boys, namely drug use . . . this response, in this situation, suggests that, in groups in which the leader's prestige is bound up in competence at enjoying esoteric 'kicks', it may well be doubted that status threat would result in aggressive behaviour. (Short & Strodtbeck, 1965, p. 194)

What is happening is that individuals whose collective identity is under threat respond by attempting to reassert that identity. The behavioural consequences of this will, however, depend on how that identity is defined and will therefore vary between different types of group. Yet if the examples given above are powerful illustrations of reputational motives they still seem to be somewhat exceptional. These reactions are presented as compensatory phenomena which only occur when identity is under threat. Our own evidence suggests that these reactions are much more routine; one must continually maintain one's reputation in order to retain group membership.

We asked those in the high delinquency group three questions which touched on this issue: Do you do things because if you did not your friends would think badly of you? Do you do things to keep in? Do you do things to show off? Of responses to the first question, 61 per cent were affirmative, 61 per cent were also affirmative to the second and 29 per cent to the third. Considering responses to the three questions together, 72 per cent answered positively to at least one. Thus, some two-thirds to three-quarters of our respondents reported intentions bound up with communicating about themselves to their fellows.

This theme recurs in other ways throughout the interviews. Delinquency within 'oppositional' groups is not just a matter of behaving appropriately but also of showing oneself to have appropriate qualities to others. Taking part in fights and acts of vandalism were ways of demonstrating one's possession of central characteristics of group life, hardness, fearlessness and independence. Given that such action is almost taken for granted in oppositional groups and therefore barely commented upon, it is rare to find comments on the self-presentational antecedents of delinquent action. Much more common, however, are comments on the consequences for one's reputation were one to refuse to participate in collective acts. The following three extracts are from interviews with different 15-year-old boys:

Int.:   What would happen if you refused to get involved in fights?
Resp.:   Think I'm chicken and I'm afraid.

Int.:   Does being in a group make you more or less likely to do things that could get you into trouble?
Resp.:   More likely. You are in a group and if somebody wants to do something you'd be as well doing it too or they'll call you chicken or something.
Int.:   Would you get drawn into fights that you wouldn't have got into on your own?
Resp.:   Yes.
Int.:   Why do you think you were drawn into them?
Resp.:   Just because you couldn't just go home. People would pick on you again and think you were soft. You have to show them you are not soft.

However the most succinct comment came from a 14-year-old girl:

Int.:   How would your friends react if they were stealing and you refused to take part.
Resp.:   Coward.

These comments may seem familiar. They are very similar in form to those presented as part of our discussion of the centrality of delinquent action which indicated that ongoing failure to participate in group activities would lead to exclusion from the group. Indeed the fact that membership of oppositional groups depends on oppositional behaviour helps explain the importance of being seen to be delinquent, of having a delinquent reputation. As a corollary we are arguing that reputation management must be seen in the context of group process. What individuals seek is not to be seen as positive in inter-individual terms but rather as representative in terms of group norms. As Patrick (1973) showed in the case of Glasgow 'razor gangs', at times the immediate objective of reputation management may be to show oneself as hard, unfeeling and savage, in fact as thoroughly unpleasant, as long as this fits the stereotype group members have of themselves.

It should be clear that the expressive and reputational facets of self-definition through delinquency are interdependent. For if, as we have shown, delinquency is a collective activity and one which is dependent on collective support, then in order to define oneself as oppositional one also needs to be accepted as such by fellow group members. Consequently, to break the rules, to fight or thieve or vandalize is simultaneously a personal expression of where one stands and a public communication designed to claim a place in the eyes of others. This interdependence of personal self-definition and public expression is well captured in the statements of two 16-year-old boys.

Int.:   Vandalizing – why do you think you have done it?
Resp.:   Just made a mark in a place. You know you were there and you are tough and that.

Int.:   Why have you vandalized things?
Resp.:   Just so people will say – there's his name again and that.

7.3.3 Delinquency and intergroup processes

Our discussion of collective factors has so far been limited to processes that are internal to the social group. However, if an individual's claim to be oppositional depends upon acceptance in an oppositional group, it is equally true that the same claim by the group as a whole depends on its relationship to other groups. As Tajfel and Turner have argued (Tajfel, 1978; Tajfel & Turner, 1979; Turner et al., 1987) the characteristics of a group can only be defined relative to other groups. Moreover, in so far as groups strive to be positively evaluated they will compete with other groups in order to prove that they better exemplify valued characteristics. It must be stressed that the behavioural outcome of this process of social differentiation will depend on the values held by the groups in question. Conventional groups may well compete on dimensions of intelligence, dilligence or trustworthiness. Oppositional groups, which can only be tough and hard in so far as they are more so than other oppositional groups will compete to see which is the toughest. The importance of such intergroup competition is illustrated in one 15-year-old boy's account of a fight:

> Int.: Fights, what happened there?
> Resp.: That was with going to discos in a big squad and the other lot said they were tougher than us and we said we were tougher than them.

Another 15-year-old boy talks in more general terms about how fights start:

> Resp.: People say come to our (housing) scheme and people from different schemes come to your scheme and start shouting gang slogans and that. That means . . .
> Int.: People pick out those who seem hard and tough and fight them?
> Resp.: Yes.

He later fleshes this out when talking of events in which he was personally involved:

> Resp.: If there is going to be a fight you usually call a boy out to fight. Whoever wins goes back with your gang like.
> Int.: Why do you think you do it? Is it someone you don't particularly like?
> Resp.: Yes. People think they are the hard man from other schemes.

As we saw in the last chapter a delinquent reputation may form part of a strategy of self-protection and redress for those who regard more formal solutions as unreliable or unavailable. But the group is also a source of unofficial protection and remedy for grievances, and relations with ingroup members are characteristically those of protection rather than aggression. Even when there is conflict within a group it is less serious or significant than conflict between groups (Patrick, 1973; Short & Strodtbeck, 1965). Correspondingly, looking after oneself is also a matter of protecting one's own group from other groups for one's own interests are bound up with those of the group.

Whether we look at it in terms of self-affirmation or self-protection, the assertion of toughness must be considered as an intergroup phenomenon and must therefore be analysed in terms of intergroup processes. As Turner and Giles (1981) have shown, people can act either in terms of their distinctive individuality or in terms of group membership and there is a considerable difference between the two. Thus one cannot extrapolate from inter-individual interaction to intergroup interaction. The fact that groups are in conflict does not mean that individuals from the two groups are necessarily personal enemies. Nor does personal friendship rule out aggression when individuals interact as group members (Hewstone & Brown, 1987). Our own interviews with 'oppositional' youth clearly show conflict to operate only at the intergroup level.

> Int.:   Does being in a group make you more or less likely to do the sort of things that get you into trouble?
> Resp. (15 year old male):   More likely. If you are with a group you might say 'There's a boy from somewhere. Go and get him.' If you are on your own you don't bother. You'd just walk past and say 'hi' to them.

> Int.:   Do you ever do things with others that you regret?
> Resp. (15-year-old male):   Yes. Standing at the shops and say somebody you know comes past and you end up fighting with them because you are with the gang.

> Int.:   What sort of things do you do when you are out with your friends?
> Resp. (16-year-old boy):   Usually stand about at the bottom of the multi (high rise block) for a while – call abuse like.
> Int.:   Do you think you are different with your friends?
> Resp.:   Yes, when you are with your friends you act tough and that. On my own I'm pretty shy.

In these fights, how individuals react to a person is determined by what group they belong to. Thus, to put it in more general terms, the way in which an individual is regarded is a matter of how the group as a whole is seen (Tajfel, 1978, 1981; Turner & Giles, 1981). If a group is seen as aggressive and hostile then its members will be treated likewise. They may, moreover, be treated as such irrespective of their immediate actions. Thus we find that fights between groups do not depend upon particular acts of provocation. Our interviewees report that they can arise from the mere encounter.

> Int.:   Is fighting to do with the gang you go around with?

Resp. (16-year-old female):   When you are with a crowd of people and you meet another kind of crowd you just start fighting.
Int.:   Were most of the groups from particular schemes?
Resp.:   It's usually schemes near about each other, Fintry and Douglas.

Int.:   How do the gang fights start?
Resp. (16-year-old male):   They just see us and start fighting.
Int.:   What would happen (when fights start)?
Resp.:   Just standing at the shops, another gang comes along and that's how the fight starts.

It is important to stress we are not suggesting that intergroup relations are inevitably aggressive – any more than we were proposing that group behaviour is inevitably destructive. In both cases behaviour is governed by stereotypic processes, though here it is a matter of the stereotypes groups have of each other rather than those they have of themselves. Thus oppositional groups may regard and treat each other in terms of threat and aggression. However, this is not how they regard conventional groups nor how such groups view each other. As previous work has shown (Patrick, 1973; Short & Strodtbeck, 1965; Willis, 1977) and as was evident in our own interviews, rebellious youth may tease, harass and bully their more conformist peers but they rarely fight them collectively. Conventional group members, far from fighting on contact, would not accept anyone who did so. A 15-year-old girl said her group would reject 'people in gangs, people who disobey the teacher and are cheeky'. A 12-year-old girl reported the rejection of 'people who smoke or stay off school, people who bully people and people who steal things'. A 15-year-old boy rejected would-be 'vandals, ones that go around shouting and starting fights', and a 12-year-old boy was inclined to reject 'people who fight and swear a lot'.

The argument that conflicts are characteristically intergroup in nature, that they stem from the stereotypical perceptions that groups have of each other rather than from personal likes and dislikes, has two important sets of consequences for the ways in which individuals come to be involved. The first has to do with ingroup pressures. If fights are unavoidable when oppositional groups meet, or are at least immanent possibilities, and if the fighting involves all members irrespective of their individual acts, then both individual and collective security depends upon group solidarity. For, if half of one's group stand aside, everyone in the group is more likely to be beaten. A 13-year-old explained his involvement in fighting in the following terms: 'If you are fighting and you are getting beat, but if there is more of you there's a better chance.'

This interdependence of individual action and group fate makes fighting quite distinct from vandalism or theft. Non-participation in these latter activities may violate group norms, it may show one to be cowardly or boring, but it does not actively let down other group members. So individuals may also get involved in fights to protect their fellow group members. As one 15-year-old boy put it, 'two groups meeting, you just jump in because you don't want your mates to be battered'. On the other hand, fellow group members may pressure the individual into joining in. We found group fighting to be the one area where individuals would be actively coerced into conformity rather than merely ignored.

> Int.:   What if (your group) were getting involved in a fight and you said 'no', what would they have done?
> Resp. (15-year-old boy):   They made you do it, forced you. If you didn't do it you'd get it back from them.

The pressure to participate does not merely come from the ingroup, however. Even if a person wishes to avoid a fight, this wish may be ignored by the outgroup. Merely as a member of another group this person becomes a target. Indeed individuals do not even have to be in a group in order to become the focus of aggression, they only have to be identified as members of another group.

> Int.:   How did you usually get involved in fights?
> Resp. (15-year-old male):   Just if somebody asks where do you come from and you say 'Lochee' and they start fighting. I've been caught twice on my own, but I got out of it. Got chased. Lots of people from the Hilltown and maybe six from Menzieshill and Linlathen. They come from the Ferry and then it starts.

In such circumstances trying not to fight is no protection. If anything it leaves the individual more vulnerable. 'You can't run away because they'd come after you so you just have to come and fight' is the observation of a 15-year-old boy. Another, asked how he got involved in fights, recalled more whimsically, 'Other people provoking me. Gang got our budgie and kept swinging the cage and wouldn't give it back. So we fought.'

Just as ingroup pressure can commit individuals to aggress against an outgroup, so outgroup assumptions can draw people into conflict without it being individually willed. This then is the second way in which the consequences of intergroup processes lead to individual involvement in fighting. But the relevance of these processes is not limited to relations between oppositional groups of peers. Such groups may be stereotyped as 'trouble' by adults in general and by teachers and the police in particular. Consequently, group members may be held responsible for group actions even when there is no personal responsibility. Various of our respondents stressed this point.

> Int.: How did you get involved in vandalizing things?
> Resp. (16-year-old female): Sometimes you didn't actually do it. But you are with somebody that is. You are just as much involved as they are but you didn't actually do it.
> Int.: How does it start?
> Resp.: Say somebody has a spray can and you are going away to spray a wall with them. If you are with them while they are standing spraying and the police come along they think you are as much involved as they are, but you might not even have touched the tin.

> Int.: Does being in a group affect how people see you?
> Resp. (12-year-old boy): Yes, if anybody is making a noise, the whole group gets blamed.

Given this, any consideration relating to fear of apprehension becomes irrelevant. If one is as likely to be damned if one does not as one is to be damned if one does, then the legal sanction loses all deterrent force within the group. This argument can be extended. Sometimes group members may meet official disapproval even when no one has committed an offence. The moral panic surrounding rebellious youth (Cohen, 1972) can be sufficient for these to be construed as a menace.

> Int.: Do you think the friends you are with affects how people see you?
> Resp. (15-year-old male): Yes, in a bad way. You get stereotyped, out for trouble. You can just stand and someone will come out and start shouting at you that you shouldn't be there and that.

> Int.: How do people see you?
> Resp. (15-year-old female): We are standing at the shops with a crowd of people and they think we are going to break windows and spray on the walls.

Int.:   How did (trouble) start?

Resp. (14-year-old male):   We didn't intentionally go out to try and do something bad – it was usually just ended up doing something bad – not intentionally. Maybe wandering around an old building site and getting caught and taken to the police station.

Thus besides there being no security for individuals who desist from collective transgressions, the group as a whole may face official disapproval whatever its behaviour. In this way stereotypic perceptions of oppositional groups go some way towards being a self-fulfilling prophecy. Even if they do not compel such groups into delinquent action, the indiscriminate use of sanctions may remove restraining factors which inhibit group members from anti-social behaviour. After all, if 'anything gets you into trouble, standing at the shops, going on a bus', as a 15-year-old boy claimed, one has little to lose by doing something that is genuinely proscribed.

7.4 Conclusions

In the course of our analysis we have shown that the mass society thesis, in which traditional approaches to delinquency are rooted, is based on a false set of assumptions about human social existence. Far from living as perpetual strangers, people largely know and are known by those with whom they interact. In this, adolescents are no different from other age groups; their lives too are lived within communities populated by kin, friends and acquaintances. In rejecting a 'mass society' description of social life we have also had to reject its conceptual tenets. Rather than regarding delinquency as evidence for the breakdown of identity and loss of rationality, we regard the commission of delinquent acts, no less than abstention from such acts, as means by which individuals define where they stand. And rather than regarding the group as the cloak of anonymity under which identity (and identifiability) evaporate, we regard the group as contributing both symbolically and practically to the achievement of identity, whether it be conventional or oppositional.

For us the group is psychologically constructive in the sense of helping the individual to find a way in the world. It is important to draw a distinction here between psychological and societal levels of analysis. The perspectives that are constructed in the group may be inimical to the social order. Indeed, delinquent acts are by definition those which violate that order and so on a societal level delinquent groups may well be defined as destructive. The danger lies in conflating the two levels, in arguing that because actions oppose a dominant view of what makes sense they therefore lack any sense. As we argued in chapter 1, opposition should not be confused with mindlessness.

It is also important to be careful with the word 'opposition'. We are not suggesting that delinquency is in any conscious way a political act. Certainly it is not intended as an attempt to undermine the status quo. The lack of interest of most adolescents in affairs of state is well established (Banks et al., 1992; Bynner & Ashford, 1994; Coffield, Borrill & Marshall, 1986). They are, on the other hand, keenly interested in their relations with the institutions which govern their everyday lives though even here it would be simplistic to regard acts of delinquency as motivated solely by subversive intentions.

We have argued that an adolescent interest in formal institutions is due to the fact that one has to know their nature in order to live with them. This nature is not self-evident. One does not 'know' the institution and then decide how to act. Delinquent action serves to define where one stands as much as it represents a reaction to that stance. We would therefore reject the popular contrast, exemplified in the difference between Sherif and Sherif (1964) and Short and Strodtbeck (1965), between delinquency as expressive and delinquency as instrumental. For us the two elements are necessarily intertwined. It is only through the expression of an oppositional stance that individuals gain the collective support to deal with antagonistic institutions and groups. Conversely the need to be tough and cynical depends upon the expression of a collective view which sees institutions of authority as an opposition.

Thus, in arguing that delinquency is oppositional, several elements are combined. First, we mean that it stems from seeing oneself in opposition to formal authority. Second, it is a means of survival in a world where authority offers, or is believed to offer, no protection. Only in conjunction with these should delinquency be seen as a means of striking at authority and only in the sense of a means of defining and managing one's social relations should delinquency be seen as political.

Delinquency as meaningful communication; delinquency as a collectively achieved form of adaptive understanding and action; delinquency as embedded in an oppositional stance. We could hardly be further from traditional approaches. However, our reason for rejecting such approaches was not only their conceptual limitations. We also argued that they failed to account for the observed character of delinquent action. It remains for us to show, in the last chapter, that our approach is more satisfactory in this respect.

8

Summing Up:
Explanation, Intervention and the
Theory of Social Control

8.1 Introduction

Our examination of 'the facts of delinquency' in chapter 3 revealed them to possess a double character. Even if the statistics are controversial and may distort the picture, it is none the less very unlikely that this picture is entirely misleading. There are differences between groups: more 14-year-olds offend than 11-year-olds, more boys than girls, more working-class youth than middle-class youth, more who are resident in inner cities than garden suburbs. At the same time there is considerable heterogeneity within groups. So, for example, if delinquency is overall somewhat more prevalent amongst working-class youth this does not mean that all or even that most working-class adolescents are delinquent. Nor should it obscure the fact that many middle-class adolescents become highly involved in delinquency. A statistically significant difference between group means should not be used to construct a generalized stereotypic image.

This double character of delinquency makes the task of explanation particularly difficult. The risk is that conceptual accounts focus on one side of the story to the exclusion of the other. Psychological accounts derived from the mass society perspective may be criticized for their exclusive attention to intra-psychic processes at the expense of the social patterning of behaviour. But to replace psychological reductionism with sociological reductionism is equally one-sided. Theories which explain delinquency in terms of macro-social factors and forces may alert us to the relevance of age, gender, class and area of residence. But they do not explain why, for instance, some girls and only certain boys are delinquent. Of course one could refine these broad categories to reduce such difficulties: much female delinquency may be down to working-class girls and much male conformism may be confined to middle-class boys.

But the use of such categories, however much they are combined and subdivided, will not eliminate variability within categories. The general point therefore remains: an adequate account of delinquency must combine rather than counterpose personal difference and social shape. It must take account of individual factors without being individualistic and recognize social determination without being socially deterministic. Our model of delinquency is aimed at fulfilling – or at least addressing – these criteria.

8.2 A General Framework of Interpretation

Delinquency is related to young people's representation of formal authority. Consequently, the distribution of delinquent acts is not related directly to social reality but rather to the processes whereby people come to perceive that reality.

We have argued that the representations which adolescents form of schools and other institutions are highly practical. They explain the nature of the institution and determine the responses which are appropriate to it. According to whether school is seen as a path to personal progress or a means of external control, one decides whether to obey teachers or challenge them, whether to spend evenings on homework or out in the streets. This practicality – the devising of strategies to cope with the world – is dependent upon the ability of representations to make sense of the individual's experience. To borrow a term from Antonio Gramsci's (1971) analysis of ideology, ideas must have a 'common-sense' validity.

If representations must 'fit' with the reality they purport to explain, we must also consider the fit between different representations that the individual may hold. For while we have emphasized the significance for delinquency of orientations to authority this is not the only way in which individuals define themselves. Important as the school and other institutions may be, there are many other relationships of significance to young people. Consequently, individuals will have a series of representations of their worlds, each of which will have implications for where those persons stand and what sorts of persons they are. It is therefore necessary to consider the relationship between these different representations. For instance, to see oneself as antagonistic to authority – as rebellious, tough and hard – may be more or less consonant with other definitions one may hold which could in turn affect one's willingness to adopt an antagonistic stance. Conversely, there may be times when a conformist stance contradicts other definitions and so becomes problematic.

In suggesting that dissonant representations may lead to problems, we are not subscribing to the argument that contradiction between elements of cognition is inherently aversive (cf. Festinger, 1957). Billig's (1987) argument that contradiction is more a condition of than an exception to human consciousness is closer to the truth. However, we would also argue that there are social conditions under which contradictions become impossible to maintain.

Many of our adolescents made clear that their conduct varied markedly from one context to another. In particular, members of our 'delinquent' sample were keen to insulate their rebellious stance from their parents. This ability to maintain incompatible definitions of the self was facilitated by the fact that the contexts in which the divergent definitions were maintained were themselves temporally, socially and physically separated. As our diary study showed, it was rare for the parents and friends of any of our sample to meet. On average the 'high' delinquents spent 0.1 periods per week in the company of both family and friends, while the figure for 'low' delinquents was 0.4 periods per week. To put it slightly differently, of the 294 interaction periods we recorded, there were only two instances of 'delinquents' being with family and friends and eight instances in which this was the case for 'non-delinquents'. Although the overall figures are small, binomial analysis shows that the more delinquent group were even more likely than the less delinquent group to keep peers and parents apart (P = 0.055).

The reason why these audiences need to be kept apart is that each is necessary to support a different self-definition and that support depends upon normatively acceptable behaviour. As long as they stay separate it is possible to behave appropriately with each, to retain the support of both and hence to maintain otherwise incompatible identities. However, should the different sources come together then one will no longer be able to act so as to maintain acceptance of one aspect of identity without jeopardizing collective support for other aspects. As characters in a French farce discover, the problem of living multiple lives lies in so managing affairs as to satisfy each set of relations without alienating the others. And as the climax of such pieces invariably reveals, when the whole cast assembles on one stage this is no longer possible.

For us the significance of contradiction is based in the collective dynamics of representation. It is problematic only in terms of its implications for collective support and that, in turn, depends on the relations between the different groups in which individuals are located. Thus the compatibility of different representations gains significance only in the context of group processes.

The analysis of group processes is important to us in another sense as well. It has been central to our position that individuals do not construct a world view in isolation. Collective support is important both to transmit ideas and also to provide the context in which they can be acted upon. In other words individuals do not spontaneously construct ideas that 'fit' their worlds. Rather, their understanding will be dependent on the ideas with which they come into contact and this in turn will depend upon the opportunities they have to become members of social groups. Practical considerations tend to limit the choice of affiliations to groups in the immediate neighbourhood and therefore the stance which individuals adopt will be affected by the distribution of conventional and oppositional groups in the close vicinity.

Bringing these various elements together we can now identify three broad factors which will bear upon the orientation to authority to which individuals incline and their ability to act upon those inclinations. The first concerns that individual's experience of formal authority, particularly in the context of the school, and the extent to which this fits with oppositional or conventional representations. The second covers the ideological relationship between these stances and other representations of significance to the individual as well as the practical relations between the different groups in which these various representations are upheld. The third and final factor has to do with the availability of collective support.

If our approach is adequate to explaining the complex pattern of delinquent action, it is necessary to show how both social structural and individual differences affect these various factors. We shall consider the two in turn.

8.3 Explaining Structural Differences

8.3.1 Age

Since our intention is to understand adolescent delinquency it is appropriate to begin by explaining why delinquent action is so much more prevalent in the years of early adolescence – in the years between 12 and 16 – than in any other period of life. We have already addressed this issue in part by arguing that this is the period of life in which formal institutions and formalized social relations assume a particular importance in the life of the individual. Delinquency flows from and is the expression of an antagonistic relation to formal authority. While this may explain the onset of delinquent action it does not in itself account for the drop-off. Why, once this antagonism is established, should offending begin to decline?

The short answer to this question is that around the age of 16 support for delinquency falls and repression increases. Let us begin with the issue of support, or to be more specific, with the collective resources which are necessary to develop and demonstrate an oppositional stance. When individuals first enter secondary school, previously formed groups are likely to be disrupted. Several lower schools will feed into the same upper school and not everyone from the same lower school will progress together. It will be some time before the group structure of the new entrants is firmly established. Thus there is some lag between entry and increased delinquency. We found it was between the first and the second year – between 11 and 12 – that delinquent activity doubled.

Once formed, this group structure is likely to stay fairly constant at least until individuals leave school. At this point groups will again be disrupted. Individuals will begin to move in different directions. Jobs or places on training schemes will be found with different employers, and leisure time too will be spent in different ways, including in courting relationships. Collective support for oppositional activity is facilitated by common involvement in an age-structured institution, the school. Those most likely to leave full time education at 16 are those previously most involved in delinquency. But departure from school also ends a daily routine which provided regular contact with like-minded peers.

As individuals come to the end of their schooling and approach adult institutions of work (or social security) another change takes place, They are increasingly treated as adults and held responsible in new ways as well as acquiring new rights. From our perspective the important change concerns the way in which people are held to account for their actions and therefore delinquency will have more serious repercussions.

In the eyes of younger adolescents it is possible to get into trouble, and even to get a police record, without any long-term consequences. Although there may be some ambiguity about the exact position, our interviews described in chapter 6 revealed that adolescents believe there are different consequences of delinquency at different ages.

This shift in accountability with age is important because, as reported in chapter 6, those young people who are more delinquent may also be cynical about the system, they may believe the future holds little for them, but they still recognize the importance of finding employment. They also recognize that jobs and a police record do not go together. One may recall here, for example, the case of the boy who first of all expressed no concern about getting a bad name or a police record, but then decided that there was indeed a contradiction between being in trouble with the police and his desire to get into the army (see p. 168). The great majority of the more delinquent youngsters we interviewed could see a connection between a bad reputation, in the form of a police record, and damaged employment prospects or other aspirations for the future.

This residual attachment to the system, even among 'High' delinquent youth, means the prospect that being caught will lead to criminalization does act as a deterrent. But if the link between being caught and criminalization is believed to hold only in late adolescence then it is a less relevant deterrent to these people when they are young. Thus we can identify a progression involving three stages for delinquent youth. As they enter the secondary school system they meet a new reality which has to be dealt with. To the extent that this system is seen as the imposition of illegitimate control then there is a second stage in which they lose any positive reasons to be good. At the same time there are few negative sanctions to stop them being bad. However, as they approach school leaving age there is a third stage in which cynicism is counterbalanced by the establishment of deterrence.

It is in the gap between the loss of positive attachment to authority and the reassertion of negative compliance – with authority in which delinquent action can flourish. Only in this gap can delinquency be an expression of opposition without carrying too high a cost. But the period from 12 to 16 is also when the collective support necessary for delinquency is most readily at hand. This combination of motive and means explains why adolescence is the age of delinquency.

8.3.2 Gender

With the rise of the women's movement in recent years a number of authors have challenged the way in which research into delinquency has dealt with the issue of gender. On the one hand many point out that much theory ignores girls completely (Campbell, 1981; McRobbie & Garber, 1975; Rosenbaum, 1989; Smart, 1977). Indeed, Chesney-Lind points out that many theorists are quite explicit about their masculine bias: 'the academic study of delinquent behaviour has, for all intents and purposes been the study of male delinquency. The delinquent is a rogue male, declared Cohen (1955, p. 140) in his influential book on gang delinquency. More than a decade later Hirschi, in his equally important book *The Causes of Delinquency* relegated women to a footnote which suggested, somewhat apologetically, that 'in the analysis that follows, the "non-Negro" becomes "white" and the girls disappear' (1969, p. 6).

On the other hand, when theory has dealt with female delinquency it has tended to emphasize the complete discontinuity between boys and girls. Campbell (1981) divides these theories into three categories. The first stresses biological and hormonal peculiarities of women; the second lays stress on women's genetic distinctiveness and the third deals with upbringing and socialization. The outcome of girls' socialization is to imbue them with desires and needs wholly different from those of boys; whereas boys seek satisfaction in social status, girls seek it in relationships (Morris, 1964); where boys want jobs 'it has been taken as axiomatic that the acquisition of a man is the only legitimate goal of females' (Campbell, 1981, pp. 79–80).

While these two tendencies might seem to be polar opposites, the one assimilating girls to theories based on boys and the other erecting a Chinese wall between the two, they actually stem from a common starting point. In both cases the reality of girls' experience is set aside, either completely ignored or else reduced to a sexist stereotype. Given these distortions it will be necessary to examine the issue of gender in more detail, for a complex task confronts us. We must challenge the view that girls are totally 'other than' boys while at the same time recognizing the specificity of girls' experience. In other words we must recognize both similarity and difference. However, for both purposes it is necessary to expand upon the traditional view of girls' lives as a solitary hunt for the perfect partner.

To start with, our research gives little support to the view that girls are solely interested in a domestic future. As the figures reported in chapter 6 reveal, when asked what they thought they would be doing when leaving school over half mentioned jobs or higher education. When asked what they would like to be doing three-quarters mentioned these destinations.

This is not meant to suggest that girls are disinterested in domestic roles. We have no reason to challenge Campbell's (1981) finding that working-class girls do aspire to being attractive wives and mothers. But it does mean it is wrong to counterpose different domains of interest.

Not only do girls have wider interests than is often assumed, they also participate more fully in social life. Campbell (1981) argued that past research on female delinquency had been particularly remiss in its failure to consider the peer group. Girls, she argues, not only join in social groups but are taking an increasingly forceful role in adolescent delinquent groups. Our research supports this view. As has been discussed at length, all adolescents irrespective of gender spend much of their time in the company of their peers, and those girls involved in delinquency are equally if not even more likely to pursue these activities in the company of others (Emler, Reicher & Ross, 1987). What is more, within delinquent groups as within non-delinquent groups, girls' descriptions of process match those of boys. We therefore concur with Campbell's argument that research on girls' delinquency 'must at last direct attention to the effect of the peer group' (1981, p. 92).

However, perhaps our most striking finding in this area is that, once the the effects of attitudes to formal authority are partialled out, the relationship between gender and delinquency all but disappears (cf. chapter 5). In other words, gender differences in levels of delinquent activity directly parallel gender differences in attitudes, and this points to both a similarity and a difference between boys and girls. On the one hand female delinquents, like their male counterparts, are distinguished from non-delinquents in their alienation from the institutions, figures and practices of formal authority. And, given equally negative views about such authority, they are equally delinquent. On the other hand, girls as a whole are much less likely to reject authority.

On the basis of these data we would argue that the processes we have been discussing in this book are not gender specific. For boys as well as for girls, delinquency is a collective activity and one which expresses a negative orientation to formal authority. The gender difference is not located in these processes but in their antecedents. In order to account for it we must ask why girls are much less willing to define themselves as oppositional.

We can begin to answer this question by recalling the meanings associated with an oppositional stance. Those individuals who adopt such a stance also intend to be perceived and are perceived as tough, hard, and unemotional. While this image is entirely consistent with the way in which men are traditionally defined in relation to women it is clearly dissonant with women's traditional relationship to men (Oakley, 1972). A woman whose actions support such an image risks failing to meet the criteria that render women attractive in heterosexual relationships (being soft, pliant, sensitive, affectionate) and thus risks exclusion from such relationships.

This may look like a simple variant of the argument that female criminality is inhibited by the female gender role (e.g. Adler, 1975). However, it differs from role theory in three important respects. First, it is not an argument that girls are locked into a domestic role. Both partnership and social position are important to girls and boys alike. Rather the issue has to do with the ways in which individuals are defined in the two spheres of activity. For males the definitions are consonant and therefore unproblematic. For females there is a dissonance which may make it difficult to reconcile the two spheres.

Second, for girls, 'reconciliation' does not necessarily mean conformism. What particular individuals do will depend on the options available to them. Where the labour market is relatively closed to girls then marriage may be a predominant aspiration and one in which an oppositional stance may well be a serious handicap. However, where employment opportunities are greater and women can gain adult status in other ways than through a man, oppositional activity is more viable.

To suggest this may seem to ignore evidence that there is no link between women's participation in the labour market and increased female crime (Box & Hale, 1984; Chapman, 1980; Jurik, 1983). However, this evidence largely relates to adult criminality and, as we have argued, the dynamics of delinquent behaviour are altered once an individual gains adult status and can be criminalized for offending. What is more, those women who are the principal beneficiaries of new employment trends are predominantly white and middle class (Naffine & Gale, 1989) and less disposed to be oppositional in the first place.

We are not proposing that entry to the workforce (or the future prospect of such entry) in itself increases girls' delinquency. Rather it will open a delinquent option to those girls who already feel hostility to formal authority. The data we have quoted do not address whether, amongst oppositional girls, alternatives to domestic labour increase the probability of delinquent action. There is at least some suggestive evidence in this regard. Sandhu and Allen (1969) found that delinquent girls were less committed to marriage, and Dorn (1983) has shown that, in situations where women have more employment opportunities, females are more willing to go out and seek excitement in public even if that means violating traditional norms of dependency on men.

Our third difference with role theory concerns the reasons why dissonance is a problem which requires resolution. For our perspective, the problem arises out of the fact that those peers with whom one appears as either oppositional or conformist also provide the population within which a partner is most likely to be found. If a girl is a 'hard case' the boys in her school and neighbourhood will know this and it is liable to make her less attractive as a long-term partner. It is the difficulty of maintaining incompatible self-definitions with a single audience rather than an internalized sense of role which renders delinquency problematic for girls.

This difficulty is important in another way when one considers the relationship between adolescents and their parents. Both males and females in our interview sample overwhelmingly mentioned parents as more important to them than anyone else. Moreover, nearly all of our respondents wished to be seen as 'good' by their parents and if they had been involved in delinquency they did not relish their parents knowing about it. There is no sex difference in the dissonance between delinquent and filial identities. There is, however, a difference when it comes to the respective opportunities of boys and girls to maintain a clear separation between the two.

A number of researchers have noted that parents keep a closer eye on daughters than on sons and that daughters are less free to go out as they choose (Hagan, Simpson & Gillis, 1987; Leonard, 1984; McRobbie & Garber, 1975). Campbell makes the point forcefully: 'one of the direct forms of social control is the fact that girls are kept at home while their older brothers are allowed to roam the streets' (1981, p. 60). Other work has recently confirmed that on the one hand teenage girls have more access to space in the home as a setting for peer sociability and on the other more of their socializing takes place in their own and friends' homes and less in public places, while more of their time is committed to domestic work (Emler & Abrams, 1989; Emler, 1989).

The implications of this are fourfold. In the first place, girls are less often on the streets, in public places and shops, which is to say in the common settings for delinquent activities. In a direct sense their opportunities to offend are limited. Second, their more limited public lives also reduce the incentive for the kind of self-protection that a delinquent identity in a delinquent group might seem to afford. Third, there will also be fewer abrasive encounters with authority. Finally, because they are more likely to congregate in homes, operating in what McRobbie and Garber (1975) call 'the culture of the bedroom', their friends are more likely to come into contact with their parents. Under these conditions it is difficult to be one thing to parents – dutiful, obedient daughter – and quite another – tough, reckless, rebellious – to peers. Consequently a dissonance between filial and delinquent identities is harder for girls to sustain.

When we argue that girls are less willing to adopt an oppositional stance because such a stance sits uneasily with other aspects of their lives we are therefore talking about more than a mismatch between ideologies. We are also referring to the practical relations in which those lives are lived; the resources available to girls, the options open to them, the connections between their various spheres of existence. We are not proposing that the four factors mentioned above are the only explanation of gender differences in delinquent action, for girls' social existence cannot be reduced to three sets of relationships however important they may be. However, we would argue that a fuller answer is to be found in applying the same principles to a richer picture of that existence, and only when female experience is given the same priority as male experience will our understanding increase. We agree fully with Chesney-Lind when she writes that 'the early insights into male delinquency were largely gleaned by intensive field observation of delinquent boys. Very little of this sort of work has been done in the case of girls' delinquency, though it is vital to an understanding of girls' definitions of their own situation, choices and behaviour' (1989, p. 25).

8.3.3 Class

If previous research on delinquency has tended to exclude the question of gender the opposite is true of class. Either implicitly or explicitly it has been assumed that working-class youth constitute the problem. This assumption is particularly apparent in the subcultural field. Whether it is due to the ecology of working-class areas (Shaw & McKay, 1931, 1942), to the preoccupations of working-class culture (Cohen, 1955) or to the absence of opportunity for working-class youth (Merton, 1957; Cloward & Ohlin, 1960), it is assumed that delinquent action is the preserve of disadvantaged males. Where other than working-class youth are considered it is to set them up as a point of contrast. Thus Sherif and Sherif (1964) provided a typology in which 'lower ranked' boys stole cars, 'middle ranked' boys borrowed them, and 'upper ranked' boys owned them.

As Chesney-Lind points out, this preoccupation with class but not gender is ironic since 'a clear relationship between social class position and delinquency is problematic, while it is clear that gender has dramatic and consistent effects on delinquency causation' (1989, p. 14). However, it would be wrong to ignore class entirely. An exclusive concentration on working-class delinquency should be challenged as strongly as the assumption that membership of the working class is intrinsically criminogenic. On the other hand, there is a relationship between social class background and involvement in delinquency which requires explanation.

Any foray into this area is inevitably dogged by the many controversies surrounding the concept of class. While some analysts have treated class in terms of how subjects themselves perceive social stratification (e.g. Centers, 1949; Warner & Lunt, 1941), on the whole analysts use their own criteria to define class positions. Different analysts use different criteria. For some, people should be allocated to class in terms of whether they command or whether they obey. For others, class should be decided according to whether a person is a worker or one for whom others work. However, as Haskell & Yablonsky (1971) point out, the great majority of American researchers define class in terms of whether people are rich or poor.

Our concern is not so much with the varying criteria analysts use to allocate people to classes as with an issue that is common to them all: how does economic class position affect understanding and action? In terms of our model of delinquency, the question can be further refined as follows: how does class affect orientations to formal authority and the opportunity to express them?

It is easy to invoke a series of class-related factors which might affect the way in which authority is viewed. These would vary from patterns of inconsistent discipline in families affected by the stresses of poverty (Patterson, 1986) to differential treatment of working-class youth by the police – causing hostility between them. Thus Roberts, in his study of *The Classic Slum* (1970) writes that: 'like their children, the poor, in general, looked upon (the policeman) with fear and dislike' (p. 100). However, given our insistence on school as the key formal institution in the lives of adolescents, it is worth concentrating on how class position may affect orientations to educational authority.

In the first place, a number of studies have proposed that there is a fundamental clash between the culture of working-class children and the culture of the school, which is essentially middle class (Willis, 1977). Working-class children are more likely to be criticized and even chastised for such things as the way they speak, the way they look and their manners. As a consequence they are likely to find authority more alien and discriminating than middle-class children. Secondly, working-class children may be indirectly penalized for their lack of resources. This may limit their ability to participate in school activities which have to be paid for or limit their ability to contribute to school fund-raising events and hence lead them to be seen as 'less committed' to the school. There is also a danger that, as the curriculum lays increasing stress on independent study work, that those without the facilities at home will suffer and hence come to see academic achievement as unjustly denied them. However, there is a third, and to our mind, far more important issue to be considered.

When working-class youth look around them, or when they consider the experience of older relations and acquaintances, they are far more likely than their middle-class counterparts to see people in unrewarding work if in work at all. Consequently they may assume that their own horizons are inherently limited whatever their exertions at school. Willis (1977), for instance, charts this assumption in some detail. In contrast, growing up in a middle-class milieu is likely to provide examples that show how good school results can make a difference (Dickinson, 1990; Emler & Dickinson, 1985). If, as we have argued, the acceptance of school authority depends upon the assumption that educational effort and educational success will be rewarded with enhanced opportunities after school, then working-class youth will be far more likely to reject this authority as illegitimate and oppressive.

So much for the inclination, how might class affect the possibilities for expressing opposition to authority? Let us start from the observation that delinquents are as keen to hide their transgressions from parents as they are to communicate them to peers. If so, then increased delinquency will be associated with decreased time spent in contact with the familial sphere. Our diary study data give some support to this argument. We saw (chapter 7) that the 'high delinquents' spent more time out of the home than the 'low delinquents' (5.8 nights per week compared to 4.2). The difference between the groups is much clearer in terms of what they do when they are out. The former spent more than twice as much time in 'hanging around' than the latter (2.3 nights a week compared to 1.1).

How and where one passes the time is likely to be related to resources. Where middle-class children may have their own rooms into which they can invite their friends, and their own televisions, videos and computers with which to entertain themselves, the working-class child is more likely to share rooms and resources with siblings and parents. Whereas more affluent teenagers may have a garden in which to play, their less affluent counterparts are unlikely to have such an option. Whereas the more privileged youth may have the money to go to cinemas, concerts and clubs, the less privileged youth will be far more limited. In sum, middle-class adolescents have opportunities which mean spending far more time where parents can see what they are getting up to or else in settings where any misdemeanours would be reported back. Working-class adolescents are far more limited to just 'hanging around' in the streets, open spaces and other domains where delinquent action could be kept from one's parents (Corrigan, 1976).

However, just being out and away from the parental gaze is unlikely to lead to delinquency in itself. Delinquent action requires the support and encouragement of like-minded peers. Therefore, we need to consider not only how the adolescent comes to be on the streets, but the availability of oppositional groups in the vicinity. This requires us to turn our attention towards a factor which is closely related to class – that is, area of residence.

8.3.4 *Area of residence*

The notion that inner cities are hotbeds of criminality is familiar enough. We have argued at length that it was the process of urbanization, the geographical differentiation of classes, which prompted the development of mass society theories, which in turn are the foundation of much work on delinquency. However, although the inclination to associate delinquency with district has a much longer history, systematic empirical investigation of the relationship largely begins with the Chicago school of social ecology. Park, Burgess and Mckenzie (1925) were interested in the characteristics of groups living in different city areas. Much subsequent research went into measuring differences between the five successive zones identified in their research. For instance, Shaw and McKay (1942) show that in zone 1 (central business district) rates of both delinquency and adult criminality are over five times higher than in zone 5 (commuter zone).

In explaining such differences between areas it is obviously important to pay close attention to class composition. However, it is equally important to avoid reducing area to class. In the first place, no area has a completely homogeneous class composition. Secondly, as the ecologists would stress, there may be considerable differences between areas with comparable class compositions. Cloward and Ohlin's (1960) assertion that social milieu has consequences over and above those of age, sex and socio-economic level is supported by the stronger correlation of delinquency with area than with class.

The most common account of the effects of area attributes them to level of social disorganization. For Shaw and McKay (1942) disorganization impedes the development of a stable neighbourhood, the control of the child and lawlessness. However, such a view is somewhat compromised by their own data which show disorganization to be highest in zone 2 but lawlessness to peak in zone 1.

Cloward and Ohlin (1960) provided one way out of this difficulty by suggesting that disorganization affects the type rather than the level of delinquency. In 'stable slum' areas the disadvantaged may learn illegitimate means to reach desired ends whereas this will not be possible in the 'disorganized slum' with the consequence that adolescents turn to malicious and negativistic behaviour. Unfortunately, this conflicts with the lack of evidence for these kinds of specialization among youthful offenders.

As has already been signalled, we see the impact of residential area upon delinquency as related to the availability of oppositional groups.

With respect to differences within urban areas, the stress lies on 'opposi-tional'. In other words, it is the comparative distribution of oppositional and conventional groups in different localities which is important. A 'critical mass' of individuals predisposed to a certain orientation will be needed in the locality before groups could form around this orientation. Given the importance of groups in adolescence, and given the difficulties in being part of groups from outside one's locality (apart from the practicalities of time, transport and money, the dangers of being attacked if from another 'scheme' also emerged in our own interviews), it follows that behaviour will be influenced by the nature of those groups on one's doorstep. With respect to urban–rural differences, the stress should be shifted to 'availability'. That is to say, where the population is relatively scattered, formation of any sort of group will be difficult. More specifically, as Geller (1980) argues, it is unlikely that there will be collective support for alternatives to the dominant social norms.

In addition, there is evidence that, in rural communities, individ-uals are more likely to be known and talked about by everybody else (Korte, 1980). If a group of teenagers were to get up to any mischief, the whole village would soon know about it. On the other hand, it may be easier to limit parental knowledge of one's behav-iour in the city. This draws us back to the issue of how far ado-lescents could pursue a delinquent reputation without their parents knowing of it. This is a consideration which not only differentiates between city and village but also between different city neighbour-hoods.

If class affects the opportunity to take advantage of organized enter-tainment, then area of residence will affect whether the resources exist to be taken advantage of in the first place. Some areas will be relatively well endowed with youth clubs, sports centres, recreational facilities, discos, cinemas and so on. In those that are not, going out means 'hanging around', loitering outside the chip shop, looking for some self-generated excitement. It is not that being out in the street leads to delinquency in and of itself. Rather it is easier to pursue an oppositional stance when one is outside the domains directly controlled by parents, authorities or other adults.

We have at least anecdotal evidence in support of such a link between lack of facilities, being on the streets and opportunity to undertake adolescent action. One of our interviewees, a 15-year-old boy, explained his own vandalism as deriving from the fact that 'there is nothing to do at nights, no community centre to go to'. Others used a similar explanation to account for delinquency in general. One 15-year-old boy simply stated 'There is nothing to do at nights.' A 16-year-old was more expansive.

Int.:   Why do you think people steal things?
Resp.:   There is nothing to do.
Int.:   And why do people vandalize?
Resp.:   Nothing to do. The community centre we've got – it is only a small place, it is not that big. There's about 300 go there at a time.

In summary, area differences in delinquency rates can be attributed to two complementary factors. The first is the degree of collective support in the locality for an oppositional stance, and this will be greater in areas of greater social deprivation. Secondly, the inclination and opportunity to express such a stance will be inversely related to time spend in domains of adult control – and hence to the wealth of public and private amenities in an area.

8.4 Explaining Individual Differences

The important thing to retain from the foregoing discussion is not so much the detail of each specific argument as the overall process of argumentation. For us, delinquency should not be seen as the expression of fixed qualities (or the lack of them). Rather, it is simultaneously an attempt to claim and a reflection of one's perceived place in the social world. Correspondingly, structural factors should not be seen as monolithic determinants of individuality. Instead, it is necessary to investigate how such factors affect one's experience and hence understanding of society. The focus must therefore lie on how structural position affects the minutiae of everyday life. How does it feed into what one does with one's time, where one goes, who one meets and the nature of one's encounters with other people and institutions? As Giddens (1973) argues of class, if social categories mean anything it is in the way that they denote systematic differences in people's practices. We do not claim to have identified all the ways in which age, gender, class and area of residence impinge upon lived experience in such a way as to affect delinquent action. Nor would we defend to the death each and every one of our suggestions as to the effects they do have – some of the claims depend upon speculative assumptions about the experience of different groups. What we would insist on, however, is an approach that aims to translate abstract categories into the concrete realities of adolescent experience. Any shortcomings in our understanding of how structural factors affect delinquency will not be rectified by abandoning that quest but rather by deepening our acquaintance with young people's lives.

Exactly the same logic can be used to explain individual differences in delinquent action. For instance, while social class may be a remote and general determinant of how adolescents spend their leisure time, the immediate decision whether to stay in or go out of an evening, and what to do once out, will be affected by a host of more idiosyncratic factors. If staying at home depends upon having one's own space, this will not only be a function of house size but also of such factors as family size and as whether one has priority in having a room by virtue of age or having no same-sex siblings. When out, having more money may make it more likely that one will pay for entertainment that is under adult supervision. However, one's choice will also be affected by the price of such facilities as well as the precise availability and proximity of free facilities.

Such considerations are not only relevant to the issue of adult supervision. They apply equally well to all the other elements that we have employed to build up a model of delinquent action. Take the core issue of orientation to institutional authority (especially the school). While school culture may, overall, be more alienating for working-class children, this will depend upon the nature of individual schools. The experience of a given person will also depend upon the individual teachers who have taught them over the years as well as the precise culture of the home. Similarly, commitment to education as a route to future success may be less for a class whose work horizons are generally more limited. However, if, as we have suggested, this is mediated through the adolescent's observation of what happened to parents, close siblings and friends, then the precise perception will vary from individual to individual. We have also seen other considerations to be of importance – such as whether the prospect of a safe job in waiting (a place in one's father's window-cleaning business or whatever) renders school performance irrelevant.

It is not our intention to go through and evaluate all such considerations in detail. Once again, the thing to retain is the logic rather than the details of explanation. Here, even more than in the case of structural differences, the aim is more to illustrate how our approach allows individual differences to be explained rather than to pretend that the issues are definitively settled. We simply want to show that it makes sense to root our investigations in how the details of individual lives impinge upon understandings of formal authority, the availability of collective support and the pattern of supervision. It is for the future to identify and examine the many factors that may be of relevance.

For the present, this approach stands in stark contrast to traditional psychological explanations of individual differences. For us, such approaches – based on the notion that delinquent action is the reflection of some chronic internal deficit – suffer both from errors of omission and of commission. Throughout this book we have challenged the notion that only internal psychological controls stand between order and anarchy. We have argued at length that an exclusive concentration on such intra-psychic variables omits the importance of social controls based on the importance of reputation and the centrality of collective support in the adolescent world.

The traditionalist could still retort that deficit models may not be the whole story, but they are certainly part of the story. Even in terms of our own approach, such models might be used to explain why individuals are anti-authority and why they choose the company of like-minded peers. However, even such a diluted position will not do. Different theorists propose many different forms of deficit. Delinquents are variously said to be less intelligent, to be morally backward, to lack social skills, to suffer from unresolved Oedipal conflicts – and a host of other things besides. However, as we have shown, none of these propositions gains more than equivocal support from the evidence. Moreover, an image of the delinquent as retard does not accord with the experience of our own research.

One incident may help illustrate this. We had been collecting some attitude data amongst our most delinquent sample and finished with some time to spare. One pupil then offered to collect up the completed forms. As this was going on a commotion arose. The boy at the centre of it claimed that he was only trying to help by collecting up the pencils we had handed out, but in so doing he was also removing pencils that belonged to his peers – and they, not surprisingly, were resisting. This was but one of several incidents in which the class played with us (an experience which will probably be familiar to most teachers – although not always with such good humour). What was interesting about these incidents has to do with the sophistication they displayed. They were not simple violations of rules. Rather they involved the subversion of officially sanctioned conduct in such a way that a legitimate account could be offered once the perpetrator was challenged – and hence punishment could be avoided. Such behaviour indicates an understanding of rules, an understanding of the consequences of violating them, an understanding that differing rule systems may come into conflict such that what is required under one is disbarred under another and, finally, considerable finesse in interpreting actions as satisfying one rule rather than violating another. Half an hour of dealing with these ploys, and anticipating how each seemingly legitimate request might be used to make mischief, was as mentally challenging as any academic discussion. These were not unskilled individuals. It was just that they used their skills in ways that authority condemns.

However, our objection is not only that deficit accounts have trouble accounting for research results, it is also that that they embody a flawed model of human psychology. It is not that individual characteristics are irrelevant, but rather that it is misleading to treat them as if they affect behaviour in isolation from other factors. Take aggressiveness: while some researchers have sought to explain this in terms of inherent tendencies of the child and others have sought to locate an explanation in styles of parenting, it would seem that both need to be included in an explanation of aggressive behaviour (Patterson, 1986; Vuchinich, Bank & Patterson, 1992). It is the way in which particular behavioural tendencies in the child are understood and responded to by the parent that affects the future behaviour of the child and hence the future interaction between parent and child. Indeed the same initial tendency may lead to fundamentally different paths of development as a function of how it is reacted to. A baby which is highly responsive and cries easily may be a problem child for some parents, but a sensitive child for others. Thus, level of physiological responsiveness may have a fundamental effect on the child's future, but that effect is entirely dependent upon how this characteristic is given meaning in the social context.

If development is a function of relationships rather than characteristics, then the implication is that people will change as soon as their relationships change. This might seem to suggest a model of human beings as akin to ping-pong balls – batted from one extreme to the other as soon as the context changes. However, this is to ignore the fact that people are not just made in the image of society but that they actively seek to make society in their own image. It is the balance between the two that is important. Where the world changes despite us, it is likely that we too will change. Where we have choice, we are likely to seek and mould contexts which confirm who we are. This is illustrated by Altemeyer's findings concerning authoritarianism. Those who have learnt negative views of oppressed groups will characteristically structure their social world so as to never have their views disconfirmed. The continuity of attitude is striking. However, when transplanted into an entirely new context where they have to interact with others in new ways – say by going to university – dramatic shifts in viewpoint can occur (Altemeyer, 1988).

This logic can be adapted to the issue of delinquency. If we want to know why individuals adopt a negative attitude to school and to the law, it is clearly important to look to the adolescent's history. Even if, as we have argued, the precise problem of how to orientate oneself to a system of formal authority is new, past experiences will be brought to bear upon it. One's encounters with other forms of authority – familial, primary school, police – and one's knowledge of others' experiences are all likely to be relevant. What is more, to the extent that it is possible, one is likely to seek out others with similar attitudes and interests (Kandel, 1978). The evidence suggests that those who are anti-authority will form groups with anti-authority peers and reject those who are pro-authority (Cairns et al., 1988; Vuchinich et al., 1992). In such circumstances the group does not create orientations to authority from nothing. Rather it amplifies them and allows their expression in delinquent action. Thus we would expect, and we find, a strong overall continuity between anti-social behaviour at age 10 and membership of anti-social groups at age 12.

However, choice of peers is never completely free. As well as wanting to be with others who share our values and beliefs we tend to go for relationships that involve least effort (Catton & Smircich, 1964). We relate to those who are most easily available either in terms of proximity (Festinger, Schachter & Back, 1950) or predictability of regular contact (Emler, 1990; Emler & Grady, 1986). There will be times when the peers who are easily available don't share the adolescent's pre-existing attitudes. Or else, moving from one place to another may disrupt one's association with peers who supported one orientation and bring one into contact with peers who support another. Examples were given in the previous chapter.

This suggests a second level at which the effects of individual characteristics are mediated by social context. Not only do such characteristics impact upon development as a function of the social significance accorded to them, but also the continuity between earlier and later development depends upon the degree of control that individuals exert over their social environment. Rather than considering individuality in the abstract, we are inexorably led back to asking about the way it contributes to the realities of everyday life.

The reason for this repeated insistence on everyday life is that such a focus allows us to avoid many of the problems that bedevil work on delinquency and in the social sciences more generally. Most importantly, it allows us to treat social structure and individual characteristics as mutually implicated in constituting a single reality rather than confronting each other as explanatory alternatives. By always looking to the ways in which either factor shapes – or is shaped by – this reality, we are led away from simple determinisms whereby one level of explanation excludes all others. Just as economists might argue that it is easy to control inflation and easy to control interest rates on their own – the real trick being to manage both – so we would argue that it is easy to provide accounts that just deal with structural differences in delinquency and equally easy to provide accounts that just deal with individual differences in delinquency. In the end our primary concern is neither with the one nor the other. Rather, it has been to provide a single model of delinquency that is capable of dealing with both. To the extent that we have been successful, our approach should have wider implications. First of all it should not just be a model, but a guide to action. As we are constantly reminded, there is nothing as practical as a good theory. Secondly, it should be relevant not just to adolescent delinquency but also to the general topic of behavioural control. We shall conclude with some brief observations concerning these practical and theoretical issues.

8.5 Implications for Intervention, Prevention and Remediation

Before discussing the solutions, it is worth reminding ourselves of the problem. As we pointed out right from the start, this is a book about mundane delinquency. We are dealing with those relatively petty acts whose significance lies in the fact that they are so widespread and therefore add up to a major social phenomenon. However, there is a tendency to discuss delinquency by reference to the exceptions. When a particularly spectacular or disturbing crime is committed by a young person, a public debate ensues as to causes and remedies for youth crime in general. In Britain, the most recent example was the murder of two-year-old Jamie Bulger by two ten-year-olds. This was held to be symbolic of a general social malaise and led to an explosion of speculation as to the causes. All the usual culprits were considered: was delinquency due to the breakdown of the family? Did it stem from the increase in single-parent families? Was lack of parental discipline, school discipline and penal discipline to blame? Most notably, it was suggested that violent videos were to blame. This was based on the fact that one such video, Child's Play 3, was found in the home of one of the accused even though there was no indication that he had ever watched it. None the less, starting from such tenuous evidence, the law on renting videos was tightened up. We would simply point out that, whatever the causes of such exceptional crimes, there is no reason to suppose that they are the same as those for petty misdemeanours. Equally, the remedies that may be appropriate for those at the extremes may be ineffective or even counter-productive for the everyday delinquent. Far from using incidents like the Jamie Bulger case to initiate a discussion about delinquency, perhaps there should be a moratorium on discussion while such emotive incidents remain in the public mind.

A second factor which affects discussion of delinquency has to do with the politics of law and order. It is impossible to separate out explanation from attributions of responsibility and blame. Any theory highlights particular antecedents of crime and, as a corollary, downplays others. In so far as one of the prime concerns of government, at least within a liberal-democratic system, is to guarantee a peaceful social order, there will be considerable official resistance to any theories which place the causes of crime in domains over which government has responsibility. Crime cannot be caused by policies on housing, education, employment or whatever. It is generally put down to individual factors or else aspects of the private domain – such as parenting. Thus, in recent years government ministers have repeatedly denied a connection between unemployment and crime – even when privately admitting it to be self-evident. Equally, governments have instituted policies in order to appear tough on law and order (the most obvious example being the introduction of harsh penal regimes for young offenders) even when their own research had told them in advance that such policies would be counter-productive.

Given such powerful pressures towards obfuscation, it is remarkably hard to gain a hearing for any balanced discussion of how delinquency should be tackled. Nevertheless, this renders the attempt all the more important. From our perspective, it is possible to put proposed solutions into three categories. First of all, there are false proposals which will at best be ineffective and may even exacerbate the problem. It should be clear by now that we have little faith in those interventions which are based on the notion that delinquents need help to remedy supposed deficits. This would include such things as attempts to raise offenders' levels of moral reasoning, social skills training and programmes to enhance intellectual growth.

On similar grounds, we would question the causal connection which is made between media violence and delinquency. The idea that watching a lot of violence will lead young people to go out and do likewise presupposes that they are acting without judgement. Though, in actual fact, theorists don't suppose that people will copy exactly what they have seen. Children who watch Tom and Jerry will not go out and try to drop cartoon grandfather clocks on cartoon mice. Children who see Clint Eastwood as 'Dirty Harry' will not seek to kill villains using large revolvers. Rather it is presupposed that children will copy the general category which the analyst terms 'violence'. But why should children take from the film what the analyst sees in the film? Why should they not construe the action in terms of some other category? Moreover, even if the viewer does see a programme or film as violent that doesn't mean that he or she will copy it. We have already noted that plenty of our non-delinquents see fighting close at hand but it makes them want to shun those involved rather than fight themselves. If that is so in real life why should individuals mechanically succumb to media representations? Once again, the assumption of a media-violence link rests on the false assumption that young people in general – and delinquents in particular – lack the ability to think for themselves. That evidence which purports to show such a link is flawed by confusing cause and effect. Delinquents may enjoy watching violence (or rather, being seen to watch violence) for it shows how hard they are. However, it does not follow that the watching makes them delinquent (Duhs and Gunter, 1988; Lande, 1993; Wiegman, Kuttschreuter and Baarda, 1992).

The one other false proposal that needs to be commented on is the idea that strict, punitive regimes, 'short sharp shocks' or other 'aversion therapies' are the solution to delinquency in general. We have already noted their popularity in certain sectors and the evidence of their failure. This is hardly surprising. On the one hand, an experience of formal authority as cold, impersonal and punitive is hardly likely to improve one's attitude towards it. On the other, to celebrate physical 'hardness', to force one into the company of others who offend and to cut one off from all other social contacts is the ideal way of ensuring that individuals will act upon this hostility. Indeed the basic premise of such regimes – that delinquents offend because they don't have an adequate fear of punishment – is a profound misreading of delinquent psychology.

The second category of solutions covers what we would call panaceas. These are proposals that might have short-term or localized impact on delinquent action but which only displace the problem elsewhere. They certainly don't provide a full solution. In one sense, the penal regimes we have just dealt with could be placed in this category. They are sometimes justified on the basis that at least people don't offend while inside. This is only partially true since inmates may and do offend against each other. None the less, the logic is that people don't offend as long as they are constrained and supervised. That may be true. The only problem is that offending may increase as soon as the bonds are removed. The same can be argued about less coercive forms of surveillance.

For instance, the use of closed-circuit cameras in public places to deter delinquency is becoming increasingly popular. They are being installed not only in large cities but also in small rural towns, not only in city centres but also on university campuses (including the roof of the building in which these words are being written). Popular though they are, they raise two questions. Firstly, won't crime simply be displaced from locations under surveillance to those which are not? Moreover, since the cameras are normally placed amongst those who can afford to pay for them, won't this cause increased misery amongst the under-privileged and increased perceptions of social inequality? This leads into the second point. Won't such schemes lead to increased hostility to privilege and authority? On the one hand, surveillance is likely to mean those who look less 'respectable' being subject to more stops and interference. More generally, Giddens (1991) makes the point that trust and surveillance are correlated such that those who we trust more are those who require less surveillance (this is certainly true of jobs). However the corollary may equally well be true: if we are kept under increased surveillance it indicates that we are trusted less. The experience of being observed by the camera eye suggests that we are thought of as potentially dangerous and disreputable. It may well increase antagonism to the authorities behind the eye.

There are other interventions which can only function as panaceas to the extent that they are limited to cosmetic as opposed to structural changes. For instance, it follows from our argument that increased provision of easily available leisure facilities will lessen the time spent hanging around on the street where delinquent action is most likely to occur. However, where such provision is simply imposed without consultation it may well be perceived as an act of social control. This will lessen the likelihood that it is used but, even if it is used, it will do nothing to undermine perceptions of antagonism to the authorities. Indeed such facilities may even be perceived as symbols of inequality and become targets of vandalism themselves. This is very different from provision which responds to local demands and is accountable to young people themselves. We are reminded of a debate which occured in the aftermath of the St. Pauls riot. Local council officials expressed their dismay at what had happened in the light of considerable spending on facilities in St Pauls. The local 'defence committee' responded that a lot of money might have been spent *on* St Pauls, but very little was spent *with* the people of St Pauls.

Perhaps the clearest example of such cosmetic panaceas comes in attempts to portray the friendly face of authority. For instance, there are many schemes which involve community policemen coming into schools and showing themselves to be kind, friendly and helpful human beings. The problem with this is that it ignores the fact that changing our views of one individual need not change our stereotype of the groups to which they belong – they can simply be dismissed as an exception to the rule (Hewstone & Brown, 1987). Moreover, as long as young people have experiences of the arbitrary use of police power elsewhere in their lives, the occasional smiling face will have little impact (Hewstone, Hopkins & Routh, 1992; Hopkins, 1994b). We are not suggesting that it is always futile to change the ways in which young people see authority. Indeed Tyler's work suggests that, to the extent that people consider judicial procedures to be legitimate, they will view judicial authority positively even when they are punished by it (Tyler, 1990). However, demonstrating legitimacy is very different from changing the tone of interactions. Such changes in appearances will only work if they reflect changes at all levels of the relationship between young people and authority.

This takes us on to our final category: enduring solutions. If delinquency is the expression of a negative orientation to formal authority – especially school authority – how is it possible to improve this orientation? To start with, it is necessary to realize that this question cannot be answered at a school level alone. In part adolescents reject school because of what they believe – and experience – of life beyond school: unemployment and drudgery in the main. Without addressing the nature of the labour market, levels of unemployment and barriers to social mobility, educational initiatives can only ever be partially effective. Perhaps the greatest error of moves towards comprehensivization was to overstate their case. The dream of the 1960s that educational opportunity would bring about equality of its own accord underestimated the extent to which the educational process itself is permeated by inequalities. These need urgent attention.

First of all, children come to the starting post on radically different terms. The later the post is set the greater these differences are likely to be. Some children will have been given the resources and the encouragement to exploit school when eventually they enter class while others will not. Feeling the odds are stacked against them may lead many children to withdraw from the game. This might explain the effectiveness of early interventions (Kazdin, 1987; Yoshikawa, 1994; Zigler et al., 1992) and especially the provision of early educational support. The most famous example of this is the Perry pre-school project (Berreuta-Clement et al., 1984) which provided one to two years of nursery education for three- to four-year-olds. Although the programme was intended primarily to enhance intellectual functioning, it had far wider effects, including on subsequent anti-social behaviour. Its effects can be interpreted as consequences of the more successful adaptation of those in the programme to formal schooling. Moreover, additional features of the programme, which included frequent home visits by teachers, may well have contributed to this adaptation in various ways. For example, these features of the programme may have helped foster conditions in which the parents developed and sustained good relations with the school and with their children's teachers. Perhaps one of the best ways of improving educational commitment and reducing delinquency would be the provision of nursery education to all those who wish to partake of it. Such a programme may be costly but it could be one of the best investments any government could make.

A good start is therefore crucial. However, it will be wasted unless matched by subsequent experience. As we have already noted, there is a worrying tendency for educational cutbacks to mean that even basic educational provision depends upon parental contribution. This is likely to reopen the inequality of educational experience that initiatives such as the Perry pre-school project helped to close. Similarly, there has been justified praise for activity-based project work introduced into the curriculum but unless resources are provided such that all children do the work on equal terms then the social cost could come to outweigh the educational advantage. Once again, this may require funding upfront, but it may save considerably more resources in the long term.

As well as ensuring that all pupils have the resources to fulfil educational tasks, it is also important that all are equally valued. One of the problems of recent moves to ever bigger schools – it is not uncommon for British high schools to exceed 1,500 pupils – is that it is easy to consign those who do badly to 'sink classes' and concentrate on achievers. The pressures to do this are exacerbated as league tables of exam results are used as a basis for evaluating schools. The danger with this is not only that it leads to a vicious circle of failure, alienation and further failure but also that it ensures that the alienated pupil only has peers who share a hostility to the school system. Smaller schools (and smaller classes) could ensure both that all pupils feel valued and also that their patterns of social support are more heterogenous. After all, there simply won't be enough troublesome pupils to dump them all together in the same class. Moreover, as Barker (1968) recognized long ago, schools as small communities that are also rich in valued roles and identities can successfully engage a larger proportion of their inhabitants.

This raises a further question of what people are valued for and also how their values can be expressed. One of the marks of our society is the separation between manual and intellectual pursuits. To have physical prowess is to be stupid and to be clever is to be soft. For those who value being hard and strong, educational values can easily appear as alien and therefore be rejected. Those who work hard are to be pitied as effete dupes. The system that tries to get one to work hard is the enemy. That, after all, is the core of Willis's conclusion from his study of working-class boys (Willis, 1977). While in part this culture may be in decline as manual labour declines (figures in *The Guardian* newspaper of 25 February 1995 show that manual labourers have fallen from 65 per cent to 51 per cent of the male labour force in the period 1971–91) it remains a significant phenomenon.

There are two ways of addressing this phenomenon. One is to ensure that physical pursuits are valued alongside intellectual pursuits. This means such things as not treating metalwork like a subject only fit for those who fail at mathematics but rather as something that is important for all. However, it must be stressed that changing values in school will mean nothing as long as the differentials continue to be expressed in radically different pay rates outside school. For such reasons it is hard to foresee rapid changes in this direction.

A second way forward, therefore, is to try and reassess the meaning of what it means to be hard and streetwise. Willis's pessimistic message is that the last laugh is taken from the boys who reject school. They may correctly see the bias in education and recognize the likelihood that they will end up in manual labour. However, by rejecting education they ensure that this becomes a self-fulfilling prophecy. Is it utopian to suppose that one could turn this message around by persuading pupils that the real way of getting one over the system is to succeed in it? Similarly, can't being hard be defined as derision for petty insults rather than bothering to batter the perpetrators? Whatever the value of these particular suggestions, the general point is that the meaning of values and beliefs is not set in stone but rather is open to interpretation and debate (Billig, 1987). To the extent that this is so, 'hard' and 'clever' might be redefined as consonant rather than contradictory. More generally, it makes sense to investigate other channels through which physical prowess can be expressed. From this perspective the 'adventure holidays' much maligned in the tabloid press seem logical and imaginative initiatives.

There is one final solution that all the evidence (if not all the theories) point to: time. At the age of 15 or 16 most delinquent action will cease. The danger is that overly draconian responses to adolescent misdemeanours will impede this decline by metaphorically and/or literally imprisoning people in a criminal milieu. There is also a danger that overly dramatic theories of delinquency will facilitate – or at least justify – such measures. One important remedy is therefore to retain balance in our theories of delinquency, to resist demonization of delinquents and to recognize that delinquent action is a fairly widespread activity amongst many people who are later seen as respectable members of the community. In that sense, we would like to see this book as partially a remedy as well as an explanation.

8.6 The Theory of Social Control

This has been a book about adolescent delinquency. We have focused on a narrow range of conduct and we have not considered either adult or childhood conduct in any detail. However, we believe that there are implications in the analysis presented here which generalize beyond the particular conditions of adolescence and touch upon our understanding of the nature of social control. The two principal concepts in social psychology's interpretation of social control have been socialization and social influence. The former has taken social control to be a matter of self-control based on psychological mechanisms incorporated into the individual personality during childhood. The latter is treated as a situationally specific means of control. However, the two have by no means been treated equally. It is socialization, and the development of a sound autonomous sense of self, which has been assigned the major role in assuring that behaviour is rationally controlled by reference to clear values. The major role assigned to social influence is that of undermining rational control and substituting mindless conformity. Our theoretical criticism of such approaches has been twofold. On the one hand, we argue that people do not only hold one set of values associated with the autonomous individual self. They may also act in terms of a collective sense of self and hence take on board the associated collective values. This is the 'social identity' side of our position. On the other hand, we argue that adherence to standards does not necessarily depend upon internalized values. It may also be assured by face-to-face interactions, personal relationships, the promise of social acceptance or the threat of social rejection. This is the 'reputational' side of our position.

What counts is the way in which the two act together. It is important to recognize that the private claim to an identity depends upon public acceptance of that claim and social support for expressing that claim. This introduces a degree of inertia into our identities, depending upon the stability of our social environments. In effect one cannot be a Catholic or socialist today and Protestant or Conservative tomorrow because one's acquaintances will not readily accept such shifting claims, any more than one can be a delinquent today and a saint tomorrow.

It is also necessary to acknowledge that the ways in which one builds a reputation – who one seeks to impress and how one seeks to impress them – will depend upon the identity to which one aspires. To try to seek acceptance from one's academic peers in the same way one seeks acceptance from fellow football fans could land one in a lot of trouble. Thus we must ask the questions 'what identity?' and 'what reputation?' together, and we must ask how each affects the other. In this final section, we draw attention to some implications of these questions for a general understanding of social control.

As long as the individual self is seen as the sole seat of values then questions of control resolve to considerations of when this self is stronger or weaker. Once we acknowledge that there may be different values associated with different senses of self then such talk of 'loss of self' and 'loss of values' becomes meaningless. Instead it becomes necessary to examine how different senses of self lead to the adoption of different values. In particular, it is necessary to lose our generic fear of the social group. Groups may certainly change the basis on which our behaviour is controlled, but they certainly don't remove it. Of course, this is not to deny that certain groups behave in extremely undesirable ways. What is more, given the power of numbers, such behaviour may be even more problematic than that of isolated individuals. However, it is important to assess correctly the location of the problem. If Nuremburg rallies promote racism it is because those who participate adopt racist ideologies, not because they have lost their minds. The phenomenon needs to be addressed at the level of social values rather than individual psychology.

It follows from our argument that one of the principal ways of affecting behavioural control is by manipulating the identities in terms of which people act. Indeed analysis of political discourse suggests that one of the main ways in which politicians seek to influence mass action is through the ways in which they define social categories: both what categories are relevant in a given situation and what values are associated with these categories (Reicher & Hopkins, in press a,b).

It is not just the politician who uses rhetorical skills to define identity and it is not just that others define who we are. In the active search for reputation, rhetorical sophistication is one of the primary prerequisites. Take the debate concerning childhood developments in the capacity for moral judgement. Extensive and sophisticated capacities of these kinds do not appear to play the direct role in self-control that has been proposed for them, so what functions do they serve? If we recognized that these are also, or perhaps primarily capacities for argument, and not just systems for thinking (and indeed the only evidence for their existence is in the moral arguments that children and adults provide in response to the questions of researchers, cf. Kohlberg, 1984; Piaget, 1932) then we can immediately anticipate a different kind function they might serve. They provide individuals with means for controlling one another, through criticism, argument and persuasion (cf. also Billig, 1987). Moral education programmes intended to develop moral reasoning abilities may produce few direct improvements in the behaviour of the individuals involved. But if they successfully enhance children's or adolescents' capacities to formulate and articulate moral criticisms they are certainly necessary to the claiming of identity and hence implicated in the process of behavioural control.

The deployment of such rhetorical skills is a vital part of our social life. It is not just in adolescence that we depend upon others. Indeed it might be argued that at least in education, progress will ultimately depend upon anonymous exams which we do alone and where performance alone should be taken into account. In adulthood, we depend upon others not only for our leisure activities but also for our progress at work. It is therefore essential that we are seen as acceptable to those we depend upon. Such judgements are more likely to be made on the basis of reputation than direct experience – although the promotional procedures in organizations may use inappropriate dimensions of reputation (Emler & Hogan, 1993). Indeed the dissemination of reputational information is one of the primary means by which communities protect themselves from the harm that could be done by accepting those who are either incompetent or hostile to their aims (Emler, 1994). To trust others with resources, power or influence means that we have to confident that they will use them in ways we approve of. The point is not only relevant to formal organizations. Any coordination in any human organization depends upon the forging of agreements (Mintzberg, 1973). Being accepted into such coordinations therefore depends upon being seen as the sort of person who can be relied upon to keep their agreements.

The task of establishing a reputation is as complex as it is vital. We must not only know what behaviours are appropriate, but we also have to be our own 'spin-doctors' – offering acceptable interpretations of our behaviour in case it should be understood in ways that damage our reputational ambitions. We have to know how to use social networks in order to 'leak' information that will bolster or defend our image. We have to be able to deploy accounting strategies that deflect the impact of actions that might seem inappropriate. Finally, all of this will be complicated should we wish to establish different reputations with different audiences: colleagues, friends, family and so on. Much of the dynamics of social control is to be explained by reference to the opportunities afforded for reputation management due to one's place in systems of social networks and by the abilities of individuals to take advantage of these opportunities.

The fact that behaviour is visible to others has been the key observation upon which our psychology of reputation has been built. It allows us to address such issues as to whom the behaviour is visible and the means by which we seek to manipulate its visibility. However, it is important to note that these issues are relevant to the matter of identity as well. Our own work shows that who we can see affects how we see ourselves. For instance, being surrounded by ingroup members is likely to increase the salience of group identity. What is more, relations of visibility will affect our ability to express such social identities. Thus, increased visibility to an outgroup will make it harder to express those aspects of ingroup identity that are unacceptable to that outgroup (Reicher, Spears & Postmes, in press). The key point, however, is that we do not wish the distinction between identity and reputational aspects of our approach to be seen as reflecting a new division between intra-psychic and social determinants of action. Instead we would stress that our social location structures our identity every bit as much as our identities structure our public action.

Final chapters are the traditional place to contemplate the wider significance of earlier and tighter discussions. They therefore run a thin line between theoretical imagination and theoretical fantasy. This has been a particularly speculative end to a speculative chapter. Our earlier discussion was mainly aimed at showing how our model of delinquency provides a possible means of explaining structural and individual differences in commission rates. Similarly, the aim of the present section is to show how our underlying assumptions provide a starting point for reorienting the study of social control. We propose that such a study might profitably be based on an analysis of identity, reputation and the structuring of both by reference to relations of visibility. This in turn depends upon overturning an even more basic assumption. Still, in today's mediatized and atomized society our acts do not pass without notice. Modernists, even post-modernists, still have friends.

References

Adelson, J. (1964) The mystique of adolescence. *Psychiatry, 27*, 1–5.

Adelson, J. (1971) The political imagination of the young adolescent. *Daedalus, 100*, 1013–50.

Adler, F. (1975) *Sisters in Crime*. New York: Mcgraw Hill.

Adler, F. (1979) Changing patterns. In F. Adler and R. Simon (eds) *The Criminology of Deviant Women*. Boston: Houghton-Mifflin.

Ageton, S.S. and Elliott, D.S. (1974) The effects of legal processing on self-concept. *Social Problems, 22*, 87–100.

Ageton, S.S. and Elliott, D.S. (1978) The dynamics of delinquent behavior: A national survey. *MTT 27552*, Project Report no. 3.

Akers, R.L., Krohn, M.D., Lauza-Kaduce, L. and Radesovich, M. (1979) Social learning and deviant behavior: A specific test of a general theory. *American Sociological Review, 44*, 636–55.

Allinsmith, W. (1960) The learning of moral standards. In D.R. Miller and G.E. Swanson (eds) *Inner Conflict and Defence*. New York: Holt, Rinehart and Winston.

Allport, F.H. (1924) *Social Psychology*. Cambridge: Houghton-Mifflin.

Allport, F.H. (1934) The J-curve hypothesis of conforming behavior. *Journal of Social Psychology, 5*, 141–83.

Allsopp, J.F. and Feldman, P.M. (1976) Personality and antisocial behaviour in school boys. *British Journal of Criminology, 16*, 337–51.

Altemeyer, B. (1988) *Enemies of Freedom*. San Francisco: Josey-Bass.

Archer, D. (1985) Social deviance. In G. Lindzey and E. Aronson (eds) *Handbook of Social Psychology*. Vol. 2, 3rd edn. New York: Random House.

Aronfreed, J. (1968) *Conscience and Conduct*. New York: Academic Press.

Asch, S.E. (1956) Studies of independence and conformity: A minority of one against a unanimous majority. *Psychological Monographs, 7*, no. 9 (Whole No. 416).

Averill, J.R. (1983) Studies on anger and aggression: Implications for theories of emotion. *American Psychologist*, November, 1145–60.

Bailey, R. (1971) *Gifts and Poison: The Politics of Reputation*. Oxford:

Blackwell.

Bandura, A. (1964) The stormy decade: Fact or fiction? *Psychology in the Schools, 1,* 224–31.

Bandura, A. (1969) *Principles of Behavior Modification.* New York: Holt, Rinehart and Winston.

Bandura, A., Ross, D. and Ross, S.A. (1963). Imitation of film-mediated aggressive models. *Journal of Abnormal and Social Psychology, 66,* 3–11.

Bandura, A. and Walters, R.M. (1959) *Adolescent Aggression.* New York: Ronald Press.

Banks, M., Bates, I., Breakwell, G., Bynner, J., Emler, N., Jamieson, L. and Roberts, K. (1992) *Careers and Identities.* Milton Keynes: Open University Press.

Barker, R.G. (1968) *Ecological Psychology.* Stanford, CA: Stanford University Press.

Barrows, S. (1981) *Distorting Mirrors.* Yale: Yale University Press.

Baumeister, R. and Tice, D.M. (1986) How adolescence became the struggle for self: A historical transformation of psychological development. In J. Suls and A.G. Greenwald (eds) *Psychological Perspectives on the Self,* vol. 3. Hillsdale, NJ: Erlbaum.

Becker, H.S. (1963) *The Outsiders.* New York: Free Press.

Berrueta-Clement, J.R., Schweinhart, L.J., Barnett, W.S., Epstein, A.S. and Weikart, D.P. (1984) *Changed Lives: The Effects of the Perry Preschool Program on Youths through Age 19.* Ypsilanti, MI: High/Scope Press.

Berti, A.E. and Bombi, A.S. (1988) *The Child's Construction of Economics.* Cambridge: Cambridge University Press.

Billig, M. (1987) *Arguing and Thinking.* Cambridge: Cambridge University Press.

Black, D. (1983) Crime as social control. *American Sociological Review, 48,* 34–45.

Blackmore, J. (1974) The relationship between self-reported delinquency and official convictions amongst adolescent boys. *British Journal of Criminology, 14,* 172–6.

Blos, P. (1962) *On Adolescence: A Psychoanalytic Interpretation.* New York: Free Press.

Blumstein, P.W. (1974) The honoring of accounts. *American Sociological Review, 39,* 551–6.

Boissevain, J. (1974) *Friends of Friends: Networks, Manipulators and Coalitions.* Oxford: Blackwell.

Bowlby, J. (1946) *Forty-four Juvenile Thieves.* London: Bailliere, Tindall and Cox.

Bowlby, J. (1969) *Attachment and Loss,* Vol. 1, Attachment. New York: Basic Books.

Box, S. (1981) *Deviance, Reality and Society.* Second edn. London: Holt, Rinehart and Winston.

Box, S. (1983) *Power, Crime and Mystification.* London: Tavistock.

Box, S. and Hale, C. (1984) Liberation/emancipation, economic marginalisation or less chivalry: The relevance of three theoretical arguments to female crime patterns in England and Wales 1951–1980. *Criminology, 22,* 473–97.

Braithwaite, J.B. and Law, H.G. (1978) The structure of self-reported delinquency. *Applied Psychological Measurement, 2,* 221–38.

Brake, M. (1973) Cultural revolution or alternative delinquency. In R. Bailey and J. Young (eds) *Contemporary Social Problems in Britain.* London: Saxon House.

Brake, M. (1985) *Comparative Youth Culture: The Sociology of Youth Cultures and Youth Subcultures in America, Britain and Canada.* London: Routledge and Kegan Paul.

Brown, D. (1974a) Cognitive development and willingness to comply with law. *American Journal of Political Science, 18,* 583–94.

Brown, D. (1974b) Adolescent attitudes and lawful behavior. *Public Opinion Quarterly, 38,* 96–106.

Brown, R. (1965) *Social Psychology.* New York: Free Press.

Brown, R.J. (1988) *Group Processes: Dynamics Within and Between Groups.* Oxford: Blackwell.

Bryant, B. and Trower, P.E. (1974) Social difficulty in a student sample. *British Journal of Educational Psychology, 44,* 13–21.

Burt, C. (1925) *The Young Delinquent.* London: London University Press.

Burton, R.V. (1963) Generality of honesty reconsidered. *Psychological Review, 70,* 481–99.

Bynner, J. and Ashford, S. (1994) Politics and participation: Some antecedents of young people's attitudes to the political system and political activity. *European Journal of Social Psychology, 24,* 223–36.

Bynner, J.M., O'Malley, P. and Bachman, J. (1981) Delinquency and self-esteem revisited. *Journal of Youth and Adolescence, 10,* 407–41.

Cairns, R.B., Cairns, B.D., Nekerman, H.J., Gest, S.D., and Gariepy, J.-L. (1988) Social networks and aggressive behavior: Peer support or peer rejection? *Developmental Psychology, 24,* 815–23.

Campbell, A. (1981) *Girl Delinquents.* Oxford: Blackwell.

Candee, D. (1975) The psychology of Watergate. *Journal of Social Issues, 31,* 183–92.

Catton, W.R. and Smircich, R.J. (1964) A comparison of mathematical models for the effect of residential propinquity on mate selection. *American Sociological Review, 29,* 522–9.

Centers, R.C. (1949) *The Psychology of Social Classes.* Princeton: Princeton University Press.

Chandler, M.J. (1973) Egocentrism and antisocial behavior: The assessment and training of social perspective taking skills. *Developmental Psychology, 9,* 326–32.

Chapman, J.A. (1980) *Economic Realities and the Female Offender.* Lexington: D.C. Heath.

Cheek, J. (1982) Aggregation, moderator variables, and the validity of personality tests: A peer rating study. *Journal of Personality and Social Psychology,* *43,* 1254–69.

Chesney-Lind, M. (1989) Girls, crime, and women's place: Towards a feminist model of female delinquency. *Crime and Delinquency, 35,* 5–30.

Chevalier, L. (1973) *Labouring Classes and Dangerous Classes in Paris during the First Half of the Nineteenth Century.* London: Routledge and Kegan Paul.

Clark, J.P. and Wenninger, E.P. (1964) The attitude of juveniles toward the legal institution. *Journal of Criminal Law, Criminology and Political Science, 55,* 482–9.

Clarke, J., Hall, S., Jefferson, J. and Roberts, B. (1976) Subcultures, cultures and class. In S. Hall and S. Jefferson (eds) *Resistance through Rituals.* London: Hutchinson.

Cleckley, H. (1976) *The Mask of Sanity.* 5th edn. St. Louis, Mo: C.V. Mosby.

Cloward, R.A. and Ohlin, L.E. (1960) *Delinquency and Opportunity.* New York: Free Press.

Cochrane, R. (1974) Crime and personality: Theory and evidence. *Bulletin of the British Psychological Society, 27,* 19–22.

Coffield, F., Borrill, C. and Marshall, S. (1986) 'Shit jobs, govvy schemes or the dole': Occupational choice for young adults in the north-east of England. In H. Beloff (ed.) *Getting into Life.* London: Methuen.

Cohen, A.K. (1955) *Delinquent Boys: The Culture of the Gang.* Glencoe, Ill.: Free Press.

Cohen, P. (1972) Sub-cultural conflict and working class community. *Working Papers in Cultural Studies, No. 2.* Centre for Contemporary Cultural Studies, University of Birmingham.

Cohen, S. (1972) *Folk Devils and Moral Panics: The Creation of the Mods and Rockers.* London: MacGibbon and Kee.

Cohen, S. (1985) *Visions of Social Control.* London: Polity Press.

Colby, A., Kohlberg, L. and collaborators (1987) *The Measurement of Moral Judgement. Volume 1: Theoretical Foundations and Research Validation.* Cambridge: Cambridge University Press.

Coleman, A. (1961) *The Adolescent Society.* Glencoe: Free Press.

Coleman, J.C. (1980) *The Nature of adolescence.* London: Methuen.

Coleman, J.C. and Hendry, L. (1990) *The Nature of adolescence.* London: Routledge.

Conger, J.J. and Petersen, A.C. (1984) *Adolescence and Youth.* New York: Harper and Row.

Cooley, C.H. (1902) *Human Nature and the Social Order.* New York: Charles Scribner's.

Cooley, C.H. (1909) *Social Organisation.* New York: Charles Scribner's.

Corrigan, P. (1976) Doing nothing. In S. Hall and S. Jefferson (eds) *Resistance through Rituals.* London: Hutchinson.

Corrigan, P. (1979) *Schooling the Smash Street Kids.* London: Macmillan.

Cronbach, L.J. (1955) Processes affecting scores on "understanding others" and "assumed similarity". *Psychological Bulletin, 52*, 177–93.

Culbertson, R.G. (1975) The effects of institutionalisation on the delinquent inmate's self-image. *Journal of Criminal Law and Criminology, 66*, 88–93.

Cymablisty, B.Y., Schuck, S.Z. and Dubeck, J.A. (1975) Achievement level, institutional adjustment and recidivism among juvenile delinquents. *Journal of Community Psychology, 3*, 289–94.

Dale, R. and Esland, G. (1977) *Mass Schooling (Open University Course E202)*. Milton Keynes: Open University Press.

Damon, W. (1983) *Social and Personality Development*. New York: Norton.

Danziger, K. (1971) *Socialization*. Harmondsworth: Penguin.

Darby, B.W. and Schlenker, B. (1982) Children's reactions to apologies. *Journal of Personality and Social Psychology, 43*, 742–53.

Demos, J. and Demos, V. (1969) Adolescence in historical perspective. *Journal of Marriage and the Family, 31*, 632–38.

Dentler, R.A. and Munroe, L.J. (1961) Social correlates of early adolescent theft. *American Sociological Review, 26*, 733–43.

Dickinson, J. (1990) Adolescent representations of socio-economic status. *British Journal of Developmental Psychology, 8*, 351–71.

Diener, E. (1979) Deindividuation, self awareness and disinhibition. *Journal of Personality and Social Psychology, 37*, 1160–71.

Diener, E. (1980) Deindividuation: the absence of self-awareness and self-regulation in group members. In P. Paulus (ed.) *The Psychology of Group Influence*. Hillsdale, NJ: Lawrence Erlbaum.

Dishion, T.J., Patterson, G.R., Stoolmiller, M. and Skinner, M.L. (1991) Family, school, and behavioral antecedants to early adolescent involvement with antisocial peers. *Developmental Psychology, 27*, 172–80.

Dodge, K.A. (1986) A social information-processing model of social competence in children. In M. Perlmutter (ed.) *Minnesota Symposium on Child Psychology*, vol. 18. Hillsdale, NJ: Erlbaum.

Donaldson, M. (1978) *Children's Minds*. London: Fontana.

Dorn, N. (1983) *Alcohol, Youth and the State*. London: Croom Helm.

Douvan, E. and Adelson, J. (1966) *The Adolescent Experience*. New York: Wiley.

Duhs, L.A. and Gunter, R.J. (1988) TV violence and childhood aggression: A curmudgeon's guide. *Australian Psychologist, 23*, 183–95.

Dunbar, R.I. (1988) *Primate Social Systems*. Beckenham: Croom Helm.

Durkheim, E. (1897) *La suicide: Etude de sociologie*. Paris: Alcan.

Durkheim, E. (1915) *The Elementary Forms of the Religious Life*. (Trans. Joseph Ward Swain). London: Allen and Unwin.

Durkheim, E. (1961) *Moral Education*. New York: Free Press (first published in 1925).

Durkheim, E. (1984) *The Division of Labour in Society*. London: Macmillan (First published in 1893).

Durkin, D. (1961) The specificity of children's moral judgments. *Journal of Genetic Psychology, 98*, 3–14.

Ekman, P. (1985) *Telling Lies: Clues to Deceit in the Marketplace, Politics and Marriage*. New York: Norton.

Elliott, D.S. and Ageton, S.S. (1980) Reconciling race and class differences in self-reported and official estimates of delinquency. *American Sociological Review, 45*, 95–110.

Elliott, D.S. and Voss, H. (1974) *Delinquency and Dropout*. Lexington, Mass.: Heath.

Elmhorn, K. (1965) Study on self-report delinquency among school children in Stockholm. In K.O. Christiansen (ed.) *Scandinavian Studies in Criminology*. London: Tavistock.

Emler, N. (1984a) Differential involvement in delinquency: Toward an interpretation in terms of reputation management. In B.A. Maher and W.B. Maher (eds) *Progress in experimental personality research*. vol. 13. New York: Academic Press.

Emler, N. (1984b) *Participation in personal networks*. Paper presented at General Meeting of the European Association of Experimental Social Psychology, Tilburg.

Emler, N. (1988) *Peer relations and accommodation to the institutional system*. Paper presented at ESRC 16–19 'first findings' Workshop, Harrogate.

Emler, N. (1989) *The social psychology of reputation*. Paper presented at European Association of Experimental Social Psychology East–West Meeting, Jablonna, Poland.

Emler, N. (1990) A social psychology of reputation. In W. Stroebe and M. Hewstone (eds) *European Review of Social Psychology*, vol. 1. Chichester: Wiley.

Emler, N. (1991) What do children care about justice: Culture and cognitive development in the development of a sense of justice. In H. Steensma and R. Vermunt (eds) *Social Justice in Human Relations*. New York: Pergamon.

Emler, N. (1994) La réputation. In S. Moscovici (ed.) *Psychologie sociale des relations à autrui*. Paris: Nathan.

Emler, N. and Abrams, D. (1989) The sexual distribution of benefits and burdens in the household. *Social Justice Research, 3*, 137–56.

Emler, N. and Dickinson, J. (1985) Children's representations of economic inequalities: The effects of social class. *British Journal of Developmental Psychology, 3*, 191–8.

Emler, N. and Fisher, S. (1981) *Gossip and the nature of the social environment*. Paper presented at the British Psychological Society Social Psychology Section Conference, Oxford.

Emler, N. and Grady, K. (1986) *The university as a social environment*. Paper presented at British Psychological Society, Social Psychology Section Annual Conference, Brighton.

Emler, N., Heather, N. and Winton, M. (1978) Delinquency and the development of moral reasoning. *British Journal of Social and Clinical Psychology, 17*, 325–31.

Emler, N. and Hogan, R. (1993) Moral psychology and public policy. In

W. Kurtines and J. Gewirtz (eds), *Handbook of Moral Development and Behaviour*, vol. 3 (Hillsdale, N.J.: Erlbaum Associates).

Emler, N. and Ohana, J. (1992) Réponses au prejudice: Representations sociales enfantines. *Bulletin de Psychologie, 45*, 223–31.

Emler, N., Ohana, J. and Moscovici, S. (1987) Children's beliefs about institutional roles: A cross-national study of representations of the teacher's role. *British Journal of Educational Psychology, 57*, 26–37.

Emler, N. and Reicher, S. (1987) Orientations to institutional authority in adolescence. *Journal of Moral education, 16*, 108–16.

Emler, N., Reicher, S. and Ronson, B. (1987) 'Young people's perceptions of the personal attributes of rule breakers and rule followers'. Unpublished manuscript, University of Dundee.

Emler, N., Reicher, S. and Ross, A. (1987) The social context of delinquent conduct. *Journal of Child Psychology and Psychiatry, 28*, 99–109.

Emler, N., Renwick, S. and Malone, B. (1983) The relationship between moral reasoning and political orientation. *Journal of Personality and Social Psychology, 45*, 1073–80.

Emler, N., Renwick, S., Reicher, S. and Heather, N. (1983) *Interpreting factorial evidence for the generality of delinquent inclination.* Unpublished Manuscript, University of Dundee.

Emler, N. and St James, A. (1990) Staying at school after sixteen: Social and psychological correlates. *British Journal of Education and Work, 3*, 60–70.

Emler, N. and St James, A. (1994) Carriers scolaires et attitudes envers l'authorité formelle. *L'Orientation Scolaire et Professionelle, 23*, 355–67.

Empey, L.T. (1982) *American Delinquency: Its Meaning and Construction.* Homewood, Ill.: Dorsey.

Endler, N. and Magnusson, D. (1976) Toward an interactional psychology of personality. *Psychological Bulletin, 83*, 956–74.

Ennis, P.H. (1967) *Criminal Victimization in the United States: Report of a National Survey.* Washington, DC: US Government Printing Office.

Erickson, M.L. (1971) The group context of delinquent behavior. *Social Problems, 19*, 114–29.

Erickson, M.L. and Empey, L.T. (1963) Court records, undetected delinquency and decision making. *Journal of Criminal Law, Criminlogy, and Political Science, 54*, 456–69.

Erickson, M.L. and Jensen, G.F. (1977) Delinquency is still group behavior. *Journal of Criminal Law and Criminology, 68*, 262–73.

Erickson, M.L., Gibbs, J.P. and Jensen, G.F. (1977) The deterrence doctrine and the perceived certainty of legal punishments. *American Sociological Review, 42*, 305–17.

Erikson, E.H. (1968) *Identity: Youth and Crisis.* New York: Norton.

Erikson, K.T. (1962) Notes on the sociology of deviance. *Social Problems, 9*, 307–14.

Eysenck, H. (1964) *Crime and Personality.* London: Routledge and Kegan Paul.

Eysenck, H.J. (1970) *Crime and Personality*. 2nd edn. London: Granada Press.

Eysenck, S.B.G. and Eysenck, H.J. (1970) Crime and personality: An empirical test of the three-factor theory. *British Journal of Criminology, 10*, 225–39.

Farrington, D.P. (1973) Self reports of deviant behaviour: Predictive and stable? *Journal of Criminal Law and Criminology, 64*, 99–110.

Farrington, D.P. (1979) Experiments on deviance with special reference to dishonesty. In L. Berkowitz (ed.) *Advances in Experimental Social Psychology*, vol. 12. New York: Academic Press.

Farrington, D.P. (1991) Antisocial personality from childhood to adulthood. *The Psychologist, 4*, 389–94.

Farrington, D.P., Biron, L. and LeBlanc, M. (1982) Personality and delinquency in London and Montreal. In J. Gunn and D.P. Farrington (eds) *Abnormal Offenders, Delinquency and the Criminal Justice System*. Chichester: Wiley (pp. 153–201).

Farrington, D.P., Osborne, S.G. and West, D.J. (1978) The persistence of labelling effects. *British Journal of Criminology, 18*, 277–84.

Farrington, D.P. and West, D.J. (1981) The Cambridge study in delinquent development. In S.A. Mednick and A.E. Baert (eds) *Prospective Longitundinal Research: An Empirical Basis for the Primary Prevention of Psychosocial Disorder*. Oxford: Oxford University Press.

Farrington, D.P. and West, D.J. (1990) The Cambridge study in delinquent development: A long-term follow-up of 411 London males. In H.J. Kerner and G. Kaiser (eds) *Kriminalität: Persönlichkeit, Lebensgeschichte und Verhalten*. Berlin: Springer-Verlag.

Feldman, M.P. (1977) *Criminal Behaviour: A Psychological Analysis*. London: Wiley.

Felson, R.B. (1978) Aggression as impression management. *Social Psychology, 41*, 205–13.

Felson, R.B. (1981) An interactionist approach to aggression. In J. Tedeschi (ed.) *Impression Managment Theory and Social Psychological Research*. New York: Academic Press.

Felson, R.B. (1982) Impression management and the escalation of aggression and violence. *Social Psychology Quarterly, 45*, 245–54.

Ferdinand, T.N. and Luchterhand, E.G. (1970) Inner city youth, the police, the juvenile court and justice. *Social Problems, 17*, 510–27.

Festinger, L. (1954) A theory of social comparison processes. *Human Relations, 7*, 117–40.

Festinger, L. (1957) *A Theory of Cognitive Dissonance*. Stanford: Stanford University Press.

Festinger, L., Schachter, S. and Back, C. (1950) *Social Pressures in Informal Groups*. Stanford: Stanford University Press.

Fischer, C. (1981) *To Dwell among Friends: Personal Networks in Town and City*. Chicago: University of Chicago Press.

Fishbein, M. and Ajzen, I. (1974) Attitudes towards objects as predictors of single and multiple behavioral criteria. *Psychological Review, 81*, 49–74.

Flavell, J.H., Botkin, P., Fry, C., Wright, J. and Jarvis, P. (1968) *The Development of Role-taking and Communication Skills in Children*. New York: Wiley.

Fleming, C.M. (1963) *Adolescence: Its Social Psychology*. London: Routledge and Kegan Paul.

Foucault, M. (1977) *Discipline and Punishment*. London: Allen Lane.

Fox, R. (1977) The inherent rules of violence. In P. Collett (ed.) *Social Rules and Social Behaviour*. Oxford: Blackwell.

Frankena, W.K. (1973) *Ethics*. Englewood Cliffs, NJ: Prentice-Hall.

Freedman, B.J., Rosenthal, L., Donahoe, C.P. Schlundt, D.G., and McFall, R.M. (1978) A social-behavioral analysis of skills deficits in delinquent and non-delinquent adolescent boys. *Journal of Consulting and Clinical Psychology, 46*, 1448–62.

Freud, A. (1937) *Ego and the Mechanisms of Defense*. London: Hogarth.

Freud, A. (1958) Adolescence. *Psychoanalytic Study of the Child, 13*, 255–78.

Freud, S. (1939) *Moses and Monotheism*. In Standard edition, vol. 23. London: Hogarth Press.

Freud, S. (1955) *Totem and Taboo*. In Standard edition, vol. 13. London: Hogarth Press (First German edition 1913).

Freud, S. (1963) *Introductory Lectures on Psychoanalysis*. In Standard edition, vols. 15 and 16. London: Hogarth Press (First German edition 1917).

Freudenberg, W.R. (1986) The density of acquaintanceship: An overlooked variable in community research. *American Journal of Sociology, 91*, 27–63.

Freudenberg, W.R. and Jones, R.E. (1991) Criminal behavior and rapid community growth: Evaluation of the evidence. *Rural Sociology, 56*, 619–45.

Funder, D.C. and Colvin, C.R. (1988) Friends and strangers: Acquaintanceship, agreement and accuracy of personality judgment. *Journal of Personality and Social Psychology, 55*, 149–58.

Furnham, A. (1984) Personality, social skills, anomie and delinquency: A self-report study of a group of normal non-delinquent adolescents. *Journal of Child Psychology and Psychiatry, 25*, 409–20.

Furth, H.G. (1980) *The World of Grown-ups*. New York: Elsevier.

Gallatin, J.E. (1975) *Adolescence and Individuality*. New York: Harper & Row.

Gallatin, J. and Adelson, J. (1971) Legal guarantees of individual freedom: A cross-national study of the development of political thought. *Journal of Social Issues, 27*, 93–108.

Gans, H.J. (1962) *The Urban Village*. New York: Free Press.

Geller, D.M. (1980) Responses to urban stimuli – a balanced approach. *Journal of Social Issues, 36*, 86–100.

Gibson, H.B. (1967) Self-reported delinquency among schoolboys and their attitudes to the police. *British Journal of Social and Clinical Psychology, 3*, 190–5.

Gibson, H.B. (1971) The factorial structure of juvenile delinquency: A study of self-reported acts. *British Journal of Social and Clinical Psychology*, 10, 1–9.

Gibson, H.B., Morrison, S. and West, D.J. (1970) The confession of known offences in response to a self-reported delinquency schedule. *British Journal of Criminology*, 10, 277–80.

Giddens, A. (1973) *The Class Structure of the Advanced Societies*. London: Hutchinson.

Giddens, A. (1991) *Modernity and Self-identity*. Cambridge: Polity.

Gillis, J.R. (1974) *Youth and History: Tradition and Change in European Age Relations*. New York: Academic Press.

Giner, S. (1976) *Mass Society*. London: Martin Robertson.

Giordano, P.C., Cernovich, S.A. and Pugh, M.D. (1986) Friendship and delinquency. *American Journal of Sociology*, 91, 1170–201.

Glaser, D. (1956) Criminality theory and behavioral images. *Sociological Review*, 61, 433–44.

Glueck, S. and Glueck, E. (1950) *Unravelling Juvenile Delinquency*. New York: Commonwealth Fund.

Glueck, S. and Glueck, E. (1968) *Delinquents and Nondelinquents in Perspective*. Cambridge, Mass: Harvard University Press.

Goddard, H.H. (1914) *Feeblemindedness: Its Causes and Consequences*. New York: Macmillan.

Goffman, E. (1959) *The Presentation of Self in Everyday Life*. New York: Doubleday.

Gold, M. (1970) *Delinquent Behavior in an American City*. Belmont, CA: Brooks/Cole.

Gough, H.G. (1965) Cross-cultural validation of a measure of antisocial behavior. *Psychological Reports*, 17, 379–87.

Gramsci, A. (1971) *Selections from Prison Notebooks*. London: Lawrence & Wishart.

Granovetter, M. (1973) The strength of weak ties. *American Journal of Sociology*, 78, 1360–80.

Grasmick, H.G. and Bryjack, G.J. (1980) The deterrence effect of perceived severity of punishment. *Social Forces*, 59, 471–91.

Grinder, R.E. (1961) New techniques for research in children's temptation behavior. *Child Development*, 32, 679–88.

Gross, A.M., Brigham, T.A., Hopper, R. and Bologna, N.C. (1980) Self management and social skills: A study with predelinquent and delinquent youth. *Criminal Justice and Behavior*, 7, 161–84.

Haan, N., Smith, B. and Block, J. (1968) The moral reasoning of young adults: Political-social behavior, family background and personality correlates. *Journal of Personality and Social Psychology*, 10, 183–201.

Hagan, J., Simpson, J. and Gillis, A.R. (1987) Class in the household: A power-control theory of gender and delinquency. *American Journal of Sociology*, 92, 788–816.

Hains, A.A. and Miller, D.J. (1980) Moral and cognitive development in delinquent and non-delinquent children. *Journal of Genetic Psychology, 137,* 21–35.

Hains, A.A. and Ryan, E.R. (1983) The development of social cognitive processes among juvenile delinquents and non-delinquent peers. *Child Development, 54,* 1536–44.

Hall, G.S. (1904) *Adolescence: Its Psychology and its Relations to Physiology, Anthropology, Sociology, Sex, Crime, Religion and Education.* 2 vols. New York: Appleton.

Hall, S. and Jefferson, T. (1976) *Resistance through Rituals.* London: Hutchinson.

Hardt, R.H. and Peterson-Hardt, S. (1977) On determining the quality of the delinquency self-report method. *Journal of Research on Crime and Delinquency, 14,* 247–61.

Hargreaves, D.H. (1967) *Social Relations in a Secondary School.* London: Routledge and Kegan Paul.

Harrell, W.A. (1979) Aggression against a remorseful wrongdoer: The effects of self-blame and concern for the victim. *Journal of Social Psychology, 7,* 267–77.

Harry, J. and Minor, W.W. (1986) Intelligence and delinquency reconsidered: A comment on Menard and Morse. *American Journal of Sociology, 91,* 956–62.

Hartshorne, H. and May, M.A. (1928) *Studies in the Nature of Character. Vol. 1, Studies in Deceit.* New York: Macmillan.

Hartshorne, H., May, M.A. and Shuttleworth, H. (1930) *Studies in the Nature of Character. Vol. 3. Studies in the Organisation of Character.* New York: Macmillan.

Hartup, W.W. (1983) Peer relations. In P.H. Mussen and M. Hetherington (eds) *Carmichael's Manual of Child Psychology,* 4th edn. New York: Wiley.

Haskell, M. and Yablonsky, L. (1971) *Crime and Delinquency.* New York: Rand McNally.

Haswell, D. (1991) *Delinquency and reputation.* Unpublished MA Thesis, University of Dundee.

Hathaway, S.R. and Monachesi, E.D. (1953) *Analysing and Predicting Juvenile Delinquency with the MMPI.* Minneapolis, Minn: University of Minnesota Press.

Hathaway, S.R., Reynolds, P.C. and Monachesi, E.D. (1969) Follow-up of the later careers and lives of 1,000 boys who dropped out of high school. *Journal of Consulting and Clinical Psychology, 33,* 370–80.

Havighurst, R. and Taba, H. (1949) *Adolescent Character and Personality.* New York: Wiley.

Heise, D.R. (1968) Norms and individual patterns of student deviancy. *Social Problems, 19,* 78–92.

Henderson, M. and Hollin, C.R. (1986) Social skills training and delinquency. In C. Hollin and P. Trower (eds) *Handbook of Social Skills Training,* vol. 1.

Oxford: Pergamon, pp. 79–101.

Hess, R.D. and Torney, J.V. (1967) *The Development of Political Attitudes in Children*. New York: Aldine.

Hewstone, M. and Brown, R.J. (1987) Contact is not enough: An intergroup perspective on the contact hypothesis. In M. Hewstone and R.J. Brown (eds) *Contact and Conflict in Intergroup Encounters*. Oxford: Blackwell.

Hewstone, M., Hopkins, N. and Routh, D. (1992) Cognitive models of stereotype change, I: Generalisation and subtyping in young people's views of the police. *European Journal of Social Psychology, 22*, 219–34.

Hinde, R.A. (1979) *Toward Understanding Relationships*. London: Academic Press.

Hindelang, M.J. (1970) The commitment of delinquents to their misdeeds: Do delinquents drift? *Social Problems, 17*, 502–9.

Hindelang, M.J. (1971) Extraversion, neuroticism and self-reported delinquent involvement. *Journal of Research in Crime and Delinquency, 8*, 23–31.

Hindelang, M.J. (1973) Causes of delinquency: a partial replication and extension. *Social Problems, 20*, 471–87.

Hindelang, M.J. (1976) With a little help from their friends: Group participation in reported delinquent behaviour. *British Journal of Criminology, 16*, 109–25.

Hindelang, M.J. (1978) Race and involvement in common-law personal crimes. *American Sociological Review, 43*, 93–109.

Hindelang, M.J., Hirschi, T. and Weis, J.G. (1981) *Measuring Delinquency*. Beverley Hills: Sage.

Hindelang, M. and Weis, J. (1972) Personality and self-reported delinquency: an application of cluster analysis. *Criminology, 10*, 268–94.

Hirschi, T. (1969) *Causes of Delinquency*. Berkeley, CA: University of California Press.

Hirschi, T. and Gottfredson, M. (1983) Age and the explanation of crime. *American Journal of Sociology, 89*, 552–84.

Hirschi, T. and Hindelang, M.J. (1977) Intelligence and delinquency: A revisionist review. *American Sociological Review, 42*, 571–87.

Hockett, C. (1958) *A Course in Modern Linguistics*. New York: Macmillan.

Hoffman, M. (1970) Conscience, personality and socialization techniques. *Human Development, 13*, 90–126.

Hoffman, M. (1977) Moral internalization: Current theory and research. In L. Berkowitz (ed.) *Advances in Experimental Social Psychology*, vol. 10. New York: Academic Press.

Hogan, R. and Jones, W.H. (1983) A role theoretical model of criminal conduct. In W.S. Laufer and J.M. Day (eds) *Personality Theory, Moral Development and Criminal Behavior*. Lexington, Mass: Lexington Books.

Hogg, M. and Abrams, D. (1988) *Social Identifications*. London: Routledge.

Hollin, C. (1989) *Psychology and Crime: An Introduction to Criminological Psychology*. London: Routledge.

Hollin, C.R. and Henderson, M. (1981) The effects of social skills training on incarcerated delinquent adolescents. *International Journal of Behavioural Social Work and Abstracts, 1,* 145–55.

Hood, R. and Sparks, R. (1970) *Key Issues in Criminology.* London: Weidenfeld and Nicolson.

Hopkins, N. (1994a) Peer group pressure and adolescent health related behaviour: Questioning the assumptions. *Journal of Community and Applied Social Psychology, 4,* 329–46.

Hopkins, N. (1994b) School pupils' perceptions of the police that visit schools: not all police are 'pigs'. *Journal of Community and Applied Social Psychology, 4,* 189–208.

Humphreys, N. (1976) The social function of the intellect. In P.P.G. Bateson and R.A. Hinde (eds) *Growing Points in Ethology.* Cambridge: Cambridge University Press.

Humphries, S. (1981) *Hooligans or Rebels? An Oral History of Working Class Childhood and Youth 1889–1939.* Oxford: Blackwell.

James, W. (1890) *Principles of Psychology.* New York: Holt, Rinehart and Winston.

Janis, I.L. (1972) *Victims of Groupthink.* Boston: Houghton-Mifflin.

Jencks, C. (1972) *Inequality.* Penguin: Harmondsworth.

Jenkins, R. (1983) *Lads, Citizens and Ordinary Kids: Working Class Youth Life-styles in Belfast.* London: Routledge and Kegan Paul.

Jennings, W.S., Kilkenny, R. and Kohlberg, L. (1983) Moral development theory and practice for youthful and adult offenders. In Laufer, W.S. and Day, J.M. (eds) *Personality Theory, Moral Development and Criminal Behavior.* Lexington, Mass: Lexington Books/D.C.Heath.

Jensen, G.F. (1972) Parents, peers and delinquent action: A test of the differential association perspective. *American Journal of Sociology, 78,* 562–75.

Jensen, G.F. (1976) Race, achievement and delinquency: A further look at delinquency in a birth cohort. *American Journal of Sociology, 82,* 379–87.

Jensen, G.F., Erikson, M.L. and Gibbs, J.P. (1978) Perceived risk of punishment and self-reported delinquency. *Social Forces, 57,* 37–58.

Jensen, G.F. and Eve, R. (1976) Sex differences in delinquency: An examination of popular sociological explanations. *Criminology, 13,* 427–48.

Johnson, J.A. (1981) The "self-disclosure" and "self-presentation" views of item response dynamics and personality scale validity. *Journal of Personality and Social Psychology, 40,* 761–9.

Johnson, R.E. (1979) *Juvenile Delinquency and its Origins.* Cambridge: Cambridge University Press.

Jones, E.E. (1990) *Interpersonal Perception.* New York: Freeman.

Jones, S.C., Knurek, D.A. and Regan, D.T. (1973) Variables affecting reactions to social acceptance and rejection. *Journal of Social Psychology, 90,* 269–84.

Jurik, N.C. (1983) The economics of female recidivism: A study of TARP women ex-offenders. *Criminology, 21,* 603–22.

Kandel, D.B. (1978) Similarity in real life adolescent friendship pairs. *Journal of Personality and Social Psychology, 36,* 306–12.

Kaplan, H.B. (1980) *Deviant Behavior in Defense of Self.* New York: Academic Press.

Kaplan, R.E. (1984) Trade routes: The manager's network of relationships. *Organisational Dynamics, 12,* 37–52.

Kazdin, A.E. (1987) Treatment of antisocial behaviour in children: Current status and future directions. *Psychological Bulletin, 102,* 187–203.

Kelly, D.H. (1975) Status origins, track position and delinquent involvement: A self-report analysis. *Sociological Quarterly, 16,* 264–71.

Kenny, D. and DePaulo, B. (1993) Do people know how others view them? An empirical and theoretical account. *Psychological Bulletin, 114,* 145–61.

Kett, J.F. (1977) *Rites of Passage: Adolescence in America 1790 to the Present.* New York: Basic Books.

Kituse, J.I. (1962) Societal reaction to deviant behavior. *Social Problems, 9,* 247–56.

Kituse, J.I. (1980) The "new conception of deviance" and its critics. In W.R. Gove (ed.) *The Labelling of Deviance.* Beverly Hills, Calif.: Sage.

Klein, M.W. (1969) On the group context of delinquency. *Sociology and Social Research, 54,* 63–71.

Klein, M. (1984) Offence specialisation and versatility among juveniles. *British Journal of Criminology, 24,* 185–94.

Kohlberg, L. (1963) The development of children's orientations toward a moral order. I: Sequence in the development of human thought. *Vita Humana, 6,* 11–33.

Kohlberg, L. (1969) Stage and sequence: The cognitive developmental approach to socialisation. In D.A. Goslin (ed.) *Handbook of Socialisation Theory and Research.* Chicago: Rand McNally.

Kohlberg, L. (1976) Moral stages and moralization: the cognitive developmental approach. In T. Lickona (ed.) *Moral Development and Behaviour: Theory, Research and Social Issues.* New York: Holt, Rinehart and Winston.

Kohlberg, L. (1984) *The Psychology of Moral Development: Vol. 2. Essays on Moral Development.* New York: Harper and Row.

Kohlberg, L. and Candee, D. (1984) The relation of moral judgment to moral action. In L. Kohlberg (ed.) *The Psychology of Moral Development: Vol. 2. Essays on Moral Development.* New York: Harper and Row.

Kohlberg, L., Scharf, P. and Hickey, J. (1972) The justice structure of the prison: A theory and an intervention. *The Prison Journal, 51,* 3–14.

Korte, C. (1980) Urban–non-urban differences in social behavior. *Journal of Social Issues, 36,* 29–51.

Kulik, J.A., Stein, K.B. and Sarbin, T.R. (1968a) Dimensions and patterns of adolescent antisocial behavior. *Journal of Consulting and Clinical Psychology, 32,* 375–82.

Kulik, J.A., Stein, K.B. and Sarbin, T.R. (1968b) Disclosures of delinquent behavior under conditions of anonymity and non-anonymity. *Journal of Consulting and Clinical Psychology, 32,* 506–9.

Lande, R.G. (1993) The video violence debate. *Hospital and Community Psychology, 44*, 347–51.

Latane, B. and Darley, J.M. (1970) *The Unresponsive Bystander: Why Doesn't He Help?* New York: Appleton-Century-Crofts.

Lazarsfeld, P.F., Berelson, B.R. and Gaudet, H. (1948) *The People's Choice.* New York: Columbia University Press.

Le Bon, G. (1947) *The Crowd: A Study of the Popular Mind.* London: Ernest Benn (first pub. 1895).

Lee, M. and Prentice, N.M. (1988) Interrelations of empathy, cognition and moral reasoning with dimensions of juvenile delinquency. *Journal of Abnormal Child Psychology, 16*, 127–39.

Leonard, P. (1984) *Personality and Ideology: Towards a Materialist Understanding of the Individual.* London: Macmillan.

Lemert, E.M. (1967) *Human Deviance, Social Problems and Social Control.* Englewood Cliffs, NJ: Prentice-Hall.

Lerman, P. (1967) Gangs, networks and subcultural delinquency. *American Journal of Sociology, 73*, 63–83.

Levine, R.A. and Campbell, D.T. (1973) *Ethnocentrism.* New York: Wiley.

Lingoes, J.C. and Guttman, L. (1967) Nonmetric factor analysis: A rank-reducing alternative to linear factor analysis. *Multivariate Behavioral Research, 2*, 485–505.

Liska, A.E. and Reed, M.D. (1985) Ties to conventional institutions and delinquency: Estimating reciprocal effects. *American Sociological Review, 50*, 547–60.

Litwak, E. and Szelenyi, I. (1969) Primary group structures and their functions. *American Sociological Review, 35*, 465–81.

Loeber, R. (1982) The stability of anti-social and delinquent behavior: A review. *Child Development, 53*, 1431–46.

Lombroso, C. (1912) *Crime: Its Causes and Remedies.* Boston: Little, Brown.

Losel, F. (1988) *On the self-report method and its application in testing elementary models of social deviance.* Paper presented at NATO Workshop on 'Self-report metholodogy in criminological research', Leuwenhorst, Netherlands.

Lynham, D., Moffitt,T. and Stouthamer-Loeber, M. (1993) Explaining the relation between IQ and delinquency: Class, race, test motivation, school failure or self-control? *Journal of Abnormal Psychology, 102*, 187–96.

McCarthy, J.D. and Hoge, D.R. (1984) The dynamics of self-esteem and delinquency. *American Journal of Sociology, 90*, 396–410.

McCord, W., McCord, J. and Zola, I.K. (1959) *Origins of Crime.* New York: Columbia University Press.

McDougall, W. (1920) *The Group Mind.* Cambridge: Cambridge University Press.

MacKinnon, D.W. (1938) Violation of prohibition. In H.A. Murray (ed.) *Explorations in Personality.* New York: Oxford University Press.

McRobbie, A. and Garber, J. (1976) Girls and subcultures: An exploration.

In S. Hall and S. Jefferson (eds) *Resistance through Rituals*. London: Hutchinson.

Markoulis, D. (1989) Testing Emler's theory. *British Journal of Social Psychology, 28*, 203–12.

Mars, G. (1981) *Cheats at Work: An Anthropology of Work-place Crime*. London: Unwin.

Matza, D. (1964) *Delinquency and Drift*. New York: Wiley.

Mays, A. (1972) *Juvenile Delinquency, the Family and the Social Group: A Reader*. New York: Longman.

Mead, G.H. (1937) *Mind, Self and Society*. Chicago: University of Chicago Press.

Mednick, S.A. and Christiansen, K.O. (1977) *Biosocial Bases of Criminal Behavior*. New York: Gardner Press.

Meier, R.F. and Johnson, W.T. (1977) Deterrence as social control: The legal and extra-legal production of conformity. *American Sociological Review, 42,* 292–304.

Menard, S. and Morse, B.J. (1984) A structuralist critique of the IQ–delinquency hypothesis: Theory and evidence. *American Journal of Sociology, 89*, 1347–78.

Merton, R.K. (1938) Social structure and anomie. *American Sociological Review, 3*, 672–82.

Merton, R.K. (1957) *Social Theory and Social Structure*. New York: Free Press.

Merton, R.K. (1968) *On Theoretical Sociology*. New York: Free Press.

Milgram, S. (1970) The experience of living in cities. *Science, 167*, 1461–68.

Miller, W.B. (1958) Lower class culture as a generating milieu of gang delinquency. *Journal of Social Issues, 14*, 5–19.

Minton, C., Kagan, J. and Levine, J.A. (1971) Maternal control and obedience in two year olds. *Child Development, 42*, 1873–94.

Mintzberg, H. (1973) *The Nature of Managerial Work*. Englewood Cliffs, NJ: Prentice Hall.

Mischel, W. (1968) *Personality and Assessment*. New York: Wiley.

Mischel, W. (1976) *Introduction to Personality*. 2nd edn. New York: Holt, Rinehart and Winston.

Mischel W. (1977) *Personality and Assessment*. 2nd edn. New York: Wiley.

Mitchell, J.C. (1969) *Social Networks in Urban Situations*. Manchester: Manchester University Press.

Mohr, G.S. and Despres, M.A. (1958) *The Stormy Decade: Adolescence*. New York: Random House.

Morash, M. (1982) Relationship of legal reasoning to social class, closeness to parents and exposure to a high level of reasoning among adolescents varying in seriousness of delinquency. *Psychological Reports, 50*, 755–60.

Morash, M. (1983) Gangs, groups and delinquency. *British Journal of Criminology, 23*, 309–31.

Morris, R. (1964) Female delinquency and relational problems. *Social Forces,*

43, 82–9.

Moscovici, S. (1976) *Social Influence and Social Change*. London: Academic Press.

Moscovici, S. (1984) The phenomenon of social representations. In R. Farr and S. Moscovici (eds) *Social Representations*. Cambridge: Cambridge University Press.

Moskowitz, D.S. and Schwartz, J.C. (1982) Validity comparison of behavior counts and rating by knowledgeable informants. *Journal of Personality and Social Psychology, 42*, 518–28.

Muller-Hill, B. (1988) *Murderous Science*. Oxford: Oxford University Press.

Murdock, G. (1973) *Culture and classlessness: The making and unmaking of a contemporary myth*. Paper delivered to symposium on 'Work and leisure', University of Salford.

Murdock, G. and McCrone, R. (1976) Consciousness of class and consciousness of generation. In S. Hall and S. Jefferson (eds) *Resistance through Rituals*. London: Hutchinson.

Musgrove, F. (1968) *Youth and the Social Order*. London: Routledge and Kegan Paul.

Mussen, P. Sullivan, L.B. and Eisenberg-Berg, N. (1977) Changes in political-economic attitudes during adolescence. *Journal of Genetic Psychology, 130*, 69–76.

Myers, D. (1982) Polarizing effects of social interaction. In M. Branstatter, J.H. Davis and G. Stoker-Kreichgauer (eds) *Group Decision Making*. London: Academic Press.

Naffine, N. and Gale, F. (1989) Testing the nexus: Crime, gender and unemployment. *British Journal of Criminology, 29*, 144–56.

Neville, R. (1971) *Play Power*. London: Paladin.

Norman, W.T. and Goldberg, L.R. (1966) Raters, ratees and randomness in personality structure. *Journal of Personality and Social Psychology, 4*, 417–43.

Nunally, J. (1978) *Psychometric Theory*, 2nd edn. New York: McGraw Hill.

Oakes, P., Turner, J. and Haslam, A. (1993) *Stereotyping and Social Reality*. Oxford: Blackwell.

Oakley, A. (1972) *Sex and Gender in Society*. London: Temple Hill.

Ollendick, T.H. and Hersen, M. (1979) Social skills training for juvenile delinquents. *Behavioural Research and Therapy, 17*, 547–54.

Oplinger, J. (1990) *The Politics of Demonology: The European Witcrazes and the Mass Production of Deviance*. Selinsgrove: Susquehanna University Press.

Ouston, J. (1984) Delinquency, family background and educational attainment. *British Journal of Criminology, 24*, 2–6.

Paicheler, G. (1988) *The Psychology of Social Influence*. Cambridge: Cambridge University Press.

Paine, R. (1967) What is gossip about? An alternative hypothesis. *Man, 2*, 278–85.

Palmonari, A., Kirchler, E. and Pombeni, M.L. (1991) Differential effects of identification with family and peers on coping with developmental tasks in adolescence. *European Journal of Social Psychology, 21,* 381–402.

Park, R.E., Burgess, E.W. and McKenzie, R.D.L. (1925) *The City.* Chicago: Chicago University Press.

Parke, R.D. (1967) Nurturance, withdrawal and resistance to deviation. *Child Development, 38,* 1101–10.

Passini, F.T. and Norman, W.T. (1966) A universal conception of personality structure? *Journal of Personality and Social Psychology, 4,* 44–9.

Patrick, J. (1973) *A Glasgow Gang Observed.* London: Eyre Methuen.

Patterson, G.R. (1982) *A Social Learning Approach: Vol. 3. Coercive Family Process.* Eugene, OR: Castilia.

Patterson, G.R. (1986) Performance models for antisocial boys. *American Psychologist, 44,* 105–11.

Pearson, G. (1983) *Hooligan: A History of Respectable Fears.* London: Macmillan.

Philips, D. (1985) A just measure of crime, authority, hunters and blue locusts: The 'revisionist' social history of crime and the law in Britain. In S. Cohen and A. Scull (eds) *Social control and the state.* Oxford: Blackwell.

Piaget, J. (1932) *The Moral Judgement of the Child.* Penguin: London.

Piaget, J. (1950) *The Psychology of Intelligence.* London: Routledge and Kegan Paul.

Piliavin, I. and Briar, S. (1964) Police encounters with juveniles. *American Journal of Sociology, 70,* 206–14.

Piliavin. I.M., Vadum, A.C. and Hardyck, J.A. (1969) Delinquency, personal costs and parental treatment: A test of a reward–cost model of juvenile criminality. *Journal of Criminal Law, Criminology and Political Science, 60,* 165–72.

Pittel, S.M. and Mendelsohn, G.A. (1966) Measurement of moral values: A review and critique. *Psychological Bulletin, 142,* 318–31.

Poole, E.D. and Rigoli, R.M. (1979) Parental support, delinquent friends and delinquency. *Journal of Criminal Law and Criminology, 70,* 188–93.

Porterfield, A. (1946) *Youth in Trouble.* Forth Worth, Texas: Leo Potisham Foundation.

Powell, G.E. (1977) Psychoticism and social deviancy in children. *Advances in Behavioural Research and Therapy, 1,* 27–56.

Quay, H.C. and Blumen, L. (1963) Dimensions of delinquent behavior. *Journal of Social Psychology, 61,* 273–7.

Radcliffe-Brown, A.R. (1952) *Structure and Function in Primitive Society.* New York: Free Press.

Reckless, W. (1967) *The Crime Problem.* 4th edn. New York: Appleton Century Crofts.

Reicher, S. (1982) The determination of collective behaviour. In H. Tajfel (ed.) *Social Identity and Intergroup Relations.* Cambridge: Cambridge University Press.

Reicher, S. (1984) The St. Paul's riot: An explanation of the limits of crowd action in terms of a social identity model. *European Journal of Social Psychology, 14*, 1–21.

Reicher, S. (1987) Crowd behaviour and social action. In J. Turner, M. Hogg, P. Oakes, S. Reicher and M. Wetherell, *Rediscovering the Social Group*. Oxford: Blackwell.

Reicher, S. (forthcoming) *The Crowd: A Study of the Social Mind*. Cambridge: Cambridge University Press.

Reicher, S. and Emler, N. (1985a) Delinquent behaviour and attitudes to formal authority. *British Journal of Social Psychology, 3*, 161–8.

Reicher, S. and Emler, N. (1985b) Moral orientation as a cue to political identity. *Political Psychology, 5*, 543–51.

Reicher, S. and Emler, N. (1986) The management of delinquent reputations. In H. Beloff (ed.) *Getting Into Life*. London: Methuen.

Reicher, S. and Hopkins, N. (in press, a) Constructing categories and mobilising masses: an analysis of Kinnock's and Thatcher's speeches in the British miners' strike, 1984–5. *European Journal of Social Psychology*.

Reicher, S. and Hopkins, N. (in press, b) Seeking influence through characterising self-categories: an analysis of anti-abortionist rhetoric. *British Journal of Social Psychology*.

Reicher, S. and Potter, J. (1985) Psychological theory as intergroup perspective: A comparative analysis of 'scientific' and 'lay' accounts. *Human Relations, 38*, 167–89.

Reicher, S., Spears, R. and Postmes, T. (in press) A social identification model of deindividuation. *European Review of Social Psychology*, vol. 6.

Reichtel, H. (1987) *The intelligence–criminality relationship: A critical review*. Reports from the Department of Psychology, Stockholm University, Supplement 66.

Reiss, A.J. and Rhodes, A.L. (1961) The distribution of juvenile delinquency in the social class structure. *American Sociological Review, 26*, 720–32.

Renwick, S. (1987) *A comparative examination of the role of social skills deficits in delinquent conduct*. Unpublished PhD Thesis, University of Dundee, 1986.

Renwick, S. and Emler, N. (1984) Moral reasoning and delinquent behaviour among students. *British Journal of Social Psychology, 23*, 281–3.

Renwick, S. and Emler, N. (1991) The relationship between social skills deficits and juvenile delinquency. *British Journal of Clinical Psychology, 30*, 61–71.

Renwick, S., Ridley, A. and Ramm, M. (1993) Deficits and dysfunctions: old assumptions revisited. Paper presented at European Conference on Clinical Psychology and Offenders, Royal Holloway and Bedford New College, April.

Rest, J. (1979) *Development in Judging Moral Issues*. Minneapolis: University of Minnesota Press.

Rich, J. (1956) Types of stealing. *Lancet, 2*, 496.

Rigby, K. and Rump, E. (1979) The generality of attitude to authority. *Human Relations, 32*, 469–87.

Rhodes, A.L. and Reiss, A.J. (1970) Apathy, truancy and delinquency as adaptations to school failure. *Social Forces, 48*, 12–22.

Roberts, R. (1970) *The Classic Slum*. Harmondsworth: Penguin.

Rook, C. (1899) *The Hooligan Nights*. London: Grant Richards (reprinted 1979, Oxford: Oxford University Press).

Root, N. (1957) Neurosis in adolescence. *Psychoanalytic Study of the Child, 12*, 320–4.

Rosenbaum, J.L. (1989) Introduction. *Crime and Delinquency, 35*, 2–5.

Rosenberg, G.J.R. and Rosenberg, M. (1978) Self esteem and delinquency. *Journal of Youth and Adolescence, 7*, 279–95.

Rosenthal-Gaffney, L. and McFall, R.M. (1981) A comparison of social skills in delinquent and non-delinquent adolescent girls, using a behavioral role-playing inventory. *Journal of Consulting and Clinical Psychology, 49*, 959–67.

Ross, L.D. (1977) The intuitive psychologist and his shortcomings: Distortions in the attribution process. In L. Berkowitz (ed.) *Advances in Experimental Social Psychology*, vol. 10. New York: Academic Press.

Ross, M. and Fletcher, G.J.O. (1985) Attribution and social perception. In G. Lindzey and E. Aronson (eds) *Handbook of Social Psychology*, vol. 2. New York: Random House.

Rothbart, M. and Park, B. (1986) On the confirmability and disconfirmability of trait concepts. *Journal of Personality and Social Psychology, 50*, 131–42.

Rumsey, M.G. (1976) Effects of defendant's background and remorse on sentencing judgments. *Journal of Applied Social Psychology, 6*, 64–8.

Runciman, W.G. (1966) *Relative Deprivation and Social Justice*. London: Routledge and Kegan Paul.

Rutter, M.C. and Giller, H. (1983) *Juvenile Delinquency: Trends and Prospects*. New York: Guilford.

Sampson, E.E. (1971) *Social Psychology and Contemporary Society*. New York: Wiley.

Sandhu, H.S. and Allen, D.E. (1969) Female delinquency: Goal abstraction and anomie. *Canadian Review of Sociology and Anthropology, 6*, 107–10.

Sarason, I.G. (1968) Verbal learning, modelling and juvenile delinquency. *American Psychologist, 23*, 254–66.

Sarason, I.G. and Ganzer, V.J. (1973) Modelling and group discussion in the rehabilitation of juvenile delinquents. *Journal of Counseling Psychology, 20*, 442–9.

Schalling, D. (1978) Psychopathy-related personality variables and the psycho-physiology of socialisation. In R.D. Hare and D. Schalling (eds) *Psychopathic Behavior: Approaches to Research*. New York: Wiley.

Schur, E. (1973) *Radical Non-intervention*. New York: Prentice-Hall.

Scott, M.B. and Lyman, S.M. (1968) Accounts. *American Sociological Review, 33*, 46–62.

Scott, J.F. (1959) Two dimensions of delinquent behaviour. *American Sociological Review, 24*, 240–3.

Scott, P.D. (1956) Gangs and delinquent gangs in London. *British Journal of Delinquent, 7*.

Senna, J., Rathus, S.A. and Siegal, L. (1974) Delinquent behavior and academic investment among suburban youth. *Adolescence, 9*, 481–94.

Shapland, J. (1978) Self-reported delinquency in boys aged 11 to 14. *British Journal of Criminology, 18*, 256–66.

Shaw, C.R. and McKay, H.D. (1931) *Social Factors in Juvenile Delinquency.* Washington, D.C.: U.S. Government Printing Office.

Shaw, C.R. and McKay, H.D. (1942) *Juvenile Delinquency and Urban Areas.* Chicago: University of Chicago Press.

Shaw, C.R. and McKay, H.D. (1969) *Juvenile Delinquency and Urban Areas.* 2nd edn. Chicago: University of Chicago Press.

Sherif, M., Harvey, O.J., White, B.J., Hood, W.R. and Sherif, C.W. (1961) *Intergroup Conflict and Cooperation: The Robber's Cave Experiment.* Norman: University of Oklahoma Book Exchange.

Sherif, M. and Sherif, C.W. (1964) *Reference Groups: Exploration into Conformity and Deviation of Adolescents.* New York: Harper and Row.

Short, J.F. (1957) Differential association and delinquency. *Social Problems, 4*, 233–9.

Short, J.F. and Nye, F.I (1957) Reported behavior as a criterion of deviant behavior. *Social Problems, 5*, 207–13.

Short, J.F. and Nye, F.I. (1958) Extent of unrecorded delinquency: tentative conclusions. *Journal of Criminal Law and Criminology, 49*, 296–302.

Short, J.F. and Strodtbeck, F.L. (1965) *Group Processes and Gang Delinquency.* Chicago: Chicago University Press.

Silberman, M. (1976) Toward a theory of deterrence. *American Sociological Review, 41*, 442–61.

Singh, A. (1979) Reliability and validity of self-reported delinquency studies. *Psychological Reports, 44*, 987–93.

Skowronski, J. and Carlston, D. (1989) Negativity and extremity biases in impression formation. *Psychological Bulletin, 105*, 131–42.

Skowronski, J. and Carlston, D. (1992) Caught in the act: When impressions based on highly diagnostic behaviours are resistant to contradiction. *European Journal of Social Psychology, 22*, 435–52.

Slaby, R.G. and Guerra, N.G. (1988) Cognitive mediators of aggression in adolescent offenders: I. Assessment. *Developmental Psychology, 24*, 580–8.

Slocum, W.L. and Stone, C.L. (1963) Family culture patterns and delinquent type behavior. *Marriage and Family Living, 25*, 202–8.

Smart, C. (1977) Criminological theory: Its ideology and implications concerning women. *British Journal of Sociology, 28*, 89–100.

Smetana, J. (1990) Morality and conduct disorders. In M. Lewis and S.M. Miller (eds) *Handbook of Developmental Psychopathology.* New York: Plenum.

Smiles, S. (1903) *Self-help.* London: John Murray.

Smith, A. (1910) *The Wealth of Nations.* London: Dent (first published 1776).

Snarey, J. (1985) Cross cultural universality of socio-moral development: A critical review of Kohlbergian research. *Psychological Bulletin, 97*, 202–32.

Spence, S.H. (1981) Differences in social skills performances between institutionalized juvenile male offenders and a comparable group of boys without offence records. British *Journal of Social and Clinical Psychology,* *20,* 163–71.

Spence, S.H. and Marzillier, J.S. (1979) Social skills training with adolescent male offenders – I. Short term effects. *Behaviour Research and therapy, 17,* 7–16.

Spence, S.H. and Marzillier, J.S. (1981) Social skills training with adolescent male offenders – II. Short term, long term and generalised effects. *Behaviour Research and Therapy, 19,* 349–68.

Steadman Jones, G. (1983) *Languages of Class.* Cambridge: Cambridge University Press.

Stein, K.B., Sarbin, T.R. and Kulik, J.A. (1968) Future time perspective: its relation to the socialization process and the delinquent role. *Journal of Consulting and Clinical Psychology, 32,* 257–64.

Sutherland, E.H. (1939) *Principles of Criminology.* Philadelphia: Lippincott.

Sutherland, E.H. and Cressey, D.R. (1970) *Principles of Criminology.* 8th edn. Chicago: Lippincott.

Tajfel, H. (1968) Social and cultural factors in perception. In G. Lindzey and E. Aronson (eds) *Handbook of Social Psychology,* vol. 3. Reading, Mass: Addison-Wesley.

Tajfel, H. (1978) *Differentiation between Social Groups.* London: Academic Press.

Tajfel, H. (1981) *Human Groups and Social Categories: Studies in Social Psychology.* Cambridge: Cambridge University Press.

Tajfel, H. and Turner, J.C. (1979) An integrative theory of intergroup conflict. In S. Worchel and W.G. Austin (eds) *Psychology of Intergroup Relations.* Chicago: Nelson-Hall.

Taylor, I., Walton, P. and Young, J. (1973) *The New Criminology.* London: Hutchinson.

Thompson, B.L. (1974) Self-concepts among secondary school pupils. *Educational Research, 17,* 41–7.

Thrasher, F.M. (1927) *The Gang.* Chicago: University of Chicago Press.

Tilly, C., Tilly, L. and Tilly, R. (1975) *The Rebellious Century: 1830–1930.* London: Dent.

Tonnies, F. (1957) *Community and Society.* New York: Harper (1st German edition, 1887).

Tracy, P.E. and Piper, E.S. (1982) *Gang membership and violent offending: Preliminary results from the 1958 cohort study.* Paper presented at annual meeting of the American Society of Criminology, Toronto.

Tracy, P.E., Wolfgang, M.E. and Figlio, R.M. (1990) *Delinquency Careers in Two Birth Cohorts.* New York: Plenum Press.

Trasler, G. (1978) Relations between psychotherapy and persistent criminality – methodological and theoretical issues. In R.D. Hare and D. Schalling (eds) *Psychopathic Behaviour: Approaches to Research.* New York: Wiley.

Trivers, R. (1971) The evolution of reciprocal altruism. *Quarterly Review of Biology, 46,* 35–57.

Trower, P., Bryant, B. and Argyle, M. (1978) *Social Skills and Mental Health*. London: Methuen.

Turiel, E. (1973) A comparative analysis of moral knowledge and moral judgment in males and females. *Journal of Personality, 44*, 195–208.

Turiel, E. (1983) *The Development of Social Knowledge*. Cambridge: Cambridge University Press.

Turner, J.C. (1991) *Social Influence*. Milton Keynes: Open University Press.

Turner, J.C. and Giles, H. (1981) *Intergroup Relations*. Oxford: Blackwell.

Turner, J., Hogg, M., Oakes, P., Reicher, S. and Wetherell, M. (1987) *Rediscovering the Social Group*. Oxford: Blackwell.

Tyler, T. (1990) *Why People Obey the Law*. New Haven, CN: Yale University Press.

Voss, M.L. (1964) Differential association and reported delinquent behavior: A replication. *Social Problems, 12*, 78–85.

Voss, M.L. (1969) Differential association and containment theory: A theoretical convergence. *Social Forces, 47*, 381–91.

Vuchinich, S., Bank, L. and Patterson, G.R. (1992) Parenting, peers and the stability of antisocial behavior in preadolescent boys. *Developmental Psychology, 28*, 510–21.

Wadsworth, M. (1979) *Roots of Delinquency: Infancy, Adolescence and Crime*. New York: Robinson.

Walberg, H.J., Yeh, E.G. and Paton, S.M. (1974) Family background, ethnicity, and urban delinquency. *Journal of Research in Crime and Delinquency, 11*, 80–7.

Waldo, G.P. and Hall, N.E. (1970) Delinquency potential and attitudes towards the criminal justice system. *Social Forces, 49*, 291–8.

Walker, L.J. (1983) Sex differences in the development of moral reasoning.: A critical review. *Child Development, 55*, 677–91.

Wallach, M.A., Kogan, N. and Bem, D.J. (1962) Group influence on individual risk taking. *Journal of Abnormal and Social Psychology, 65*, 75–86.

Wallerstein, J.S. and Wyle, C.J. (1947) Our law-abiding law-breakers. *Probation, 25*, 107–12.

Wallis, C.P. and Maliphant, R. (1967) Delinquent areas in the county of London: Ecological factors. *British Journal of Criminology, 7*, 250–84.

Walzer, M. (1970) *Obligations*. Cambridge, Mass: Harvard University Press.

Warner, W.L. and Lunt, P.S. (1941) *The Social Life of a Modern Community*. New Haven: Yale University Press.

Weber, M. (1947) *The Theory of Social and Economic Organisations*. New York: Free Press.

Weis, J. (1973) *Delinquency among the Well-to-do*. Unpublished PhD dissertation, University of California.

Weis, J.G. (1971) Dialogue with David Matza. *Issues in Criminology, 6*, 33–53.

Weiss, D.S. (1979) The effects of systematic variations in information on judges' descriptions of personality. *Journal of Personality and Social Psychology, 37*, 2121–36.

Wellman, B. (1979) The community question: the intimate networks of East Yorkers. *American Journal of Sociology, 84,* 1201–31.

Wells, L.E. and Rankin, J.H. (1983) Self-concept as a mediating factor in delinquency. *Social Psychology Quarterly, 46,* 11–22.

West, D.J. (1982) *Delinquency: Its Roots, Careers and Prospects.* London: Heinemann.

West, D.J. and Farrington, D.P. (1973) *Who Becomes Delinquent?* London: Heinemann.

West, D.J. and Farrington, D.P. (1977) *The Delinquent Way of Life.* London: Heinemann.

Wiatrowski, M.D., Hansell, S., Massey, C.R and Wilson, D.L. (1982) Curriculum tracking and delinquency. *American Sociological Review, 47,* 151–60.

Wiegman, O., Kuttschreuter, M. and Baarda, B. (1992) A longitudinal study of the effects of television viewing on aggression and prosocial behaviour. *British Journal of Social Psychology, 31,* 147–64.

Wiggins, J.S. (1973) *Personality and Prediction: Principles of Personality Assessment.* Reading, Mass: Addison-Wesley.

Willis, P. (1977) *Learning to Labour: How Working Class Kids Get Working Class Jobs.* Farnborough: Saxon House.

Wilmott, P. (1966) *Adolescent Boys of East London.* London: Routledge and Kegan Paul.

Wilson, E.O. (1975) *Sociobiology: The New Synthesis.* Cambridge, Mass.: Belknap/Harvard.

Wilson, H. (1980) Parental supervision: A neglected aspect of delinquency. *British Journal of Criminology, 20,* 203–35.

Winslow, R.W. (1967) Anomie and its alternatives: A self-report study of delinquency. *Sociological Quarterly, 8,* 468–80.

Wirth, L. (1938) Urbanism as a way of life. *American Journal of Sociology, 44,* 3–24.

Wolfgang, M., Figlio, R. and Sellin, T. (1972) *Delinquency in a Birth Cohort.* Chicago: University of Chicago Press.

Yablonsky, L. (1962) *The Violent Gang.* New York: Macmillan.

Yoshikawa, H. (1994) Prevention as cumulative protection: Effects of early family support and education on chronic delinquency and its risks. *Psychological Bulletin, 115,* 28–54.

Young, M. and Willmott, P. (1957) *Family and Kinship in East London.* Harmondsworth: Penguin.

Zigler, E., Taussig, C. and Black, K. (1992) Early childhood intervention: A promising prevention for juvenile delinquency. *American Psychologist, 47,* 997–1006.

Zimbardo, P. (1969) The human choice: individuation, reason and order versus deindividuation, impulse and chaos. In W.J. Arnold and D. Levine (eds) *Nebraska Symposium on Motivation,* vol. 17. Lincoln, Neb: University of Nebraska Press.

Zweig, F. (1961) *The Worker in an Affluent Society.* London: Heinemann.

Author Index

Subject Index

academic attainment, 157–8, 159, 161, 170
accounting conventions, 128–9
adolescence, 47–59
  as crisis period, 23, 48
  modern concept of, 20–1
  sexuality in, 50–1
  vulnerability in, 9, 21, 48–9, 52, 53, 58–9
age and delinquency, 3–4, 73–5, 92–3, 153, 169, 205–6
aggression, 73–4, 89, 91, 120, 148, 195–9
  and impression management, 135, 141, 149
aggressiveness, 220
anomie, 38
anonymity and crime, 16, 18–19, 123
  see also mass society thesis
area of residence, 77–8, 215–17
Aristotle, 20
attachment
  to the collective, 38
  to parents, 31, 51, 134–5
attitudes
  to authority, 150, 164, 167, 183, 226
  content of, 153,
  and peer relations, 221
  related to delinquency, 151–4,
  to rules, 101–2,
attribution, 72

Beccaria, Cesare, 16
Bentham, Jeremy, 16
Binet, Alfred and measurement of intelligence, 26
biological basis of crime, 26–7
bureaucracy, school as, 159, 162
bureaucratic relations, 144, 159

careers
  aspirations, 166–7
  expectations, 164–5,
cities, criminogenic conditions of life in, 13–14, 15–18, 39, 67, 108–9, 123
  see also anonymity, mass society thesis, urban-rural differences
civil disobedience, 35
cognitive development, 31–2
commercial relations, 145
community
  in Durkheim's theory, 13, 37
  in mass society theory, 13
  romanticization of, 15, 18
  urban, 109
  J-curve distribution of, 85
  see also honesty, experimental measures of
conditioning, 27
  classical, 28
  operant, 28–9
conformity, 8, 13, 37
control theory, 99, 133–5, 152, 157–8, 159